Systemic Implications of Transatlantic Regulatory Cooperation and Competition

World Scientific Studies in International Economics
(ISSN: 1793-3641)

---

15 World Scientific
Studies in
International
Economics

Systemic Implications of Transatlantic Regulatory Cooperation and Competition

Simon J Evenett

University of St Gallen, Switzerland

Robert M Stern

University of Michigan, USA

 World Scientific

NEW JERSEY · LONDON · SINGAPORE · BEIJING · SHANGHAI · HONG KONG · TAIPEI · CHENNAI

Published by

World Scientific Publishing Co. Pte. Ltd.

5 Toh Tuck Link, Singapore 596224

USA office: 27 Warren Street, Suite 401-402, Hackensack, NJ 07601

UK office: 57 Shelton Street, Covent Garden, London WC2H 9HE

British Library Cataloguing-in-Publication Data
A catalogue record for this book is available from the British Library.

SYSTEMIC IMPLICATIONS OF TRANSATLANTIC REGULATORY COOPERATION AND COMPETITION
World Scientific Studies in International Economics — Vol. 15

ISBN-13 978-981-283-848-3
ISBN-10 981-283-848-1

Typeset by Stallion Press
Email: enquiries@stallionpress.com

Printed in Singapore.

Contents

Preface

This volume is a collection of the revised papers that were originally presented at a conference entitled "Systemic Implications of Transatlantic Regulatory Cooperation and Competition" that was held at the University of Michigan's Gerald R. Ford School of Public Policy on May 8–9, 2008. The motivation for the conference stemmed from the observations that regulations and enforcement decisions that may at first appear to have only a domestic impact can have substantial spillover effects on other nations' economies. Experience has shown time and again that there is no reason to expect that these effects are always confined to jurisdictions at the same level of development. Governments on both sides of the Atlantic recognize this, yet their responses in many policies are not aligned — sometimes deliberately so. This creates a complex regulatory landscape that appears to be the product of both cooperation and competition, and which can often only be fully understood by looking through a number of disciplinary lenses.

The presentations of the papers at the conference were shorter than the academic norm so as to facilitate discussion among the participants that included the authors as well as a number of practitioners with policy-making and business expertise. We are particularly grateful to James Sanford, former Deputy Assistant Secretary for European Affairs, in the Office of the US Trade Representative, who attended the conference and provided many useful comments and insights on the issues being addressed.

Funding for the conference was provided by the German Marshall Fund of the United States and by the University of Michigan Department of Economics, Center for International Business Education, Center for European Studies, Law School, William Davidson Institute, and the Ford School International Policy Center. We wish to thank the late Faith Vlcek for her assistance in the administration of the conference arrangements and Judith Jackson for her assistance with the manuscript editing and preparation of the conference volume.

Simon J. Evenett and Robert M. Stern
St. Gallen and Ann Arbor
February 23, 2010

Chapter 1

Condemned to Cooperate?

Simon J. Evenett
University of St. Gallen

Robert M. Stern
University of Michigan

1. Introduction

In our interdependent world surely further cooperation on policymaking between large economic blocs, such as the United States (US) and the European Union (EU), is inevitable? And does not the recent global economic crisis point to the necessity of transatlantic economic cooperation in establishing a less volatile foundation for the world economy? Furthermore, cannot a transatlantic partnership provide the stimulus necessary to address long-standing global challenges — such as completing the Doha Round of multilateral trade negotiations — and nascent ones, such as climate change?

Sentiments such as these are expressed frequently on both sides of the Atlantic, yet rarely do they translate into concrete policy decisions.[1] The contrast between the rhetoric and results has become so stark that it is about time to ask whether it is really the case that the United

---

[1] Recognition of the limited prospects for further transatlantic cooperation — at least in the near term — has been given as one of the reasons for US President Obama's decision not to attend the EU–US summit in May 2010. Whether the European reaction to this decision spurs the identification of joint projects across the Atlantic remains to be seen.

1

States and the European Union are "condemned to cooperate," as former European Commissioner McGreevy put it? The purpose of this volume is to revisit the assumptions and arguments used to advance transatlantic solutions to common problems. For what class of societal problems is a transatlantic approach the optimal response?

One might immediately ask "optimal for whom?" The world economy is no longer bipolar (or tripolar, if one includes Japan), so the question arises as to whether transatlantic initiatives might come at the expense of other nations or compromise established multilateral principles of state conduct? Therefore, in assessing the merits and prospects of transatlantic cooperation at the beginning of the second decade of the twenty-first century, it is not enough to understand the internal logic of transatlantic cooperation but also its systemic consequences. The chapters in this volume — written by experts drawing upon different sectoral expertise and intellectual traditions — attempt to do exactly that.

The emphasis on the systemic consequences of potential transatlantic cooperation should appeal to those policymakers and analysts that are not solely concerned with European and American decision-making. If the reasons for the paucity of transatlantic cooperation in recent years can be established and those reasons turn out not to be particular to European and North American circumstances, then they may reveal something about the likelihood of successful forms of policy cooperation between other poles of the world economy.

At a time when multilateral approaches to global problem solving appear to be falling short (witness the ongoing Doha Round of trade negotiations and the discord at the climate change conference in Copenhagen in December 2009), interest is bound to grow in other forms of international cooperation and the temptation of some economic poles to "forge ahead" in small groups may grow. The recent experience with transatlantic cooperation might be salutary in this regard.

The remainder of this introductory chapter is organized as follows. The next section discusses the multi-faceted relationship between economic interdependence, transatlantic cooperation, and multilateralism. In so doing a number of questions are raised that are picked up in subsequent chapters of the book. The third section summarizes the main findings of chapters that follow. As will become clear, there is no "corporate" view on the merits and prospects of transatlantic cooperation from the contributors to this book; rather the objective was to see where the logic of various arguments for cooperation would take us. This approach enables readers to see where transatlantic means best serve different policy objectives. The final section offers some concluding remarks on the wider significance of some of the findings of this volume for economic and regulatory cooperation among major trading nations in what remains of the first quarter of the twenty-first century.

2. Economic Interdependence, Transatlantic Cooperation, and Multilateralism

2.1. *From economic interdependence to the Merkel Initiative*

It is customary to start most discussions on transatlantic cooperation on economic matters by referring to a barrage of statistics that point to the degree of interdependence between the economies of the European Union and the United States.[2] From these statistics it is typically asserted that "much is at stake" in properly managing transatlantic economic relations.

Moreover, one or two significant events are typically referred to — at the current time it might refer to the apparent global economic recovery and the goal of avoiding widespread resort to protectionism as well as the need to rewrite the regulations of the financial sector so as to avoid another sharp downturn, like that experienced in 2008 and 2009 — and the imperative for transatlantic cooperation is established, or so we are told. In some accounts the subtle juxtaposition

---

[2]For such a barrage see pages 3 and 4 of Stokes and Paeman (2009, pp. 3–4). As part of the background research for this chapter, the degree of economic interdependence, as reported in Stokes and Paeman and in comparable publications, was confirmed. Sapir's chapter in this volume presents some of the key statistics in an appendix table.

of the shared interests in the postwar years with the future uncertainties associated with the shift of economic power to Asia and appeals to "leadership" and "vision"[3] further bolsters the diplomatic and geopolitical case for transatlantic initiatives.

Business interests often appeal to the costs of fragmented markets — or the consequences of more open markets, that is, economies of scale, greater incentives to innovate, and less time and money spent on regulations — to make the corporate case for closer transatlantic cooperation. From time to time, some have gone further and made the case for a transatlantic free trade area or at least for widespread mutual recognition of national regulations. Reference here is typically made to a widely publicized study by the Organisation for Economic Co-operation and Development (OECD, 2005) that included estimates of 2.5% and 3% per capita income gains for Americans and Europeans from the widespread elimination of tariffs and non-tariff barriers.[4]

Ever since the conclusion of the Uruguay Round of multilateral trade negotiations, and with the fall of the Berlin Wall ending the ideological competition over national economic systems, the above arguments have been employed to foster closer transatlantic economic ties. For example, in 1995 European and American leaders agreed on a

---

[3] It not being clear what these terms actually mean.

[4] More recent estimates of the effects of transatlantic elimination of tariffs can be found in Erixon and Pehnelt (2009) (essentially of the order of 7–18 billion euros for welfare and 1.5–4.5% for bilateral trade volumes). Their colleague, Sally (2009), concludes on the basis of these numbers and other considerations that:

> Nevertheless, tariff elimination on its own might not be worth the candle. Large political capital would be needed to deliver quite modest gains, while sidelining the WTO and perhaps undermining multilateral rules. Rather a shallow-integration agreement should be seen as a stepping-stone to a much bigger prize, a "deep-integration" TAFTA that would tackle non-tariff barriers and seriously liberalise trade in goods, services and investment. Gains from regulatory liberalisation would be much, much larger, especially in services. But this is precisely where the major technical and political obstacles lie, as the TEC record shows. The advantage of doing a deal on tariffs is that it might, finally, generate momentum to tackle regulatory barriers.

New Transatlantic Agenda which included proposals for the creation of a Transatlantic Market Place. There were similar such announcements at the transatlantic summits that followed.

The most recent — and arguably most extensive — initiative saw the creation of the Transatlantic Economic Council (TEC) in 2007. This was part of the Framework for Advancing Transatlantic Economic Integration that was signed by US and EU leaders at a summit in 2007. Much of the impetus for this initiative came from the German government that held the Presidency of the EU Council at the time, and is often referred to as the Merkel Initiative. This initiative has the following three objectives:

1. To remove or reduce prevailing non-tariff impediments to transatlantic commerce.
2. To amicably and expeditiously resolve current and future commercial disputes between the US and the EU.
3. To establish joint EU–US approaches to certain commercial matters of global importance.

With these ends in mind, consultations by EU and US officials have been held in various fora, including the TEC, between peer agencies, and in the High Level Regulatory Cooperation Forum.[5] Reports on the resulting consultations have been prepared for subsequent EU–US summits. A typical example of the latter is the "TEC Report to the EU–US Summit 2008: Review of progress under the framework for advancing transatlantic economic integration between the European Union and the United States of America" (EU–US 2008). This report noted that the TEC had established procedures for working with stakeholders, which includes legislators, that influence regulatory processes and laws on both sides of the Atlantic. As many of the authors in this volume will make clear, the involvement of legislators is critical to further progress.

---

[5]This Forum comprises the heads of regulatory agencies on both sides of the Atlantic (or their representatives) and engages in the exchange of views on best practices.

Many incremental steps — often involving processes by and initiating dialogue between regulators — were listed in this report, EU–US (2008). Perhaps the best known step was the decision in November 2007 by the US Securities and Exchange Commission (SEC) to end the requirement that foreign companies employing the International Financial Reporting Standards (IFRS) need to reconcile their accounts with the US Generally Accepted Accounting Principles (GAAP). The report also lists the 2007 "Open Skies" accord between the US and the EU as an accomplishment; doing so highlights a difficulty in interpreting the TEC's accomplishments, as this negotiation was already underway when the TEC was created.[6] The report also describes how certain longstanding disputes between the EU and the US are being dealt with.[7]

In reviewing the assessments of the Merkel Initiative, it is striking how cautious many are about the accomplishments to date, what it

---

[6]This raises, of course, the question as to what is the counterfactual. In the absence of the TEC would the conclusion of the Open Skies Accord, for example, have been impossible? In general, when interpreting the contribution of the Merkel Initiative it is surely a mistake to infer that every instance of regulatory cooperation since April 2007 can be credited to this Initiative. Surely some cooperation, even if more limited, would have occurred in the absence of this initiative.

[7]For example, on the ongoing poultry dispute between the US and EU, the report notes:

At the TEC meeting in November 2007, the subject of the treatment of poultry meat with pathogen reduction substances was discussed. The European Commission has undertaken to act on this issue before the next EU–US Summit, after receiving scientific advice. In this sense, the Commission consulted the European Food Safety Authority on the possible effects of the treatment on antimicrobial resistance and the Scientific Committee on Health and Environment and the Scientific Committee on Emerging and Newly Identified Health Risks on the environmental risk and on the risk of emergence of microbial resistance associated with the use of these substances. The Commission has reviewed these scientific opinions and, in the light of those opinions, which provide no scientific basis for the continuation of the import ban, it will in the coming weeks come forward with a proposal for allowing the use of pathogen reduction treatments for poultry meat in the EU Member States and in imported poultry products. In line with its previous commitment, the Commission will actively solicit Member State and European Parliament support and will make best endeavours to achieve the final adoption of the relevant EU legislation before the next TEC meeting, planned for autumn 2008.

takes to make progress, and likely future progress.[8] Even the officials associated with the TEC process do not downplay some of the challenges ahead. For example, the conclusion to the report referred to above (EU–US 2008) includes the following statement:

> The TEC's working arrangements have proved to be a successful innovation which has given new political impetus to EU–US economic cooperation with the objective of overcoming disagreements. A number of goals identified in the 2007 Framework have been achieved in the first year of its work. However, much remains to be done. The first year has confirmed that regulatory cooperation and economic integration entail arduous technical work to be successful and require the continued attention of and commitment by the political leadership to press for progress. This is a long-term project (page 25).

Prominent supporters of further transatlantic cooperation too are dissatisfied with the rate of progress under the Merkel Initiative. Stokes and Paeman (2009), for example, argue:

> While the TEC has advanced some transatlantic regulatory cooperation, it has not produced the deeper economic integration that is its core purpose. The reasons for failure are many. Most important, the effort has lacked a broad strategic vision. The transatlantic dialogue has far too often allowed itself to be stymied by disagreements on technical trade issues, most recently over safety standards for poultry.

As will become clear, some of the contributors to this volume offer tougher assessments of the TEC and point to structural reasons for its limited success.

Adding to concerns about the lack of progress has been the perception that the Obama administration is unsure what to make of the TEC process. Apparently, the TEC has support at high levels within the current US administration, yet no clear agenda for it has been established. Vague suggestions have been made to focus on longer-term, more forward-looking issues, which could be read as either an

---

[8]This caution is all the more striking when contrasted with the optimistic remarks about the probability and benefits of completing the Doha Round of multilateral trade negotiations.

attempt to develop a grander vision for transatlantic economic relations or an attempt to avoid the difficult choices associated with resolving certain ongoing transatlantic disputes. The apparent desire on the Obama administration's part to appoint labor union representatives to the Group of Advisors of the TEC is perhaps the only concrete process-related suggestion made to date, and may well provide more evidence of the influence of the American labor movement over US trade policy. Overall, a sense of drift prevails. In situations such as these it may make sense to revisit the very foundations of transatlantic interdependence and national decision-making processes to see what, if any, basis they provide for deeper transatlantic cooperation. The purpose of the remainder of this section is to do exactly this.

2.2.   *Economic interdependence and the case for transatlantic cooperation*

It is often argued that the high levels of economic interdependence *per se* imply that there is "much at stake" (presumably a large economic payoff) to transatlantic collaborative initiatives. Surely this is the wrong way to motivate such collective action. After all, low levels of trade between the US and the EU could be indicative of high barriers to trade and supportive of a case for transatlantic liberalization of commerce. What matters is not the prevailing level of interdependence or the size of trade barriers *per se*, but the impact that changes in policies on one side of the Atlantic could have on the welfare of parties living on the other side of the Atlantic. Since this argument applies to cases where the welfare impact is positive or negative, the identification of policy changes — and combinations of policy changes — likely to generate substantial impact is central to identifying potentially meaningful transatlantic cooperation.

On top of this welfare filter, of course, must be added a political economy filter. Namely, bearing in mind any differences in the effectiveness of interest groups in the domestic policymaking process, the basis for any "deal" between the US and the EU must then be identified. This in turn raises the question as to whether more can be accomplished by bundling (sometimes unrelated) issues together to form an acceptable package to both parties — or establishing a sequence of initiatives that over time effectively delivers such a package — rather than dealing with each issue sequentially. A related concern here is that an interest group (potentially including a group of state officials) might try to hold up the deal-making process in order to advance a single matter.

On the basis of these considerations, it would seem that one necessary condition for a successful transatlantic initiative is that a number of higher impact potential policy innovations be identified before the process begins, combinations of which may provide the basis for a deal as the initiative unfolds over time. Different permutations may limit the likelihood of hold-up. In addition, whatever process is adopted will have to accommodate the inevitable unanticipated events that disrupt policymakers' plans, and in this case may alter the basis of future cooperative initiatives.

However, in thinking through the relationship between economic interdependence across the Atlantic and the case for transatlantic cooperation, given the paucity of the latter in the recent past, how did the former arise? This question is important because it points to alternative initiatives that may have the effect of promoting both transatlantic economic interdependence and welfare in the EU and in the US.

Since no transatlantic free trade agreement has been signed, the only policy instruments that can be credited with promoting the prevailing transatlantic economic ties are the clutch of prevailing bilateral investment treaties and the multilateral trade accords negotiated initially at the General Agreement on Tariffs and Trade (GATT) and now at the World Trade Organization (WTO). Rising incomes and similar per capita incomes no doubt account for some of the growth of transatlantic trade too.

Moreover, transatlantic economic ties have proved to be remarkably robust over time. Sharp diplomatic disputes (such as over the merits of invading Iraq for a second time) did not lead to a deterioration in commercial policy relations. Particularly contentious commercial policy disputes between the EU and the US have been taken to the WTO's Dispute Settlement mechanism and *even in cases when one party has disliked the outcome* such outcomes have not spread unduly to other aspects of commercial policymaking, or markedly affected diplomatic relations more generally.

While it is certainly the case that extant multilateral trade accords and bilateral investment treaties are far from complete — that is, they do not prevent every form of discrimination or bias against foreign commercial interests — at a minimum these accords do embody principles that, by and large, appear consistent with how governments on either side of the Atlantic would prefer to see their commercial interests treated by the other. It would seem, then, that to make the case for a bilateral transatlantic approach it is necessary to establish that *in the absence of prevailing constraints at the multilateral level* the EU and US would have taken binding global trade accords much further. The latter provides a further filter for identifying policies and state practices where a collaborative transatlantic initiative would generate value-added (over multilateral approaches).[9]

That transatlantic interdependence has strengthened so much over time in the absence of significant transatlantic commercial initiatives outside of the multilateral trading system has another implication. Surely the benchmark — against which any transatlantic initiative is compared — should build in a natural intensification of transatlantic commerce over time? How much growth in trade, investment, etc., would have to be established empirically. Postwar experience would suggest that a zero growth benchmark for no policy change is inappropriate. Hence, the hurdle that a proposed transatlantic initiative should pass before being taken forward is probably more stringent than some analysts imply. Again, the point is to clearly establish the value-added of a transatlantic initiative, bearing in mind the existence of other negotiating fora and supply-side developments.

Moreover, the fact that firms often have more than one way to enter a foreign market implies that the removal of a barrier on any one mode of entry into a foreign market may merely induce a substitution between modes of entry. Under these circumstances the impact of a

---

[9]This is not the same thing as demonstrating that such an initiative has no adverse effects on other trading partners.

transatlantic initiative on commercial flows is likely to be larger than that on welfare — and, of course, it is the latter that ultimately matters. For sure, the reform may create a lower cost mode of entry (that enhances efficiency on standard economic metrics), however, the benefits to consumers may be slight (as they are already served by the foreign firms in question) and the net impact on measured interdependence, ambiguous (as one form of interdependence — exports, say — diminishes as another grows — such as foreign direct investment).

Having discussed the different ways in which the prevailing, high levels of economic interdependence across the Atlantic begs questions concerning the appropriate design and evaluation of transatlantic commercial initiatives, attention now turns to the potential relationships between such initiatives and the multilateral trading system.

2.3. *The impact of transatlantic initiatives on the multilateral trading system, and vice versa*

One matter analyzed in many of the contributions to this volume is the systemic consequences of previous and potential future transatlantic initiatives. Specifically, what are the potential relationships between the multilateral trading system, as embodied by the World Trade Organization agreements and associated secretariat and dispute mechanisms, and transatlantic initiatives on commercial and regulatory policies? Here the goal is to sketch out the two-way nature of that relationship.

The experience of the United States and the European Commission in working within the existing WTO structures and initiatives has arguably provided some of the impetus for a transatlantic initiative. Delays in completing the Doha Round of multilateral trade negotiations, the emphasis on agricultural subsidy and tariff cuts in those negotiations and their sensitivities in Washington DC and in national capitols in Europe, plus the end of the US's and EU's dominance of multilateral trade talks may have added to the perceived benefits of cooperating in a different forum.

The current set of multilateral disciplines — which effectively define the boundaries or reach of the WTO — may also be seen as inadequate in dealing with some of the pressing commercial policy challenges facing firms as they do business across the Atlantic. After all, the existing WTO accords were negotiated on the basis of an agenda agreed in 1986, nearly a quarter of a century ago. Much business practice and technology has changed since then — and in certain situations existing multilateral accords may provide no basis upon which to resolve international disputes or to guide policy choice. This argument should not be taken too far. While it is true that there are not specific WTO accords on every aspect of government behavior relating to modern business practices, the WTO accords do embody key principles (such as national treatment and most favored nation treatment) that could usefully guide transatlantic cooperation. In sum, it would be going too far to assert or assume that inter-governmental cooperation outside the WTO — transatlantic or, for that matter, other — as being or having to be completely uninformed by multilateral trade principles.

Still, it would be remiss to ignore the long-standing concerns about the consequences of bilateral and regional trade reform. The potential for a transatlantic initiative to discriminate in favor of firms located inside[10] the EU and the US against firms located elsewhere triggers worries about trade and investment diversion and the associated loss in efficiency in the allocation of resources. Perhaps more worrying would be the adoption of common standards by the EU and the US — or mutual recognition of each other's standards — that involved unnecessary costs for firms from third parties to comply with. These standards could be related to technical matters (e.g., voltage used) or to health and safety matters. Given the low levels of tariffs on transatlantic manufacturing trade, concerns about standards setting and the symmetric enforcement of standards are probably of greater commercial relevance.

The prospect of EU and US producers and officials setting standards for half of the world economy is unlikely to be welcomed in

---

[10]With cross-border investment, of course, such discrimination could involve an overseas subsidiary of an EU or US multinational being disadvantaged compared to an EU- or US-based subsidiary of a firm headquartered in a third country. This is a reminder that acting on simplistic notions of who is "us" and who is "them" is a recipe for likely harming some of one's own commercial interests!

the growing manufacturing powerhouses of Asia; not only are the latter bound to feel that whatever standards set were not chosen with their circumstances in mind, they are also likely to resent the outlays demonstrating compliance with those standards. Of course, such Asian firms may be tempted to set their own technical standards and the like, and force EU- and US-based exporters to pay adoption costs. This is not the place to review the steps that countries can take to limit the unnecessary costs associated with the adoption of technical and other standards; still, the principle of limiting and avoiding such costs, where possible, should be borne in mind.

Even though much of the economic literature on preferential trade reform has emphasized the adverse consequences of violating the most favored nation principle, it should be acknowledged that bilateral and plurilateral cooperative initiatives can be implemented on a non-discriminatory basis. Some may think it naïve that two trading blocs — such as the US and EU — would automatically grant the same privileges to third parties, receiving nothing in return. However, two considerations may persuade policymakers to implement measures in a non-discriminatory manner. The relevance of each consideration is likely to vary across regulations and policy area. First, the cost of maintaining two regulatory regimes (one for EU–US firms and associated commerce and one for third parties) may be large compared to the apparent benefits of discrimination. Second, US and EU firms may have subsidiaries in third countries that they do not want to see discriminated against when supplying customers on either side of the Atlantic. For both reasons, non-discriminatory approaches ought to be considered.

The resolution of transatlantic disputes is another purported benefit of EU–US cooperation. This too has ambiguous systemic consequences. On the one hand, the resolution of a dispute and putting an end to the associated discord is, on the face of it, desirable. (Indeed, many diplomats may view the absence of discord in and of itself a desirable outcome.) However, the terms upon which a dispute is settled are important, especially if they are at odds with existing multilateral principles and obligations. Furthermore, by stopping a dispute from being resolved by the WTO's Appellate Body, useful precedents may be forgone.[11] The latter argument applies, however, to any instance when two or more WTO members settle a case, and therefore cannot be elevated into a specific disadvantage of EU–US cooperation.

Another form of transatlantic cooperation that could have implications for the multilateral trading system is when the European Community (EC) and US develop common positions on matters that are — or could be placed — on the WTO agenda.[12] It has been argued that this would help forge common positions on matters that the rising powers of Asia and elsewhere may take different views on — or on issues that are new to the rest of the WTO membership. Without doubting that a combined EC and US position on a matter may look impressive — and indeed carry some diplomatic heft — however, it is important to remember that the WTO proceeds on the basis of consensus and that, as the Doha Round has amply demonstrated, the leading emerging markets plus certain groups of smaller developing countries have effectively exercised vetoes in the past and can do so in the future.

Worse, to the extent that a joint EC–US position is seen to demonstrate that both parties really want an issue addressed, then others may demand a higher price in order to acquiesce to the joint demands of the EC and US. Procedural factors may exacerbate the price paid. For example, even if the EC and US were able to persuade WTO members to launch a negotiation on a plurilateral accord on a matter of interest to them, the WTO membership may then demand the right to review, and potentially veto, the final accord. Avoiding that outcome may involve the EC and US "paying" again in negotiating capital.

---

[11]According to some trade diplomats the rulings of the WTO's Appellate Body do not have precedential value. However, since that Body is comprised of judges that sit for many years they are probably not minded to contradict their earlier rulings. In which case each ruling may help WTO members predict how the Appellate Body might rule in similar, subsequent cases. By settling a dispute, so the argument goes, the WTO Appellate Body is denied the opportunity to develop a precedent, or reinforce an existing one.

[12]A variant on this argument is that an accord between the EC and US on some commercial matter that is regarded as successful and not particularly harmful to third parties may — at some later point in time — become a model or template for a plurilateral or multilateral accord.

In short, given the bizarre zero-thinking that has erupted from time to time during the Doha Round negotiations, no strong assumptions of negotiating strength or numbers converting into positive outcomes seem warranted. Consequently, one might be doubtful of the likelihood that any transatlantic initiatives translate ultimately into plurilateral or multilateral accords, unless as part of some grand bargain.

The purpose of this sub-section has been to highlight the multi-faceted, two-way nature of the relationship between transatlantic commercial initiatives and the multilateral trading system. Reducing this matter to one of potential trade diversion and trade creation (which could be important) overlooks other important potential determinants and consequences of transatlantic cooperation. Indeed, some of the enduring impetus for such cooperation is driven by frustrations with multilateral decision-making processes.

2.4. *Transatlantic cooperation and cosmopolitan regulation*

Much of the cooperation mentioned in proposals for transatlantic initiatives relates not to formal trade barriers (such as tariffs, quotas, investment restrictions and the like) but to cooperation between regulators on both sides of the Atlantic. Here progress has been slower and less ambitious than many have liked (as witnessed by the statements of senior governmental officials and business associations). Yet there are fundamental reasons for this outcome that do not appear to have been taken on board, let alone addressed.

The starting point is to recall that since the 1980s there has been a systemic trend towards the creation of regulators that are supposed to be independent of both central government executive and of the legislature. Arguments about "taking politics out of regulation" were advanced in support of this trend. These contentions are not without merit. After all, the objectivity, predictability, and even-handedness of regulatory decision-making is likely to be compromised by interventions by politicians on behalf of specific interested parties. Ring-fenced budgets, agency officials with fixed terms and limited opportunities for reappointment, and the like were supposed to limit the opportunities for political interference.

What the creators of independent regulators probably did not anticipate was the fact that — as international economic interdependence grew — then regulatory decisions were likely to have knock-on effects in other jurisdictions. Likewise, market outcomes and welfare at home are likely to be affected by regulatory decisions abroad. Moreover, most independent regulators were established with legal mandates that made them responsible for matters within their national borders; it is as if their responsibilities ceased at the border. While these matters account for the potential for adverse knock-on effects from national regulatory decision-making, it is the absence of any obligation on the part of an independent regulator to cooperate that typically prevents the identification and implementation of mutually advantageous solutions. Cosmopolitan regulation, that is, regulation that takes account of knock-on effects across borders, is thereby frustrated. The creation of independent regulators may have solved one problem (that of political interference in domestic regulatory matters) but the manner of its implementation has created another problem in a globalized world.

The problem is made worse by the fact that firms in a given sector will make investment and other longer-term plans on the basis of the regulatory structure overseeing their sector. So while some firms may wish their sectoral regulator took a more cosmopolitan approach (perhaps because those firms seek to tap more opportunities in foreign markets), other firms may be less willing to see regulations that might enhance competition from abroad. If conforming with a regulator's rulings requires outlays by firms, then once a firm has made those outlays it may be very reluctant to see any reform in which subsequent potential entrants to the sector have to pay less — or no — such outlays. The corporate constituency for cosmopolitan regulation may in effect be smaller than originally thought.

To the extent that the regulators cherish their powers and prerogatives, then they may be reluctant to forgo their rights to review certain commercial practices, plans, etc., as part of an international accord. Regulators typically have mandates that involve non-price and non-efficiency matters, such as security of supply, safety, etc. In which case, regulators can play to the public's and politicians' fears about such matters, in an attempt to justify retaining full national control over regulation.

In sum, it would be naïve to suppose that there is some simple technical fix that will unleash a lot more cooperation between regulators on both sides of the Atlantic. Policymakers and analysts should be cognizant of the interests of regulators and incumbent firms in preserving the status quo, that is, in resisting cosmopolitan regulation that takes account of those cross-border knock-on effects that are almost inevitable in a world of relatively integrated markets. Put another way, transatlantic initiatives that are designed without making changes to the mandates and incentives of national regulators are likely to see limited results.

3. Contributions to this Volume

Experts from both sides of the Atlantic, from different sectors of the economy, and from different disciplines contributed to this volume, many making reference to the themes summarized above. In his chapter on banking, for example, De Grauwe implicitly takes a problem-and-solution approach, identifying the regulatory structure and implied international cooperation necessary to reduce the probability of a future banking crisis along the lines of what was witnessed in 2007 and 2008 (Chapter 2). Here the appropriate international initiatives are global rather than transatlantic.

Sapir, in contrast, sees a role for transatlantic cooperation on rebuilding the institutions of global economic governance and promoting liberalization of trade and investment barriers at the global level (Chapter 3). Sapir's review of prior transatlantic cooperation usefully highlights the pitfalls facing policymakers and argues that future cooperation will need to take account of the rise of the emerging powers in the developing world.

The menu of binding and non-binding options facing policymakers on both sides of the Atlantic is usefully described and analyzed in the chapter by Shaffer and Pollack (Chapter 4). Interestingly, they argue that even when the EU and US agree on an approach to regulation they are not in a position anymore to ensure that such approaches are accepted without question by other, smaller parties. Asymmetric distributional consequences are often relevant to the design of cross-border regulatory initiatives.

The systemic consequences of transatlantic cooperation are further analyzed by Hoekman and Nicita (Chapter 5). They examine the consequences of different possible transatlantic initiatives for the trading patterns of developing countries. While they do not doubt the Merkel Initiative would generate some gains (especially if administrative costs at and behind the border could be reduced), they argue that US–EC cooperation to complete the Doha Round would have the greatest payoff to the world economy.

Chapters on different sectors and types of regulatory instrument follow. Wilber and Eichbrecht (Chapter 6) show the complex web of different regulations on safety, environment, and energy confronting automobile makers in the US and the EU. The desire to exploit economies of scale and to limit regulatory uncertainty provide the rationale for transatlantic cooperation. These rationales appear to have been accepted and the authors show what progress has been made in establishing so-called global technical regulations. Still, in their view, there is much more that can be accomplished.

The potential for cooperation and discord on the enforcement of competition law is the subject of Chapter 7 by Anderson. He reviews the record of transatlantic cooperation on competition law, including the occasional sharp disagreements, and notes the tendency for the jurisdiction with the stricter interpretation to prevail. Looking forward, like Sapir, he emphasizes the rise of the emerging economies (in particular China and India) and the potential for disagreements as global transactions are reviewed by many more competition agencies. Anderson is doubtful of the benefits of bilateral cooperative instruments and advances the WTO principle of national treatment as a useful benchmark for national enforcement agencies.

The challenges in promoting transatlantic cooperation in chemicals are described by Quick (Chapter 8). The unilateral adoption of the REACH initiative by the European Commission and member states in 2003 put an end, he argues, to any hopes of regulatory cooperation and convergence — unless there is a profound change in the value judgments underlying regulatory design. Still, in the near-term he does see value in encouraging — where possible — transatlantic cooperation in the drafting of new regulations. Moreover, given the central role that legislators play in shaping regulatory structures, by resolving transatlantic disputes the TEC could build the confidence of legislators, which in turn might open the door for closer cooperation over time.

Accounting practices are the subject of Chapter 9 by Nölke. As noted earlier, one of the instances of transatlantic cooperation hailed by officials relates to the changes in rules on "reconciliation" that foreign firms face from the US Securities and Exchange Commission. Nölke explains why the continental European nations were prepared to accept this change, given the differences in their corporate governance structures with Anglo-Saxon economies. Opposition has grown since this rule was announced, and Nölke draws out its consequences in potentially limiting future transatlantic cooperation. This case study, therefore, reminds readers that transatlantic cooperation is not static and that regress is possible as well as progress.

Regulatory cooperation and competition in pharmaceuticals is the subject of Chapter 10 by Maskus and He. The multifaceted nature of national regulatory regimes is described, as is the evolution of bilateral, regional, and transatlantic cooperation. The authors identify tangible successes in cooperating over drug approval processes, which they argue have created savings for incumbent firms. More cooperation is possible, however. The authors identify differences in national propensities to develop new pharmaceuticals as a reason for divergent approaches to regulatory matters, reinforcing the point that national regulatory structures are outcomes of national political-economy processes and, in turn, this conditions the likely degree of transatlantic cooperation.

4. Concluding Remarks

In drawing the findings together, one starting point might be to ask what the prospects are for transatlantic economic cooperation in the near to medium term? If potential economic gains adjusted by the likelihood of successful conclusion of negotiations and subsequent implementation is the metric to guide policymaking, then the prospects do not look good. As in many potential reforms, the likely gains from successful implementation are positively correlated with the height of the obstacles to reform in the first place. Apart from a few tariff peaks, tariff rates on transatlantic trade are at low levels, where the ultimate gains from liberalization have been shown to be small.[13] In contrast, reforms to service sector regulations and other inside-the-border policies are likely to be much larger, but the combination of incumbent firms keen to stave off additional competition and national regulators jealous of their prerogatives make cooperative initiatives harder to pull off.

Seen in this light, a litmus test for evaluating the likely impact of any future transatlantic initiative is the determination of heads of governments and ministers to take on the vested interests, regulators, and the legislators that support those interests and the existing regulation that does so much to fragment national markets across the Atlantic and, for that matter, within Europe. Otherwise, transatlantic initiatives will probably be confined to "putting out fires" associated with bilateral commercial disputes between the EU and the US as well as to developing, where possible, joint proposals for matters of serious international or global interest, such as completing the Doha Round and climate change negotiations. (And, as argued earlier, the EU and US may find in some fora that the negotiating price of pursuing a joint initiative is too high. Therefore, even when the US and EU's interests are aligned, joint initiatives will not necessarily be taken forward.) All this bodes poorly for transatlantic economic cooperation, at least in so far as it takes current modalities as a starting point.

But should defenders of the multilateral trading system and those third parties that fear being harmed by transatlantic initiatives be relieved? On the face of it the likelihood of significant new forms

---

[13]Where tariffs do remain high — as in agriculture and products facing import competition from developing countries — there are domestic incumbents on both sides of the Atlantic that are very effective in defending their privileged positions.

of discrimination arising from transatlantic initiatives seems small. Yet the factors responsible for this outcome (the difficulties in liberalizing services vis-à-vis goods commerce, the presence of non-cosmopolitan independent regulators, etc.) are just at work on either side of the Atlantic. Indeed, these factors stymie closer and far-reaching economic cooperation, whether it be bilateral, regional, or multilateral. The current constraints on transatlantic policymaking may be those that will subsequently bite in other fora, which in turn has implications for how far the current wave of regional integration can really go, the likely outcome of any cooperative initiatives between the rising economic powers of Asia and elsewhere, and the likely scope of any future multilateral trade negotiations.

Perhaps the ultimate lesson from disappointing recent transatlantic economic cooperation is that the next phase of economic integration, if there is to be one, will be so intrusive of national regulatory and governance processes that national leaders will have to prize integration and its consequences over many other (possibly worthy) goals, will have to strengthen trade ministries and governing coordinating bodies so as to ensure that major economic policy and regulatory initiatives are aligned with the goal of integration, and be prepared to set aside the objections of many interests (producer, bureaucratic, and possibly some consumer) that to this day continue to benefit from fragmented markets.

References

Erixon and Pehnelt (2009). Fredrik Erixon and Gernot Pehnelt "A New Trade Agenda for Transatlantic Economic Cooperation" ECIPE working paper. September. Available at http://www.ecipe.org/publications/ecipe-working-papers/a-new-trade-agenda-for-transatlantic-economic-cooperation/PDF

EU–US (2008). *TEC Report to the EU-US Summit 2008: Review of progress under the framework for advancing transatlantic economic integration between the European Union and the United States of America.* Available at http://ec.europa.eu/enterprise/policies/international/files/tec_progress_en.pdf

OECD (2005) "The Benefits of Liberalising Product Markets and Reducing Barriers to International Trade and Investment: The case of the United States and the European Union", *OECD Economics Department Working Paper* No. 432.

Sally (2009). Razeen Sally. "A Transatlantic Free Trade Area?" 4 December 2009. ECIPE blog. Available at http://www.ecipe.org/blog/a-transatlantic-free-trade-area

Stokes and Paeman (2009). Bruce Stokes and Hugo Paeman. *The Transatlantic Economic Challenge. A Report of the Global Dialogue between the European Union and the United States.* Centre for Strategic and International Studies. Washington, D.C.

Chapter 2

The Banking Crisis: Causes, Consequences and Remedies

Paul De Grauwe

University of Leuven and CESifo

The paradigm that financial markets are efficient has provided the intellectual backbone for the deregulation of the banking sector since the 1980s, allowing universal banks to be fully involved in financial markets, and investment banks to become involved in traditional banking. There is now overwhelming evidence that financial markets are not efficient. Bubbles and crashes are an endemic feature of financial markets in capitalist countries. Thus, as a result of deregulation, the balance sheets of universal banks became fully exposed to these bubbles and crashes, undermining the stability of the banking system. The Basel approach to stabilize the banking system has as an implicit assumption that financial markets are efficient, allowing us to model the risks universal banks take and to compute the required capital ratios that will minimize this risk. I argue that this approach is unworkable because the risks that matter for universal banks are tail risks, associated with bubbles and crashes. These cannot be quantified. As a result, there is only one way out, and that is to return to narrow banking, a model that emerged after the previous large-scale banking crisis of the 1930s but that was discarded during the 1980s and 1990s under the influence of the efficient market paradigm.

1. The Basics of Banking

In order to analyze the causes of the banking crisis it is useful to start from the basics of banking.[1] Banks are in the business of borrowing short and lending long. In doing so they provide an essential service

---

[1]A very useful book is Goodhart and Illing, (2002).

to the rest of us, i.e., they create credit that allows the real economy to grow and expand.

This credit creation service, however, is based on an inherent fragility of the banking system. If depositors are gripped by a collective movement of distrust and decide to withdraw their deposits at the same time, banks are unable to satisfy these withdrawals as their assets are illiquid. A liquidity crisis erupts.

In normal times, when people have confidence in the banks, these crises do not occur. But confidence can quickly disappear, for example, when one or more banks experience a solvency problem due to non-performing loans. Then, bank runs are possible. A liquidity crisis erupts that can also bring down sound banks. The latter become innocent bystanders that are hit in the same way as the insolvent banks by the collective movement of distrust.

The problem does not end here. A devilish interaction between liquidity crisis and solvency crisis is set in motion. Sound banks that are hit by deposit withdrawals have to sell assets to confront these withdrawals. The ensuing fire sales lead to declines in asset prices, reducing the value of banks' assets. This in turn erodes the equity base of the banks and leads to a solvency problem. The cycle can start again: the solvency problem of these banks ignites a new liquidity crisis and so on.

The last great banking crisis occurred in the 1930s. Its effects were devastating for the real economy. After that crisis the banking system was fundamentally reformed. These reforms were intended to make such a banking crisis impossible. The reforms had three essential ingredients. First, the central bank took on the responsibility of being the lender of last resort. Second, deposit insurance mechanisms were instituted. These two reforms aimed at eliminating collective movements of panic. A third reform aimed at preventing commercial banks from taking on too many risks. In the US this took the form of the Glass-Steagall Act which was introduced in 1933 and which separated commercial banking from investment banking.

Most economists thought that these reforms would be sufficient to produce a less fragile banking system and to prevent large-scale banking crises. It was not to be. Why? In order to answer this question it is useful to first discuss "moral hazard."

In most general terms, moral hazard means that agents who are insured will tend to take fewer precautions to avoid the risk they are insured against. The insurance provided by central banks and governments in the form of lender of last resort and deposit insurance gives bankers strong incentives to take more risks. To counter this, authorities have to supervise and regulate, very much like any private insurer who wants to avoid moral hazard will do.

And that is what the monetary authorities did during most of the post-war period. They subjected banks to tight regulation aimed at preventing them from taking on too much risk. But then something remarkable happened.

2. The Efficient Market Paradigm

From the 1970s onwards, economists were all gripped by the intellectual attraction of the efficient market paradigm. This paradigm which originated in academia also became hugely popular outside academia. Its main ingredients are the following:

First, financial markets efficiently allocate savings towards the most promising investment projects, thereby maximizing welfare. Second, asset prices reflect underlying fundamentals. As a result, bubbles cannot occur, and neither can crashes. History was reinterpreted, and those of us who thought that the tulip bubble in the 17th century was the quintessential example of a price development unrelated to underlying fundamentals were told it was all fundamentally driven (see Garber (2000)).

The third ingredient of the efficient market paradigm is the capacity of markets for self-regulation. The proponents of this paradigm told us that financial markets can perfectly regulate themselves and that regulation by governments or central banks is unnecessary, even harmful, for as we all know bureaucrats and politicians always screw things up. All this led Greenspan to write these poetic words in his autobiography: "authorities should not interfere with the pollinating bees of Wall Street" (Greenspan (2007)).

The efficient market paradigm was extremely influential. It was also captured by bankers to lobby for deregulation. If markets work so beautifully there was no need for regulation anymore. And bankers achieved their objective. They were progressively deregulated in the US and in Europe. The culmination was the repeal of the Glass-Steagall act in 1999 by the Clinton administration. This allowed commercial banks to take on all the activities investment banks had been taking, e.g., the underwriting and the holding of securities; the development of new and risky assets like derivatives and complex structured credit products. Thus, banks were allowed to take on all the risky activities that the Great Depression had taught us could lead to problems. The lessons of history were forgotten.

The efficient market paradigm provided the intellectual backing for deregulation of financial markets in general and the banking sector in particular. At about the same time financial markets experienced a burst of innovations. Financial innovations allowed the designing of new financial products. These made it possible to repackage assets into different risk classes and to price these risks differently. It also allowed banks to secuterize their loans, i.e., to repackage them in the form of asset backed securities (ABSs) and to sell these in the market.

This led to the belief, very much inspired by the optimism of the efficient market paradigm, that securitization and the development of complex financial products would lead to better spreading of risk over many more people, thereby reducing systemic risk and reducing the need to supervise and regulate financial markets. A new era of free and unencumbered progress would be set in motion.

An important side effect of securitization was that each time banks sold repackaged loans, they obtained liquidity that could be used to extend new loans, which later on would be securitized again. This led to a large increase in the credit multiplier. Thus, even if the central bank tightly controlled the money base, credit expansion could go on unchecked with the same money base. The banking sector was piling up different layers of credit on top of each other allowing agents to speculate in the asset markets. All this undermined the control of central banks on expansion of credit in the economy.

3.   Are Financial Markets Efficient?

Deregulation and financial innovation promised to bring great welfare improvements: better risk spreading; lower costs of credit, benefiting firms who would invest more and benefiting millions of consumers who would have access to cheap mortgages. Who could resist the temptation of allowing these market forces to function freely without the interference of governments?

The trouble is that financial markets are not efficient. I illustrate this lack of efficiency in the two dimensions that matter for the stability of the banking sector.[2] First, bubbles and crashes are an endemic feature of financial markets. Second, financial markets are incapable of regulating themselves. Both failures would, in the end, bring down the new banking model that has been allowed to emerge and that was predicated on financial markets being efficient.

3.1.   *Bubbles and crashes are endemic in financial markets*

Nobody has written a better book on the capacity of financial markets to generate bubbles and crashes than Kindleberger in his masterful *Manias, Panics and Crashes*.[3] Kindleberger showed how the history of capitalism is littered with episodes during which asset markets are caught by a speculative fever that pushes prices to levels unrelated to fundamental economic variables. But the lessons of history were forgotten.

Let us look at some of the bubbles and crashes that littered financial markets during the last twenty–five years. Take the US stock market during 2006–2008. We show the Dow Jones and the Standard and Poor's in Figure 1.

---

[2]The empirical evidence against the efficiency of financial markets has been building up over the last decade. For useful overviews see Shleiffer (2000) and Shiller (2000).
[3]See Kindleberger (2005). Chancellor (1999) also provides a vivid account of the many bubbles and crashes in the history of financial markets.

28   P. De Grauwe

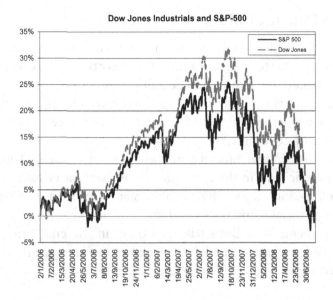

Figure 1:   The Dow Jones and the S&P 500 2006–2008.

Source: Yahoo Finance.

What happened in the US economy between July 2006 and July 2007 to warrant an increase of 30% in the value of stocks? Or put differently: in July 2006, US stock market capitalization was $11.5 trillion. One year later it was $15 trillion. What happened to the US economy to make it possible that $3.5 trillion was added to the value of US corporations in just one year? During the same year, GDP increased by only 5% ($650 billion).

The answer is: almost nothing. Fundamentals like productivity growth increased at their normal rate. The only reasonable answer is that there was excessive optimism about the future of the US economy. Investors were caught by a wave of optimism that made them believe that the US was on a new and permanent growth path for the indefinite future. Such beliefs of future wonders can be found in almost all bubbles in history, as is made vividly clear in Kindleberger's book.

Then came the downturn with the credit crisis. In one years' time (July 2007 to July 2008) stock prices dropped by 30%, destroying $3.5 trillion of value — the same amount as the one that had been

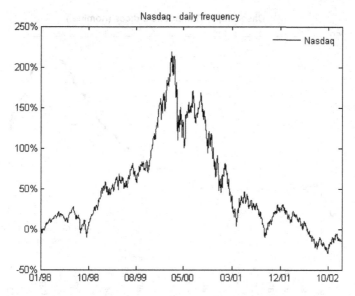

Figure 2:   Index of share prices, Nasdaq, 1999–2002.

Source: Yahoo Finance.

created the year before. What happened? Investors finally realized that there had been excessive optimism. The wave turned into one of excessive pessimism.

There were many other episodes of bubbles and crashes in the stock markets in many different countries. The most famous one was probably the IT-bubble at the end of the 1990s that had the same structure of extreme euphoria followed by depression. We show the evolution of the Nasdaq during 1999–2002 that illustrates this phenomenon in Figure 2. In one years' time the IT-shares tripled in value, and lost all of it the next year.

A similar story can be told about the US housing market. Figure 3 shows the Case-Shiller house price index from 2000 to 2008. During 2000–2007, US house prices more than doubled. What happened with economic fundamentals in the US warranting a doubling of house prices in seven years' time? Very little. Again the driving force was excessive optimism. Prices increased because they were expected to increase indefinitely into the future. This was also the expectation

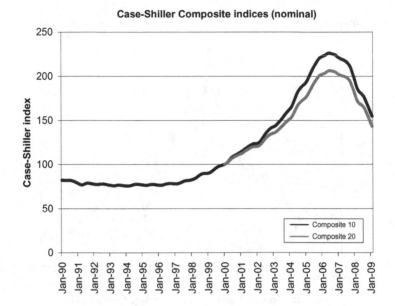

Figure 3:   Case-Shiller housing price index, 2000–2008.

Source: Standard & Poor's.

that convinced US consumers that building up mortgage debt would not create future repayment problems.

Bubbles and crashes also occurred in foreign exchange markets. Figures 4 and 5 illustrate this. They show the bubbles of the dollar (against the DM) in the 1980s and 1990s, respectively. What happened in the 1980s in the US economy to warrant a doubling of the price of the dollar against the DM (and other currencies) from 1980 to 1985? Almost nothing. Economic fundamentals between the US and the European currencies were somewhat different but these differences were dwarfed when compared to the movements of the dollar. What did happen was that the markets were gripped by euphoria about the US economy. It happened again in the second half of the 1990s when fairy tale wonders of the US economy were told. Then came the crash and the euphoria instantly made place for pessimism.

These episodes illustrate the endemic nature of bubbles and crashes in capitalist systems. They happened in the past and will continue to occur in the future.

DEM-USD 1980-87

Figure 4: US dollar vs. the DM (1980–1987).

Source: De Grauwe and Grimaldi (2006).

The fact that financial markets are continuously gripped by speculative fevers leading to bubbles and crashes would not have been a major problem had banks been prevented from involving themselves in financial markets. However, the deregulation of the banking sector that started in the 1980s fully exposed the banks to the endemic occurrence of bubbles and crashes in asset markets. Because banks were allowed to hold the full panoply of financial assets, their balance sheets became extremely sensitive to bubbles and crashes that gripped these assets. Banks' balance sheets became the mirror images of the bubbles and crashes occurring in the financial markets.

This is shown in a spectacular way in Figure 6. It illustrates how the balance sheets of the major European banks have exploded since the start of the decade, reflecting the various bubbles that occurred at that time (housing bubble, stock market bubbles, commodities bubbles).

While commercial banks were increasingly involving themselves in financial markets and thus taking over activities that were reserved for investment banks, the opposite occurred with investment banks. The

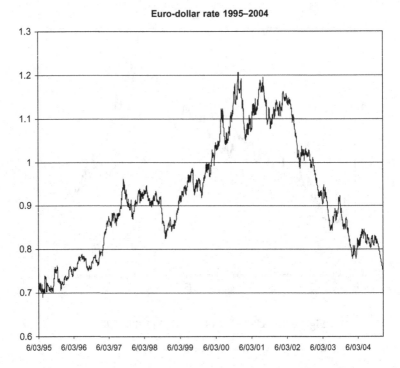

Figure 5:   US dollar vs. the DM (1995–2004).

Source: De Grauwe and Grimaldi (2006).

latter increasingly behaved like banks, i.e., they borrowed short and lent long, thereby moving into the business of credit creation. To give an example: investment banks (e.g., Lehman Brothers) moved into the business of lending money to hedge funds and accepted stocks or other securities as collateral. They then went on and lent that collateral to others so as to make extra money. Thus, investment banks had become banks in that they were creating credit. In the process they created an unbalanced maturity structure of assets and liabilities. Their assets were long-term and illiquid while their liabilities had a very short maturity. Note the historical analogy between the gold smiths who accepted gold as collateral for loans and ended up lending out the gold, thereby becoming banks. All this (the gold smiths in the past and the investment banks today) was done in a totally unregulated environment.

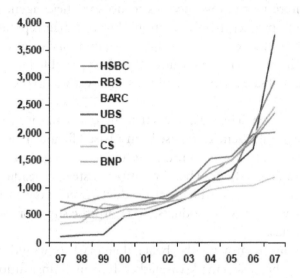

European Financials' Balance Sheets
Total Assets, $ bn

Figure 6: Balance sheets of various major European banks.

Source: Bloomberg.

Thus, as a result of deregulation a double movement occurred: commercial banks moved into investment bank territory and investment banks moved into commercial bank territory. This led to a situation in which both the commercial banks and the investment banks built up a lethal combination of credit and liquidity risks.

3.2. The mirage of self-regulation of financial markets

A centerpiece of the efficient market theory was that financial markets were capable of self-regulation, making government regulation redundant. And since bureaucrats lack the expertise and the incentives to regulate, government regulation was seen as harmful.

Two mechanisms were seen as central in making self-regulation work. One was the role of rating agencies; the other was the use of mark-to-market rules.

Rating agencies, so we were told, would guarantee a fair and objective rating of banks and their financial products. This is so because it was in the interest of rating agencies to do so. These agencies were large and had to protect their reputation. Without their reputation the value of their rating would be worthless. So, contrary to government bureaucrats, the rating agents would do the best possible job to ensure that banks created safe financial products because it was in their interest to do so.

It did not happen. The reason was that there was massive conflict of interest in the rating agencies. These both advised financial institutions on how to create new financial products and later on gave a favorable rating to the same products. Their incentives, instead of leading to the creation of sound and safe financial products, were skewed towards producing risky and unsafe products. So far for the superior incentives of rating agencies.

The other mechanism in the belief that markets would regulate themselves was the idea of mark-to-market. If financial institutions used mark-to-market rules the discipline of the market would force them to price their products right. Since prices always reflected fundamental values, mark-to-market rules would force financial institutions to reveal the truth about the value of their business, allowing investors to be fully informed when making investment decisions.

The trouble here, again, was the efficiency of markets. As we have illustrated abundantly, financial markets are regularly gripped by bubbles and crashes. In such an environment mark-to-market rules, instead of being a disciplining force, worked pro-cyclically. Thus, during the bubble this rule told accountants that the massive asset price increases corresponded to real profits that should be recorded in the books.

These profits, however, did not correspond to something that had happened in the real economy. They were the result of a bubble that led to prices unrelated to underlying fundamentals. As a result mark-to-market rules exacerbated the sense of euphoria and intensified the bubble.

Now the reverse is happening. Mark-to-market rules force massive write-downs, correcting for the massive overvaluations introduced the years before, intensifying the sense of gloom and the economic downturn.

Thus, the promise of the efficient market paradigm that financial markets would self-regulate was turned upside down. Unregulated financial markets carried the seeds of their own destruction.

4. Unintended Consequences of Regulation

The fact that financial markets do not regulate themselves does not mean that government regulation always works wonderfully. During the 1980s and 1990s attempts were made at imposing capital ratios for banks in all developed countries. This was achieved in the Basel Accords (Basel I and II). It had disastrous consequences because of regulation arbitrage.

Basel I was based on a risk classification of assets and forced banks to set capital aside against these assets based on their risk. For example, Basel I put a low risk weight on loans by banks to other financial institutions. This gave incentives to banks to transfer risky assets (e.g., structured products) which were given a high risk weight by the Basel I regulation off their balance sheets. These assets were transferred in special conduits. The funding of these conduits, however, was often provided by the same or other banks. As a result, bank funding of their activities increasingly occurred through the interbank market. Banks were investing in high risk assets, directly or indirectly, and obtained funding from the interbank (wholesale) market. In contrast to the deposits from the public, these interbank deposits were not guaranteed by the authorities. The building blocks of a future liquidity crisis were put into place.

Figure 7 illustrates the phenomenon. It shows the ratios of total assets to deposits (from the public) of the five largest banks in a number of countries in 2007. I observe that total assets of banks were more than twice the size of the deposits. Put differently, in all these countries deposits from the public funded less than half of banks' assets. Funding was increasingly done in the (volatile) wholesale market. As a result, banks created large leverage effects, i.e., they increased their return on

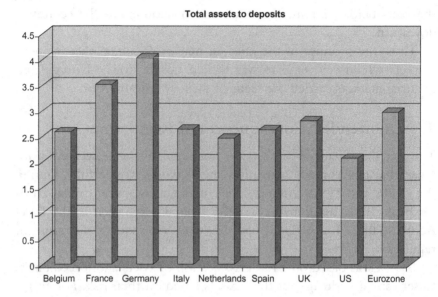

Figure 7: Ratio of banks' total assets to deposits (top 5 banks in each country), in 2007.

Source: Bankscope, Eurostat.

capital by massive borrowing. Unfortunately, they failed to price the large liquidity risks implicit in such leveraging.

Another case of regulatory arbitrage would have equally dangerous consequences. This arbitrage occurred because Basel I made it possible for banks to treat assets that are insured as government securities. As a result, Basel I gave these assets a zero risk weight. This feature was fully exploited by banks and led to the explosion of the use of CDS (credit default swaps) which insured the credit risk of banks' financial assets. In so doing, it created the illusion in the banking system that the assets on their balance sheets carried no or a very low risk.

This turned out to be wrong. The reason, again, has something to do with inefficiencies in financial markets. Financial models used to price CDS are based on the assumption that returns are normally distributed. There is one general feature in all financial markets, however, and that is that returns are not normally distributed. Returns have fat tails, i.e., large changes in the prices occur with a much greater

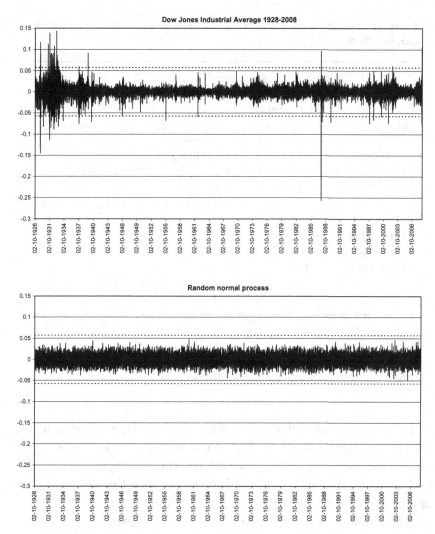

Figure 8: Normally distributed returns and observed daily returns in foreign exchange market.

probability than the probability obtained from a normal distribution. This fat tail feature is itself intimately linked to the occurrence of bubbles and crashes. The implication of this is that models based on normal distributions of returns dramatically underestimate the probability of large shocks.

Table 1: Six largest movements of the Dow-Jones industrial average in October 2008.

A *non-normal* October		
Date	Percentage Change[1]	Average Frequency under Normal Law[2]
07/10/2008	–5.11%	Once in 5,345 Years
09/10/2008	–7.33%	Once in 3,373,629,757 Years
13/10/2008	11.08%	Once in 603,033,610,921,669,000,000,000 Years[3]
15/10/2008	–7.87%	Once in 171,265,623,633 Years
22/10/2008	–5.86%	Once in 117,103 Years
28/10/2008	10.88	Once in 73,357,946,799,753,900,000,000 Years[3]

[1] Daily returns from 01/01/1971 — to 31/10/2008 (*Source*: Datastream).
[2] The mean of the distribution is set to zero and the standard deviation computed over the whole sample (St. Dev. = 1.032%).
[3] This is a vastly longer period than the age of our universe.

I show an example of this phenomenon in Figure 8. This shows the daily changes (returns) of the Dow Jones Industrial since 1928 (upper panel), and compare these observed returns with hypothetical ones that are generated by a normal distribution with the same standard deviation (lower panel). The contrast is striking.

I have added dotted horizontal lines. These represent the returns five standard deviations away from the mean. In a world of normally distributed returns, an observation which deviates from the mean by five times the standard deviation occurs only once every 7000 years (given that the observations are daily). In reality (upper panel) such large changes occurred 74 times during an 80-year period.

The models used to price credit default swaps and many other complex financial products massively underestimated this tail risk. They did not take into account that financial markets are regularly gripped by bubbles and crashes producing large changes in asset prices. Table 1 illustrates how spectacularly wrong one can be when one uses standard finance models that routinely assume normally distributed returns. I selected the six largest daily percentage changes in the Dow Jones Industrial Average during October 2008 (which was a month of unusual turbulence in the stock markets), and asked the question: how frequently do these changes occur, assuming that these events are normally distributed? The results are truly astonishing. There were two daily changes of more than 10% during the month. With a standard deviation of daily changes of 1.032% (computed over the period 1971–2008) movements of such a magnitude can occur only once every 73 to 603 trillion billion years. Yet it happened twice during the same month. A truly miraculous event, for finance theorists living in a world of normally distributed returns. The other four changes during the same month of October have a somewhat higher frequency, but surely we did not expect these to happen in our lifetime.

Our conclusion should be not that these events are miraculous but that our finance models are wrong. By assuming that changes in stock prices are normally distributed, these models underestimate risk in a spectacular way. As a result, investors have been misled in a very big way, believing that the risks they were taking were small. The risks were very big.

In addition, there were no incentives to price this tail risk because there was an implicit expectation that if something very bad would happen, e.g., a liquidity crisis (a typical tail risk), central banks would provide the liquidities. This created the perception in banks that liquidity risk was not something to worry about.

5. On Causes and Triggers

The fundamental cause of the banking crisis is a structural one. Deregulation made it possible for commercial banks to also perform the activities of investment banks, and for investment banks to also perform activities of commercial banks (i.e., to borrow short and to lend long). This had the effect of allowing these institutions to combine liquidity and credit risks in an uncontrolled way. When these risks are mixed too much, they create an explosive cocktail that will explode sooner or later. In this sense, the subprime crisis was just a trigger. If the subprime crisis had not erupted, another solvency problem would have done the trick of setting in motion the devilish interaction between solvency and liquidity crises.

A lot has been made of the low interest rate policies pursued for too long by the US Federal Reserve after 2001 as a cause of the credit crisis. There can be no doubt that this policy helped to produce a bubble in the US housing market, and in so doing contributed to the credit crisis. The point we want to stress here is that this policy led to a banking crisis because the banking sector was allowed to create lethal combinations of credit and liquidity risks. Even without the easy money policies pursued by the US, a banking crisis would have erupted sooner or later.

The same can be said of another factor that is often invoked as an important cause of the credit crisis, i.e., the international current account imbalances. Asian countries accumulated large current account surpluses during the last decade matched mainly by the large current account deficits of the US. This imbalance was the result of large saving surpluses in Asian countries that were channeled to (mainly) the US. Thus, the Asian savings surpluses made it possible to finance the dissaving of the US private and government sectors and helped to fuel a consumption boom in the US. Again, there is no doubt that these macroeconomic imbalances have created problems. But it is difficult to see how they are responsible for a banking crisis. After all, the essence of banking is to channel saving surpluses from those who want to save to those who want to spend. Banking thrives on these "imbalances." Without these imbalances there would be no banking. These imbalances may have contributed to bubbles in the US but these bubbles led to a banking crisis because banks were allowed to fully participate in them.

6.   The Reaction of the Authorities

The authorities of the major developed countries have reacted to the crisis by using three types of instruments.

First, central banks have performed massive liquidity infusions to prevent a liquidity crisis from bringing down the banking system. Second, governments have introduced state guarantees on interbank deposits aimed at preventing a collapse of the interbank market which would almost certainly have led to large-scale liquidity crisis. Third, governments have reacted to bank failures by massive recapitalizations of banks, and in a number of cases by outright nationalizations.

It must be said that these interventions have been successful in that they have prevented a collapse of the banking system. The issue that arises here however, is whether these interventions will suffice to avert future crises and to bring the banking system back on track so that it can perform its function of credit creation.

The fundamental problem banks face today is that their balance sheets are massively inflated as a result of their participation in consecutive bubbles. As asset prices tumble everywhere, banks face a period during which their balance sheets will shrink substantially. This process is unlikely to be a smooth one.

The massive deleveraging of the banking system will give strong incentives to banks not to extend new loans, thereby dragging down the real economy. How far and how long this will go, nobody knows. It is not inconceivable that this leads to a long and protracted downward movement in economic activity.

7. Short-term Solutions

The solutions in the short-term will invariably involve a return of Keynesian economics. First and foremost, governments will have to sustain aggregate demand by increased spending in the face of dwindling tax revenues. Large budget deficits will be inevitable and also desirable. Attempts at balancing government budgets would not work, as it would likely lead to Keynes' savings paradox: as private agents attempt to increase savings, the decline in production and national income actually prevents them from doing so. This paradox can only be solved by government dissaving.

Second, in the process of recapitalizing banks, governments will substitute private debt for government debt. This also is inevitable and desirable. As agents distrust private debt, they turn to government debt which is deemed safer. Governments will have to accommodate this desire. (See Minsky (1986) on this).

8. Long-term Solutions: A Return to Narrow Banking

Preventing the collapse of the banking system and making it function again are daunting tasks in the short run. Equally important is to start working on the rules for a new banking system. There are two ways to go forward. One can be called the Basel approach, the other the Glass-Steagall approach.

The Basel approach accepts as a *fait accompli* that banks will go on performing both traditional and investment bank activities. This approach then consists in defining and implementing rules governing the risks that these banks can take. Its philosophy is that a suitable analysis of the risk profile of the banks' asset portfolios allows for calculating the required capital to be used as a buffer against future shocks in credit risk. Once these minimum capital ratios are in place, credit risk accidents can be absorbed by the existing equity, preventing banks from going broke and thereby avoiding the devilish spillovers from solvency problems into liquidity problems.

This approach has failed. As was argued earlier, it was first implemented in the Basel 1 accord, but was massively circumvented by banks that profited from the loopholes in the system. Basel 2 attempted to remedy this by allowing banks to use internal risk models to compute their minimum capital ratios. The underlying assumption was that scientific advances in risk analysis would make it possible to develop a reliable method of determining minimum capital ratios.

This approach at managing risks of banks does not work and will never do because it assumes efficiency of financial markets; an assumption that must be rejected.[4] Banks that fully participate in

---

[4] There is a second reason why it will not work and that is conflict of interests. Supervisors should not trust complex risk models produced by bankers because the latter have a strong incentive not to reveal their true risk exposures.

the financial markets subject themselves to the endemic occurrence of bubbles and crashes. These lead to large tail risks that with our present knowledge cannot be quantified. In addition, when a liquidity crisis erupts, usually triggered by solvency problems in one or more banks, the interaction between liquidity and solvency crises is set in motion. No minimum capital ratio can stop such a spiral. Perfectly solvent banks capable of showing the best capital ratios can be caught by that spiral eliminating their capital base in a few hours. The Basel approach does not protect the banks from this spiral (a tail risk). In addition, there is no prospect for gaining substantial knowledge about tail risks in the near future. The Basel approach must be abandoned.

This leaves only one workable approach. This is a return to the Glass-Steagall Act approach, or put differently, a return to narrow banking in which the activities banks can engage in are narrowly circumscribed. In this approach, banks are excluded from investing in equities, derivatives and complex structured products. Investment in such products can only be performed by financial institutions and investment banks which are forbidden from funding these investments by deposits (either obtained from the public or from other commercial banks).

In a nutshell, a return to narrow banking could be implemented as follows. Financial institutions would be forced to choose between the status of a commercial bank and that of a investment bank. Only the former would be allowed to attract deposits from the public and from other commercial banks, and to transform these into a loan portfolio with a longer maturity (duration). Commercial banks would benefit from the lender of last resort facility and deposit insurance, and would be subject to the normal bank supervision and regulation. The other financial institutions that do not opt for commercial bank status would have to ensure that the duration of their liabilities is on average at least as long as the duration of their assets. This would imply, for example, that they would not be allowed to finance their illiquid assets by short-term credit lines from commercial banks. Thus, while commercial banks would be barred from engaging themselves in the activities of investment banks, the reverse would also hold, i.e., investment banks would not be allowed to borrow short and to lend long, thereby not taking on liquidity risks.

Thus, we would return to a world where banking activities are tightly regulated and separated from investment banking activities. This also implies that commercial banks would not be allowed anymore to sell (securitize) their loan portfolio. The reason is that securitization does not eliminate risk for the banks. Rather, the contrary is true. First, when a commercial bank repackages loans it is difficult to eliminate its liability associated with these loans. And as we have seen, when a credit risk materializes, these secuterized loans reappear on the balance sheets of the banks, greatly increasing their risks and undermining their capital base. Second, as argued earlier, securitization leads to a build-up of the credit pyramid. When a bank secuterizes a loan, it obtains new liquidities that can be used to grant new loans, which in turn can be used to secuterize further. As a result, a credit expansion is made possible which occurs outside the supervision and control of the central bank (which, however, will be called upon to buy these assets when it becomes the lender of last resort). Put differently, securitization allows the credit multiplier to increase for any given level of the money base provided by the central bank. Credit gets out of control, endangering the whole banking system, including the central bank. It is worth stressing the latter point. The massive credit expansion made possible by securitization also endangers the balance sheet of the central bank. This is so because in times of crisis, the central bank is called upon to function as a lender of last resort. As a result, it will be faced with the need to accept secuterized assets that were created by banks as collateral. Allowing banks to secuterize thus means that the central bank takes on a substantial part of the risk.

The preceding argument also implies that the "originate and distribute model" that banks have increasingly used in the recent past must be abandoned. Recent proposals to save it by requiring banks to hold a fraction of the secuterized assets on their balance sheets are inappropriate as they do not eliminate the risk arising from the multiplication of credit described in the previous paragraph.

To conclude: banks take extraordinary risks that are implicitly insured by the central bank in the form of lender of last resort. The central banks have the right to impose upon banks that they minimize credit risks. These cannot be eliminated completely, but they can certainly be contained by severely restricting the nature of the loans that banks can grant.

A return to narrow banking will necessitate a cooperative international approach. When only one or a few countries return to narrow banking, the banks of these countries will face a competitive disadvantage. They will lose market share to banks that are less tightly regulated. As a result, they will have forceful arguments to lobby domestically against the tight restrictions they face. In the end, the governments of these countries will yield and the whole process of deregulation will start again.

9.   Conclusion

The paradigm that financial markets are efficient has provided the intellectual backbone for the deregulation of the banking sector since the 1980s. Deregulation has made it possible for banks to be fully involved in financial markets. As a result, these banks combine the activities of traditional banks and investment banks. In addition, the total absence of regulation of investment banks has made it possible for these institutions to move in the direction of commercial banking in the sense that they became institutions that, like traditional banks, fund their long-term assets by short-term liabilities. This double movement, i.e., commercial banks moving into investment bank territory and investment banks moving into commercial bank territory, has led to a situation in which both the traditional banks and the investment banks built up a lethal combination of credit and liquidity risks.

There is now overwhelming evidence that financial markets are not efficient. Bubbles and crashes are an endemic feature of financial markets in capitalist countries. Thus, as a result of deregulation, the balance sheets of banks became fully exposed to these bubbles and crashes. As a result, banks which by their very nature are subject to liquidity risks added large amounts of credit risks onto their balance sheets; an explosive cocktail. Investment banks that traditionally take on a lot of credit risk (exposed as they are to the vagaries of financial markets), added the liquidity risks typically reserved for traditional banks to their balance sheets.

The Basel approach to stabilize the banking system has as an implicit assumption that financial markets are efficient, allowing us to model the risks banks take and to compute the required capital ratios that will minimize this risk. I have argued that this approach is unworkable because the risks that matter for banks are tail risks, associated with bubbles and crashes. These cannot be quantified. As a result, there is only one way out, and that is to return to narrow banking, a model that emerged after the previous large-scale banking crisis of the 1930s but that was discarded during the 1980s and 1990s under the influence of the efficient market paradigm. Application of this model will lead to a situation in which activities of commercial and investment banks are strictly separated.

References

Chancellor, Edward (1999). *Devil Take the Hindmost: A History of Financial Specula-tion*. New York: Farrar, Straus and Giroux.

De Grauwe, Paul, and Marianna Grimaldi, (2006). *The Exchange Rate in a Behavioural Finance Framework*. Princeton University Press.

Garber, Peter (2000). *Famous First Bubbles: The Fundamentals of Early Manias*. Cambridge, Mass: MIT Press.

Goodhart, Charles, and Gerhard Illing (eds.) (2002). *Financial Crises, Contagion, and the Lender of Last Resort: A Reader*. Oxford University Press.

Greenspan, Alan (2007). *The Age of Turbulence: Adventures in a New World*. London Penguin Books.

Kindleberger, Charles (2005). *Manias, Panics, and Crashes*, 5th Ed. New York: Wiley.

Minsky, Hyman (1986). *Stabilizing an Unstable Economy*. New York: McGraw-Hill.

Shiller, Robert (2000). *Irrational Exuberance*. Princeton University Press.

Shleifer, Andrei (2000). *Inefficient Markets: An Introduction To Behavioral Finance (Clarendon Lectures in Economics)*. New York: Oxford University Press.

Chapter 3

The Political Economy of Transatlantic Regulatory Cooperation and Competition: A (Unofficial) View from Europe

André Sapir

Professor of Economics, ECARES
Université Libre de Bruxelles
Senior Fellow, Bruegel
asapir@ulb.ac.be

1. Introduction

In January 2007, at the start of the German presidency of the European Union (EU) and the G-8, Chancellor Merkel declared her intention to seek a "new transatlantic partnership" with the United States (US). In an interview with the Financial Times, she stated that:

> At the forthcoming EU–US summit we want to talk about ever-closer economic co-operation. Our economic systems are based on the same values. The EU and the US have sophisticated patent legislation. We have regulatory mechanisms governing our financial markets. We should be looking for ways to keep developing these together at a transatlantic level. We must watch out that we do not drift apart, but instead come closer together, where there are clear advantages for both sides. For example, it causes unnecessary friction for patent rules in the US to be structured differently from those in the EU. I think our economies can save a lot of money and effort, in stock market share offerings, for instance, or in setting technical standards. We face the same tough competition from Asian markets and from Latin America in the future. We must join forces and co-operate, for instance in the fight for better intellectual property protection in the global market. (*Financial Times*, 2007).

At the annual EU–US summit held in Washington in April 2007, Chancellor Merkel, President Bush and European Commission (EC) President Barroso signed the "Framework for Advancing Transatlantic Economic Integration between the European Union and the United States of America." Key elements of this framework were the adoption of a work programme of cooperation and the establishment of the Transatlantic Economic Council (TEC) to "oversee, guide and accelerate" the implementation of this work programme. The TEC is a permanent body co-chaired by two top officials, Allan Hubbard, the senior White House economic adviser (replaced by Daniel Price in December 2007), and EC vice-president Günter Verheugen.

The creation of the TEC was hailed in Brussels as a huge achievement, opening "a new era for transatlantic economic integration." The first meeting of the Council, held in Washington in November 2007, was regarded by the European Commission as

> …a milestone that will further strengthen the economic partnership between two economic giants, the EU and the US. Enhancing our economic cooperation is of the utmost importance for both of us and should especially be aimed at reducing unnecessary administrative and regulatory burdens for businesses and in the long term [for] consumers. (Europa, 2007).

Outside official circles, two views have accompanied the so-called "Merkel initiative" and the launch of the TEC. One maintains that the initiative adds little to previous efforts to strengthen transatlantic ties, and that it would not survive beyond the end of the German presidency of the G-8 in December 2007. The other view argues instead that the Merkel initiative is really different from previous transatlantic efforts, if only because the EU and the US face new and similar global challenges that necessitate stronger bilateral ties. The purpose of this chapter is to evaluate these two opposing views.[1]

---

[1]This paper does not cover a discussion of EU–US relations in the context of the financial crisis, which would deserve an essay on its own.

2. The New Transatlantic Economic Partnership: Hype or Hope?

Attempts to promote transatlantic economic integration are not new. The first attempt came in the early 1960s, just after the creation of the European Economic Community, when the US administration proposed the creation of a North Atlantic Free Trade Area (NAFTA). The idea re-emerged in the early 1990s under the label Transatlantic Free Trade Area, or TAFTA, the acronym NAFTA having meanwhile been taken by the North American Free Trade Agreement. The impetus this time came from Europeans who feared that the end of the Cold War might result in disengagement by Americans from Europe and the collapse of NATO. Although politically motivated, TAFTA encountered strong economic opposition on both sides of the Atlantic, which eventually led to the creation of the less ambitious New Transatlantic Agenda (NTA) in 1995.[2]

The NTA essentially ignores the more contentious conventional trade barriers (such as those in agriculture), focusing instead on regulatory issues, including competition policy. It involves three forums — the Transatlantic Legislators' Dialogue (TLD), the Transatlantic Consumer Dialogue (TACD) and the Transatlantic Business Dialogue (TABD) — which bring legislative, consumer and business leaders together with high-level officials from Europe and America with a view to promoting transatlantic regulatory cooperation.

Likewise, the New Transatlantic Economic Partnership launched by Chancellor Merkel aims to reduce regulatory obstacles in key economic sectors, including industrial products, energy, intellectual property, financial markets and emerging technologies. Like its predecessor, the new initiative relies on the TLD, the TACD and the TABD to reach out to the main stakeholders and give a voice to their concerns. However, it contains a major innovation, the Transatlantic Economic Council, the high-level political body tasked with reporting progress and problems to the EU and US leaders at their annual summit. The TEC is

---

[2]Meanwhile, the acronym TAFTA has also been taken. It now refers to the Thailand–Australia Free Trade Area, which entered into force in 2005.

assisted by a Group of Advisers, consisting of the co-chairs of the three transatlantic dialogues.

Thus, the Merkel initiative can be seen as an attempt to revive the moribund New Transatlantic Agenda launched in 1995 by adding a potentially crucial new element, the Transatlantic Economic Council. The TEC has met twice so far, once in November 2007 in Washington and once in Brussels in May 2008, a few weeks ahead of the 2008 annual EU–US summit. Progress so far has been slow but not entirely insignificant.[3] However it has hit a difficult roadblock on a subject that hardly qualifies as a "key economic sector," but is illustrative of the difficulty on the European side to deliver on the regulatory agenda.

At the second TEC meeting, the EU co-chair and EC vice-president, Günter Verheugen, promised that the Commission would put forward a proposal to lift the 1997 EU ban on the import of US chlorinated poultry. The US side regarded the lifting of the ban as a test case for the credibility of the Transatlantic Council. Two weeks later, the European Commission (EC) did submit the proposal to the Standing Committee on Food Chain and Animal Health. However, the Committee voted to keep the ban on US poultry imports, with 26 EU member states rejecting the EC proposal. According to EU comitology rules, the Commission's proposal will go to the Agriculture Council, which is likely to follow the advice of the Standing Committee. In the meantime, at the June 2008 EU–US summit it was stressed that that in order "to fulfill the TEC's mandate of creating a barrier-free transatlantic market, it is essential that both sides follow through on their commitments...."

What the poultry situation illustrates is that when the Commission, which alone represents the EU on the TEC, is not ultimately responsible for EU regulation, it may be unable to deliver on its commitment in the TEC, thereby putting the new transatlantic regulatory agenda in

---

[3]See the Transatlantic Economic Council's Report to the EU–US Summit 2008, "Review of Progress Under the Framework for Advancing Transatlantic Economic Integration Between the European Union and the United States of America".

doubt. Unfortunately, this situation is common. In fact, the opposite case is the exception.

Competition policy is really the only area where the Commission acts as the (sole) EU regulator. This is also the only policy area where the EU has exclusive competence, and where the Commission has been granted unconditional delegation by the member states.[4] In this area, therefore, the Commission has exceptional authority to conclude regulatory agreements with foreign partners like the United States.

The Commission enjoys far-reaching powers of extraterritoriality in the enforcement of EU competition rules.[5] Unilateral exercise of such power clearly risks creating serious tensions with countries where large companies are headquartered, and which are the most likely target of EU antitrust action. The United States is obviously the prime country concerned. There have been a number of instances where the Commission has acted to block a merger between two US-based companies (i.e., Boeing/McDonnell Douglas, and General Electric/Honeywell) or sought to prevent the abuse of dominant power in the EU market by US-based corporations (i.e., Intel, Microsoft and Qualcom), which could have resulted in serious EU–US disputes. In fact, no major clash has occurred on account of the excellent formal cooperation between the EU and US competition regulatory authorities initiated in the early 1990s.

The main obstacle to extending the competition policy example to other areas is the lack of a single regulator and hence of a single voice on the European side.

The difficulty for Europe to negotiate with foreign partners on regulatory matters is well illustrated by the situation in financial markets, one of the areas singled out in the New Transatlantic Economic Partnership. Becht and Correia da Silva (2007) show that Europe's international role in this area is often severely impeded by its inability to adopt EU-wide regulation. A noteworthy exception is in the field of accounting, where the EU was instrumental in promoting the

---

[4]See Coeuré and Pisani-Ferry (2007).
[5]See Bertrand and Ivaldi (2007).

creation of an international standard and in making it compulsory for all EU-listed companies.

To a large extent, therefore, Europe's ability to negotiate in the regulatory area with foreign partners like the United States is a function of its internal organization. Where the Commission is the EU regulator — basically, only in competition policy — it can deliver. Where it is not the ultimate EU regulator, but the Commission is nonetheless the single external EU voice, for instance because the issue has a trade policy angle — like in the poultry case — it can make international commitments, but only conditionally on the approval of the member states who are, then, the actual EU regulators.

Can the European Union overcome the structural weakness of its internal organization and be a reliable partner in international regulatory negotiations, or does the increasing number and diversity of its member states suggest that this impediment will remain a permanent feature of the EU?

Two factors suggest that progress is the more likely of the two options, and particularly that it is more likely today than it was at the beginning of the 1990s, when the transatlantic regulatory agenda was launched. The first is that the EU has changed substantially since then; the second is that the world has changed equally.

3. New EU and a New World[6]

In the last 20 years or so, Europe has changed greatly: it has expanded from 12 to 27 members, created a unified internal market, and introduced a single currency, the euro. The European Union (EU) is now the largest economic entity in the world, with half a billion people and a gross domestic product (GDP) slightly larger than that of the United States. Its presence in the world economy is potent: it is the largest exporter and the second largest importer (behind the US) of goods; the largest exporter and importer of services; the largest importer of energy; the largest donor of foreign aid; the second largest source of

---

[6]This and the next section draw heavily on Sapir (2007a).

foreign direct investment (FDI) and the second largest destination of FDI (behind the US); and the second largest destination of foreign migrants (also behind the US). See Table 1.

The EU's presence in the world economy manifests itself not only through trade, capital and migratory flows but also via an intense regulatory activity. It is, if not the main, at least the second, most important regulatory power in the world in just about every area, including: competition policy, where EU authorities have taken the lead in certain aspects of antitrust; environmental protection, where the EU is the proponent of regulation against global warming; money, with the euro being the second largest international currency in the world (behind the US dollar); and financial market regulation, with European markets also ranking number two in the world (again behind the US).

The world economy has also changed a great deal during the past 20 years. By far the most important development is globalization, which is characterized by the emergence of a number of developing countries with the technological capability to supply increasingly sophisticated ranges of manufactured goods and services. These emerging economies are located essentially in Asia and Latin America and include new global powers — China, India and Brazil — with huge populations and very rapid economic growth. As shown in Table 2, the emerging countries now account for nearly 30% of world GDP (measured at Purchasing Power Parity), whereas the EU and the US each account for only roughly 20%. The BRICs alone (i.e., Brazil, Russia, India and China) are as large as the EU-27 or the United States.

The upshot is that "Europe and the global economy" has become the central theme of the European narrative for the 21st century. In 2007, on the occasion of the 50th anniversary of Europe and the celebration of a peaceful European political order, heads of state and government proclaimed that the EU is an effective response to major global challenges, which allows Europeans to "shape the increasing interdependence of the global economy and ever-growing competition on international markets according to [their] values". Many leaders like EC President Barroso declared that the new raison d'être of the EU is "to use its collective weight to shape globalization" in order "to help

Table 1: Indicators of size and openness, EU25 and US, 2005.

Size	EU25	USA	Openness	EU25	USA
		Macroeconomics			
Share of World GDP (current US$)	30	28	—	—	—
Share of World GDP (PPP)	20	20	—	—	—
		Trade			
Share of World Trade*	18.1	16.7	Trade as a Share of GDP*	19.2	20.8
		Energy			
Energy Consumption (TFC)	16.8	21.6	Share of Imports in Energy Consumption	72.1	42.2
		Environment			
CO_2 Emissions	15.5	22.9	—	—	—
		Development			
Share of Official Development Assistance	52%	26%	Share of ODA in GDP	0.41	0.22
		Finance			
Share of World Financial Markets**	22	46.9	Share of Foreign Assets in Total Holdings***	33.1	10.2
		Migration			
Share of World Immigration****	20.9	20.2	Share of Foreign-Born in Population*****	8.6	12.9

Source: Coeuré and Pisani-Ferry (2007) based on various official sources.
*Intra-EU25 trade excluded.
** Sum of stock market capitalization and domestic debt securities issued by the private sector.
*** Intra-EU25 foreign asset holdings excluded.
**** Share of world foreign born population, including intra-EU25 migration.
***** Intra-EU25 migration included.

Table 2: Europe, the United States and the World, 2007.

	Population (2007) (% of world)	GDP at PPP (2007) (% of world)	GDP per head (2007) (EU27 = 100)	GDP growth (1998–2007) (% per annum)
European Union (27)	7.6	22.7	100.0	2.4
(Euro area)	(4.9)	(16.1)	109.7	(2.1)
United States	4.6	21.3	154.0	3.1
EU neighbors*	10.5	10.4	34.0	4.2
(Russia)	(2.2)	(3.2)	(49.4)	(5.4)
Other advanced	4.4	14.7	111.7	1.8
(Japan)	(2.0)	(6.6)	(112.8)	(1.3)
Emerging economies**	61.0	28.6	15.6	6.1
(China)	(20.3)	(10.8)	(17.8)	(9.1)
(India)	(17.3)	(4.6)	(8.9)	(6.6)
(Brazil)	(2.9)	(2.8)	(32.6)	(2.4)
Other developing***	11.8	2.3	6.9	4.3
World	100.0	100.0	33.6	4.1
Memo items:				
G7****	11.2	43.5	130.4	2.4
BRICs*****	42.7	21.4	16.8	7.8

Source: own computations based on IMF (2008) updating the table in Sapir (2007a).
* Rest of Europe (including Russia and other CIS countries), Middle East and North Africa.
** Developing Asia and Latin America.
*** Sub-Saharan Africa.
**** Canada, France, Germany, Italy, Japan, United Kingdom and United States.
***** Brazil, Russia, India and China.

Europeans prosper in a globalised world" and "to create a new and better global order."

4.   Prospects for the New Transatlantic Agenda

The EU and the United States are the two largest economic entities in the world. Their economic relationship, therefore, matters a great deal not only to themselves but also to the world at large.

The bilateral EU–US trade relationship — the largest in the world — takes place essentially within the framework of the multilateral trading system. Although there are naturally some trade frictions between the two partners, the bilateral relationship runs quite smoothly. In fact, out of 171 trade disputes brought to the WTO during the period 2000–2006, seven were complaints by the US against the EU and 13 by the EU against the US, which makes an average of only three transatlantic disputes per year. Granted, some of them (such as the Airbus-Boeing case) are fairly significant, but they are nonetheless relatively minor in the overall scheme of things.

What is special about the EU and the US is that they jointly continue to be the "regulators of the world." Even though together they only account for 40% of world GDP (at PPP) and world trade and a little more than 10% of world population, they probably produce around 80% of the international norms and standards that regulate world markets, including the dollar and the euro. Although this leadership is bound to diminish as new powers emerge and become more assertive, it is likely to persist for a few decades, because China, India and the other emerging powers are still far from having developed at home the set of elaborate legislation and institutions that are essential for them to be effective regulators. In fields like competition policy, product and financial markets regulation, or technical standards, the US and the EU are and will remain advantaged by their development level, their experience and the size of their markets. Even Japan, a country of comparable development, has not really challenged their leadership in this area.

Will the EU and the US act separately or even as rivals on the global regulatory scene or will they cooperate with each other and with the new global powers? Regulatory competition is certainly positive as a way to identify the best rules. Nonetheless, the EU and the US cannot escape the fact that they both have a vital role to play in setting the rules for the world economy. In the 21st century, however, they can no longer act alone and will need to involve new global powers.

In recent years, the EU and the US have each sought to export their regulatory rules. The common approach has been to include regulatory requirements in bilateral or regional free trade agreements (FTAs) that principally seek reciprocal preferential trade access. There has been a proliferation of FTAs centered on the EU and the US. Initially, most of the FTAs were with countries in the relative vicinity of the EU or the US: the Americas for the United States, and Eastern Europe, the Middle East North America or Sub-Saharan Africa for the European Union. In a second phase, the two hubs went on to sign agreements in each other's "backyard": for instance, the EU with Mexico and Chile, and the United States with Jordan and Morocco.

The latest, and most significant, development is the drive by the EU and the United States to enter into FTAs with emerging Asian economies, many of which are engaged in bilateral negotiations with Asian partners, including China and Japan. The US has already concluded an agreement with Singapore in 2004 and negotiated one with Korea in 2007. The EU started negotiating an FTA with Korea in May 2007 and with India in June of that year.

Clearly, the proliferation of FTAs is a phenomenon that is by no means limited to trade agreements that involve the EU and the United States. There are also many FTAs among countries in Africa, Asia or Latin America. Nonetheless, the fact that the EU and the US are the two largest trading blocs in the world implies that FTAs centered on them pose a far greater systemic challenge to the WTO than any other FTA.

This competitive attitude between the EU and the US in terms of gaining preferential market access and extending regulatory rules to emerging countries manifests itself beyond the signature of FTAs. In competition policy, for instance, the EU maintains different forms of cooperation with various countries, including China to whom the Commission currently provides technical assistance for preparing its first comprehensive competition policy law, which it hopes will be similar to EU competition policy.

In financial market regulation, the EU was the first to adopt in 2005 the International Financial Reporting Standards (IFRS) as the required accounting standard for companies listed in its territory, and the EU has been successfully pushing for their adoption by other countries. The IFRS, whose aim is to harmonize financial reporting in a world of cross-border trade and investment, has already been, or soon will be, adopted by over 100 countries, including Australia, Canada, China, Hong Kong and Russia. The IFRS is a rival to the Generally Accepted Accounting Principles (GAAP) used by the United States and other systems of national standards in major countries, such as India and Japan, where the IFRS is currently not permitted. All these countries are, however, considering recognition of the IFRS as an acceptable set of standards for at least some of the companies listed on their markets.[7] In the end, therefore, the IFRS may actually emerge as the set of standards for global accounting rules.

Clearly, one of the main objectives of the New Transatlantic Economic Partnership initiative is for the EU and the US to change gear and adopt a more cooperative attitude at a time when their global economic leadership is more and more called into question by the emergence of new economic powers.

This view was recently articulated by members of the Commission on Transatlantic Leadership in the Global Economy, convened by the Atlantic Council of the United States, which declared that[8]:

> The United States and the European Union [have not] proven adept at providing leadership in this modern economy. They have too often been divided, sometimes acting as rivals...[N]ow [they] face a serious challenge — the international economic system from which they have prospered so much now hangs in the balance. If they do nothing, the global economy may well fracture — regional arrangements will divide the world into blocs, protectionism and economic nationalism will rise, and the governing institutions will fade into irrelevance. Only with stronger and broader leadership will the global economy continue to be open and stable in the face of the pressures of globalization and economic nationalism.

For the members of the Transatlantic Commission, the EU and the US need to move on two separate, but complementary, fronts. First, they must help rebuild global economic governance by ensuring that all the essential economic players have a stake in the process and are

---

[7] See Véron (2007).
[8] Burwell (2007).

effectively engaged in it. Second, they must promote the development of a new approach to reducing the remaining barriers to trade and investment, with the eventual goal of creating a global market. In their view, as a first step in this direction, the EU and the US should negotiate a series of agreements, including a framework regulatory accord along the lines suggested by Chancellor Merkel, aimed at creating a barrier-free transatlantic market.

Although these various transatlantic initiatives are clearly and rightly couched in the language of the new global economic environment, their ultimate objective is nonetheless somewhat ambiguous. Do they constitute a last-ditch effort to maintain the superiority of the transatlantic incumbent powers against the inevitable rise of new global giants? Or, instead, do they amount to a genuine attempt on the part of America and Europe, who founded the global economic institutions after the Second World War, to share power with the newcomers in order to ensure that these institutions continue their mission of ensuring a world economy of peaceful interdependence?

To put it differently: will bilateral transatlantic regulatory cooperation pave the way for genuine multilateral cooperation?

In the case of competition policy the answer seems to be "yes." The EU and the US were instrumental in the creation, in 2001, of the International Competition Network (ICN), an informal network of antitrust agencies from about 80 developed and developing countries that addresses practical antitrust enforcement and policy issues of common concern. Its aim is to bring "antitrust enforcement into the 21st century. By enhancing convergence and cooperation, the ICN promotes more efficient, effective antitrust enforcement worldwide." But exactly how far cooperation will go is hard to say at the moment.

What is clear is that, at least for a while longer, the EU and the US will continue to dominate the formulation of global rules. But whether they cooperate or compete, the consequences will be huge not only for them but also for the global economy. Bilateral cooperation could pave the way for a new age of global economic governance involving all major actors, old and new alike. By contrast, competition between the EU and the US might result in fragmented rules of the global game and possibly in fights between the two protagonists over alliances with emerging powers that would be detrimental to all countries.

5. Conclusion

As Pollack *et al.* (2002) already noted several years ago, however desirable, transatlantic regulatory cooperation faces many obstacles. First, in many areas, US regulators have greater regulatory independence than their European counterparts, and may therefore resist what they might perceive as an attempt to compromise domestic regulatory standards. Second, transparency and administrative law requirements differ significantly between the two sides of the Atlantic. Third, multi-level governance is a problem that afflicts both sides, not just the EU. In many areas, US states enjoy as much regulatory power vis-à-vis Washington as EU member states do vis-à-vis Brussels. Last, neither the EU nor the United States appear willing to compromise their regulatory sovereignty in the name of transatlantic cooperation. "[I]ndeed, even the most successful experiment in transatlantic regulatory cooperation, that in competition policy, is predicated explicitly on each side's ability to cooperate without any substantial change in its domestic regulatory *objectives and procedures*" (Pollack *et al.*, 2002, p. 37, emphasis added).

Does the "Merkel initiative" provide any hope of surmounting these obstacles? The answer is: Yes and No. The good news is that regulatory cooperation is now viewed as both a political and an economic necessity, and that it is supported by a high-level permanent body, the Transatlantic Economic Council, which reports directly to the principals — on the EU side, the president of the European Council and the president of the EC. The bad news is that regulatory competition between the EU and the US is spreading like wildfire via FTAs with emerging economies, and that cooperation between the two "regulators of the world" is genuinely difficult because the EU and US are both multi-level governance systems with different regulatory objectives and procedures.

References

Becht, Marco and Luis Correia da Silva (2007). External financial markets policy: Europe as global regulator? In *Fragmented Power: Europe and the Global Economy*, André Sapir (ed.), Bruegel: Brussels.

Bertrand, Olivier and Marc Ivaldi (2007). Competition policy: Europe in international markets. In *Fragmented Power: Europe and the Global Economy*, André Sapir (ed.), Bruegel: Brussels.

Burwell, Fran (2007). Transatlantic leadership for a new global economy, Policy Paper, Atlantic Council of the United States: Washington, D.C.

Coeuré, Benoît and Jean Pisani-Ferry (2007). The governance of the European Union's international economic relations: how many voices? In *Fragmented Power: Europe and the Global Economy*, André Sapir (ed.), Bruegel: Brussels.

Europa (2007). VP Verheugen chairs first meeting of Transatlantic Economic Council on 9th November. Press Releases RAPID, IP/07/1662, November 8.

Financial Times (2007). Interview with Angela Markel, January 2. Available at: http://www.ft.com/cms/s/φ/fd3d43φ-9a5b-11db-bbd2-φφφφ779e2340.html

Horn, Henrik, Petros Mavroidis and André Sapir (2010). Beyond the WTO: An anatomy of EU and US preferential trade agreements. *World Economy*, 29, 1451–1581.

Pollack, Mark *et al.* (2002). *The Political Economy of the Transatlantic Partnership*, Report prepared by the RSCAS Transatlantic Programme for and with the contribution of Her Majesty's Treasury (UK) and Ministry of Finance (The Netherlands), European University Institute: Florence.

Sapir, André (2007a). Europe and the global economy, in Sapir (2007b).

Véron, Nicolas (2007). *The Global Accounting Experiment*. Bruegel Blueprint Series, Bruegel: Brussels.

Chapter 4

How Hard and Soft Law Interact in International Regulatory Governance: Alternatives, Complements and Antagonists*

Gregory C. Shaffer
Melvin C. Steen Professor of Law
University of Minnesota Law School
shaffer@umn.edu

Mark A. Pollack
Professor of Political Science
Temple University
mark.pollack@temple.edu

1. Introduction

There has been a considerable amount of legal scholarship regarding the use of "hard" and "soft" law in international governance, written

*We thank John Bronsteen, Manfred Elsig, Brett Frischmann, Tom Ginsburg, Daniel Halberstam, Terence Halliday, Kal Raustiala, Joel Trachtman and Spencer Waller for their comments, as well as the participants at a conference at the University of Michigan entitled "Systemic Implications of Transatlantic Regulatory Cooperation and Competition" on May 8, 2008; at a panel on Transnational Legal Orders at the Law and Society Association conference on May 30, 2008; and at a workshop at Loyola University Chicago School of Law on May 7, 2008. We thank Melissa Beckman, Mathew Bills, Mathew Fortin and Kisa Patel for their research assistance. All errors of course remain our own.

from legal positivist, normative, and political economy perspectives. Within the legal academy, hard law generally refers to legal obligations of a formally binding nature, and soft law to law that is not formally binding but may nonetheless exercise significant influence on behavior. Other social scientists slightly vary these definitions of international hard and soft law, viewing international legal instruments as lying along a hard-soft law continuum in terms of different features, such as the law's precision, obligation and delegation to a third-party for dispute resolution, each of which can be of a harder and softer nature.[1] Much of this literature assesses the relative functional attributes and deficiencies of hard and soft law instruments as alternatives for international governance, as well as how these instruments can be combined sequentially as mutually reinforcing complements to lead to greater international cooperation over time. The literature on hard and soft law, in turn, has influenced our understanding of transatlantic economic cooperation, in which the United States (US) and the European Union (EU) have undertaken a wide range of agreements, both bilateral and multilateral, and largely of a soft law variety.

The existing scholarly literature on hard and soft law can be divided into three camps: legal positivists, rationalists and constructivists.[2] All three of these camps predominantly view hard and soft law as interacting in complementary ways, but they have different starting points. Many legal positivists question if soft law can be considered to be law at all because it is not legally binding, but, in any case, they view it at best as an inferior instrument whose only rationale is to serve as a stepping stone to hard (real) law. Rationalists, in contrast, contend that states choose between hard and soft law instruments depending on the level of commitment that they wish to make. Since rationalists find that both hard and soft law can be advantageous to states in different circumstances, neither should be judged to be superior. For example, rationalists contend that because soft law is less costly for states to negotiate and less costly to their sovereignty, states will prefer it in situations of uncertainty where they need to learn more about the intentions of

---

[1] See Abbott and Snidal (2000) and discussion in Section 2.1.

[2] A full explication of these three modes of scholarship and their approaches to hard and soft law interaction is set forth in Section 2.3.

the other parties or about the underlying technical issues. Constructivists, in contrast to rationalists, maintain that state interests are formed through socialization processes of interstate interaction which soft law can facilitate. They thus favor soft law instruments for their capacity to generate shared norms and a sense of common purpose and identity. Many constructivists also focus on the role of non-state actors who only have soft law instruments available and who use these instruments to catalyze change in international law and national regulatory practice. As with legal positivists, both rationalists and constructivist scholars contend that soft law can lead to hard law and, once formed, can help to further elaborate hard law, resulting in progressive cycles of law-making leading to greater regulatory cooperation.

For the purposes of this chapter, we will remain agnostic as to which of these three camps most accurately captures the nature of hard and soft law and their relative advantages, although we have our own views in this respect.[3] We will remain agnostic because our primary purpose in this chapter is to reveal what is missing in the analysis of all three camps because of their focus on hard-soft law interaction only in complementary terms. We make two central claims. Our first and primary claim is that international hard and soft law instruments (or, for that matter, any legal instruments that vary in their soft and hard law characteristics) can serve not only as alternatives or as complements but indeed as antagonists, working at cross-purposes with each other. Hard and soft law *may* interact as complements, we argue, but only under certain conditions, including most notably the absence of significant distributive conflict among parties to such agreements. Under other conditions, however, which we identify as the existence of distributive conflicts and of pluralistic regime complexes, hard and soft law may interact in an antagonistic fashion. In this sense, the existing literature may be accused of selection bias, focusing on those issue-areas in which distributive conflict is low and where the interaction of hard and soft law is correspondingly largely complementary.

---

[3]Neither of us are legal formalists, and both of us can be viewed primarily as rationalists because of our focus on actors and their interests, although our approach is of a soft rationalist variant which takes seriously constructivist insights.

Our second claim is that this antagonistic interaction between hard and soft law has particular implications in a fragmented international system, affecting the very nature of international hard and soft law regimes and their purported advantages. We will show how the interaction of hard and soft law regimes can lead to the "hardening" of soft law regimes, resulting in more strategic bargaining and reducing their purported advantages of consensus-building through information-sharing and persuasion, and the "softening" of hard law regimes, resulting in reduced legal certainty and predictability.

The chapter is in five parts. Section 2 provides an overview of the existing literature regarding the definitions of hard and soft law (Sec. 2.1), the relative attributes and deficiencies of hard and soft law as alternatives (Sec. 2.2), and how hard and soft law can act as complements, leading to greater cooperation (Sec. 2.3). Section 3 provides the background theoretical context for assessing the roles and interaction of hard and soft law in international regulatory governance as alternatives, complements and antagonists, namely the role of US and EU economic and institutional power (Sec. 3.1), the role of distributive conflict between the US, EU and third countries (Sec. 3.2), and the challenges posed by international regime fragmentation (Sec. 3.3). Section 4 assesses how, in the presence of distributive conflicts and fragmented regime complexes, hard and soft law can just as likely act as opposing tools aimed to counter each other's influence, focusing on the US/EU dispute over genetically modified foods as an illustrative case study.

Section 5 then sets forth three hypotheses regarding how hard and soft law instruments interact in international governance, and, in particular, the conditions under which they work in a complementary or opposing manner. Our first two hypotheses concern the impact of US and EU cooperation and rivalry on how international hard and soft law regimes interact. We contend that where the US and EU agree on a regulatory approach, in particular because distributive conflict between them is weak or absent, we are more likely to see hard and soft law work as complements in an evolutionary manner, consistent with the existing literature (Sec. 5.1). In contrast, where the US and EU disagree on a regulatory approach, we are more likely to see hard and soft law work in opposition to each other, especially where there are distributional consequences which spur the US and EU to attempt to advance their perspectives in different international regimes (Sec. 5.2). Given the fragmented nature of the international system, the US and EU will attempt to advance their interests in those regimes that they find to be most favorable to their positions. In such settings, we argue, soft law regimes may be "hardened" through their links to other regimes, losing the purported soft law advantages of flexibility and informality, while hard law regimes such as the World Trade Organization's dispute-settlement process may be "softened." The United States and the European Union are not the only actors, however, capable of strategically manipulating hard and soft law regimes. Hence, even where the US and EU agree on a regulatory approach, smaller states can also use hard and soft law strategies to attempt to thwart US and EU aims, again choosing regimes more favorable to their positions in a fragmented international system (Sec. 5.3). However, the US and EU have significant advantages because of their market power and resources, and they can attempt to play smaller countries off of each other, including through bilateral negotiations.

We conclude that scholars and policymakers need to recognize more explicitly that there are often real distributive conflicts in international regulatory relations, resulting in conflicts between hard and soft law instruments and regimes. We find that this development is not necessarily to be lamented, but rather reflects a maturation of international law, which is responding to global developments in a world of diverse regulatory competences in which regulation in countries and in diverse international regimes mutually affect each other. This chapter's findings call for future research regarding how international hard and soft law instruments and regimes interact in different contexts.

2. The Canonical Literature on International Hard and Soft Law: Their Attributes as Alternatives and their Interaction as Complements

We begin with an overview of scholarship concerning the definitions of hard and soft law, and this scholarship's assessment of the various attributes and deficiencies of hard and soft law as alternatives. We create a typology of this literature into three camps, each of which predominantly views hard and soft law to act as complements, leading to greater international cooperation. We here provide the background for our argument that the existing literature exhibits a selection bias as regards how hard and soft law interact.

2.1. *Definitions of hard and soft law*

To assess how hard and soft law interact in international governance, we must first define these terms. Here there is much disagreement in the existing literature. Many legal scholars use a simple binary binding/non-binding divide to distinguish hard from soft law.[4] Positivist legal scholars tend to deny the very concept of "soft law," since law by definition is "binding."[5] Rational institutionalist scholars respond that "the term 'binding agreement' is a misleading hyperbole" when it comes to international affairs, but they still find that the language of "binding commitments" matters in terms of signaling by states of the seriousness of their commitments, such that non compliance will entail greater reputational costs.[6] Constructivist scholars, in contrast, focus less on the binding nature of law at the enactment stage, and more

---

[4]See the leading study by Shelton (2000), which settles for this distinction. See also Reininke and Witte (2000, p. 76) ("soft law as used herein means normative agreements that are not legally binding"); Snyder (1993, p. 32) ("soft law consists of "rules of conduct which, in principle, have no legally binding force but which nevertheless may have practical effects"); and Klabbers (1996, p. 168) (advocating retention of the "traditional binary conception of law").

[5]Klabbers takes a positivist approach, arguing that "law can't be more or less binding" so that the soft law concept is logically flawed. Klabbers (1996, p. 181). Prosper Weil takes a normative approach, arguing that the increasing use of soft law represents a shift pursuant to which international law norms vary in their relative normativity, and he finds that this trend "might destabilize the whole international normative system and turn it into an instrument that can no longer serve its purpose." Weil (1983, p. 423).

[6]Lipson (1991, p. 508). See also Raustiala (2005) and Guzman (2005, 2008). Guzman (2005, p. 591) states that "an agreement is soft if it is not a formal treaty." He finds that states rationally choose soft law because they wish to reduce the cost to their reputation of potentially violating it in light of uncertainty.

on the effectiveness of law at the implementation stage, addressing the gap between the law-in-the-books and the law-in-action. They note how even domestic law varies in terms of its impact on behavior, so that binary distinctions between binding "hard law" and non-binding "soft law" are illusory.[7] They find that the very concept of "binding" international law is highly suspect as an operational concept. At the international level where centralized institutions are typically missing, most observers realize that "most international law is 'soft' in distinctive ways."[8]

Working within the rationalist perspective, Kenneth Abbott and his coauthors have defined legalization in international relations as consisting of a spectrum of three factors: (i) precision of rules; (ii) obligation; and (iii) delegation to a third-party decision-maker.[9] International regimes vary in the extent of their legalization along these dimensions, which can give them a "harder" or "softer" legal character. In this respect, hard law "refers to legally binding obligations that are precise (or can be made precise through adjudication or the issuance of detailed regulations) and that delegate authority for interpreting and implementing the law."[10] International trade law, at least formally, comes closest to this ideal type, although as we will see, it too is soft (or can become soft) in certain areas.[11]

By contrast with this ideal-type of hard law, soft law can be defined as a residual category: "The realm of 'soft law' begins once legal arrangements are weakened along one or more of the dimensions of

---

[7]Some scholars accuse legal formalists of "elite ignorance" and "non-knowledge of the social." See, for example, Goodrich (2000, p. 150).

[8]Abbott and Snidal (2000, p. 421).

[9]Abbott *et al.* (2000). Abbott and Snidal work within a "rational design" approach to international institutions, in Koremenos, Lipson, and Snidal (2001). See also Guzman (2008).

[10]Abbott and Snidal (2000, p. 37).

[11]See our discussion in Section 4 below. In addition, from a formal perspective, international trade law does not have independent enforcement power. Rather, WTO panels authorize a winning party to withdraw equivalent concessions, in an amount determined by the panel, in the event of non compliance by the losing party.

obligation, precision and delegation."[12] Thus, if an agreement is not formally binding, it is soft along one dimension. Similarly, if an agreement is formally binding but its content is vague so that the agreement leaves almost complete discretion to the parties as to its implementation, then the agreement is soft along this second dimension. Finally, if an agreement does not delegate any authority to a third-party to monitor its implementation or to interpret and enforce it, then the agreement again can be soft because the parties can discursively justify their acts in legalistic terms with less consequence, whether in terms of reputational costs or other sanctions.

Some scholars with sociological, constructivist leanings have questioned the characterization of law in terms of these three attributes (precision, obligation and delegation) because it distracts from how law operates normatively.[13] They likely do so because of their opposition to a presumption among legal positivists and rational institutionalists that "hardness" means binding rules interpreted and enforced by courts. In other words, their counterparts in interdisciplinary debates in international relations — realist and rationalist institutionalist scholars — tend to discount the efficacy of soft law because it creates no binding obligation on states who can thus ignore it at their whim in light of their interests. For example, Richard Steinberg contends, from a realist perspective, that "most public international lawyers, realists and positivists,

---

[12] Abbott and Snidal (2000, p. 38).

[13] See e.g., Finnemore and Toope (2001) (taking a more sociological perspective, and critiquing Abbott et al.'s formal definition of legalization because it obscures how law and legal norms actually operate in practice). We also recognize that these formal definitions can obscure the relative roles of "hard" and "soft" law in sociological terms — that is, from the way law and norms operate in the world, which indeed is what interests us. Binding dispute-settlement can be ignored or simply reflect existing power asymmetries, so that "hard" law may in fact not be so "hard" in practice. Similarly, softer forms of law can be much more transformative of state and constituent conduct, which should be the real measure of law's impact in the world. Despite these caveats, we believe that hard/soft distinction does capture something important about the making and implementation of international law, and we find the distinction to be particularly useful for our analyses of how hard and soft law regimes and instruments interact.

consider soft law to be inconsequential."[14] Similarly, Andrew Guzman maintains, from a rational institutionalist perspective, that "soft law represents a choice by the parties to enter into a weaker form of commitment."[15] Guzman and Steinberg focus on states' pursuit of predetermined interests. They do not address how states may change those interests through transnational processes of interaction, deliberation and persuasion coordinated through international institutions.

Constructivists, in contrast, explicitly address how international regimes can lead states to change their perceptions of state interests.[16] International law scholars frequently take such an approach. For example, Abraham and Antonia Chayes contend, "what is left out of the institutionalist account is the active role of the regime in modifying preferences, generating new options, persuading the parties to move toward increasing compliance with regime norms, and guiding the evolution of the normative structure in the direction of the overall objectives of the regime."[17] Similarly Harold Koh stresses the "internalization" processes to which international law gives rise through iterative processes involving interpretation over time,[18] and Thomas Franck stresses the compliance pull of international law that is deemed legitimate in its procedures.[19] From the constructivist perspective, soft law mechanisms can be as or more effective than hard law by creating settings in which states engage in open-ended discussions to reach better and more effective policy because they are less wary of rigid hard law consequences.

---

[14]Steinberg (2002, p. 340).

[15]Guzman (2005, p. 611).

[16]Ruggie (1998).

[17]Chayes and Chayes (1993, p. 229); see also Franck (1990) (on the "compliance pull" of law); and Koh (1998) (on "internalization" processes).

[18]The transnational legal process theory of Harold Koh addresses how states internalize legal norms through repeated "interaction," including through the work of non-state actors, resulting in new "interpretation," which is "internalized" within states at the domestic level. Koh (1998).

[19]Franck (1990).

In sum, the typology used by Abbott and Snidal does not prejudge these instruments' relative value. Rather, the typology simply characterizes different instruments which actors may choose in terms of their precision, binding legal obligation and delegation along a continuum. We find this typology and continuum to be particularly useful for our analyses of how hard and soft law instruments and regimes *interact*, and thus we adopt the definition of Abbott and Snidal for our purposes.

2.2.   *Advantages and disadvantages of hard and soft law as alternatives*

States and private actors have increasingly used a wide range of instruments having a relatively harder or softer legal nature in terms of precision, obligation and delegation to advance their aims. These instruments offer different advantages and disadvantages in different contexts, involving factors at the domestic and international levels. They are sometimes used alone and sometimes combined dynamically over time, resulting in a complex hybrid of hard and soft law instruments. In this section, we address the use of hard and soft law instruments as alternatives in light of their respective attributes and deficiencies before turning to an assessment of how they interact.

The quantitative growth in the use of international hard and soft law instruments reflects the breadth and intensification of economic globalization, by which we mean "a process of widening, deepening and speeding up of worldwide connectedness, in particular in the economic sphere."[20] The very emergence of the soft law concept reflects the multiplication of producers of international law in this context, including not only foreign ministries, but also sector-specific transgovernmental networks, supranational bureaucracies, multinational corporations and business associations, and international non-governmental organizations.[21] These groups generally do not have the authority to create binding international law in a traditional sense, which is reserved to

---

[20]We adapt this definition from Held *et al.* (1999, p. 2).
[21]Robilant (2005, p. 500).

states, yet they use non-binding instruments to advance their policy goals, instruments which may be subsequently transformed into binding hard law, at either the national or international levels.[22]

Private actors can also work with and through states to create binding hard law. As John Braithwaite and Peter Drahos find in their masterful study of thirteen areas of global business regulation, business actors frequently play leading roles. First, Braithwaite and Drahos find that "state regulation follows industry self-regulatory practice more than the reverse."[23] Janet Levit's recent work on the law of documentary letters of credit provides an excellent example.[24] Second, corporate actors enroll states to advance their aims. In this respect, Braithwaite and Drahos find that "US corporations exert more power in the world system than corporations of other states because they can enroll the support of the most powerful state in the world."[25]

As an institutional form, hard law features many advantages. In particular, rationalist scholars find that:

- Hard law instruments allow states to commit themselves more credibly to international agreements. Hard law instruments make state commitments more credible because they increase the cost of reneging, whether on account of legal sanctions or on account of the costs to a state's reputation where it is found to have acted in violation of its legal commitments.[26]
- Hard law treaties are more credible because they can have direct legal effects in national jurisdictions (being "self-executing"), or they can require domestic legal enactment. Where treaty

---

[22]Functional state agencies, however, will play the leading roles in areas within their competence, which can result in hard law. Braithwaite and Drahos (2000, pp. 479–485).

[23]Braithwaite and Drahos (2000, p. 481).

[24]Levit (2008).

[25]Braithwaite and Drahos (2000, p. 482).

[26]States are arguably particularly concerned with their reputation for compliance. Andrew Guzman contends that states' calculus over the reputational costs of non-compliance is the primary factor for explaining state compliance with international law. Guzman (2005). See also Abbott and Snidal (2000) and Lipson (1991, p. 508).

obligations are implemented through domestic legislation, they create new tools that mobilize domestic actors, increasing the audience costs of a violation and thus making their commitments more credible.[27]

- Hard law instruments solve problems of incomplete contracting by creating mechanisms for the interpretation and elaboration of legal commitments over time.[28]
- Hard law instruments better permit states to monitor and enforce their commitments, including through the use of dispute-settlement bodies such as courts.[29]

States, as well as private actors working with and through state representatives, thus tend to use hard law where the benefits of cooperation are great and the potential for opportunism and its costs are high.[30] To control for the risks of opportunism, they can create third-party monitoring and enforcement mechanisms, as under the WTO committee, trade policy review and dispute-settlement systems. These monitoring and enforcement mechanisms reduce the transaction costs of subsequent interstate interaction through providing an ongoing forum for interpreting, applying, enforcing and elaborating agreed rules.[31]

Yet hard law also entails significant costs. It can create formal commitments that restrict the behavior of states, thus infringing on national sovereignty in potentially sensitive areas. As a result, it can encourage states to bargain fiercely and at length regarding the legally binding commitments into which they are entering which will continue to apply over time. Because states are more likely to drag out negotiations over legally binding commitments, the use of hard law can increase contracting costs. In addition, hard law agreements can be more difficult to amend to adapt to changing circumstances. Therefore writing detailed binding agreements may be wasteful because it can force states to plan

---

[27] Abbott and Snidal (2000).
[28] Abbott and Snidal (2000).
[29] Abbott and Snidal (2000, p. 38).
[30] Abbott and Snidal (2000, p. 429).
[31] Abbott and Snidal (2000, p. 430).

for contingent events that may not occur, and can lead to undesired rigidity or prevent agreement altogether.[32] Soft law, in contrast, can be adapted, amended and replaced more easily because its provisions are non-binding and thus no single state or group of states can block its amendment.

Defenders of soft law argue that soft law instruments offer significant offsetting advantages over hard law. They find, in particular, that:

- Soft law instruments are easier and less costly to negotiate.
- Soft law instruments impose lower "sovereignty costs" on states in sensitive areas.
- Soft law instruments provide greater flexibility for states to cope with uncertainty and learn over time.
- Soft law instruments allow states to be more ambitious and engage in "deeper" cooperation than they would if they had to worry about enforcement.
- Soft law instruments cope better with diversity.
- Soft law instruments are available to non-state actors, including international secretariats, sub-state public actors such as administrative agencies and business associations and non-governmental organizations.[33]

Abbott and Snidal, for example, contend that states use soft law where contracting costs increase, whether because of the number of parties involved, factual uncertainty, domestic ratification challenges, politically charged issue-areas or distributional asymmetries. They note how, in these contexts, "states can limit their legal obligation through hortatory language, exceptions, reservations and the like," such as safeguard and rebalancing clauses under the WTO.[34]

---

[32] Abbott and Snidal (2000, p. 433). Trubek, Cottrell, and Nance (2006). These arguments also support the use of soft law in purely domestic settings as advocated by the "new governance literature." See Scott and de Búrca (2006).

[33] For good discussions on the purported strengths of soft law, see e.g. Lipson (1991, pp. 500–501, pp. 514–527) (discussing the strengths of "informal agreements"); Raustiala and Victor (1998, pp, 684–686); Hillgenburg (1999, pp. 501, 504); Abbott and Snidal (2000, pp. 38–39); Trubek, Cottrell and Nance (2006); Kirton and Trebilcock (2004); and Sindico (2006, p. 832).

[34] Abbott and Snidal (2004, p. 54).

Both rationalist and constructivist scholars recognize the potential advantages of soft law instruments, but they do so in different ways. While rationalist-oriented scholars focus on the reduction of contracting and sovereignty costs under soft law, constructivist scholars stress how soft law can "facilitate constitutive processes such as persuasion, learning, argumentation, and socialization."[35] While rationalist scholars note the importance of soft law instruments for generating information leading to common understandings in situations of uncertainty, constructivist scholars contend that soft law instruments can help states to develop common norms and a sense of a collective enterprise. For both rationalists and constructivists, then, soft law can create mechanisms for parties to learn about consequences before obligations are made binding. This process occurred under the Montreal Protocol for Protection of the Ozone, an agreement to protect a global commons, the earth's atmosphere. Soft law instruments can bring a broad array of participants together, as under a framework convention, in a process that over time permits them to gain trust, leading to harder obligations in the future.[36]

Soft law instruments, nonetheless, have obvious disadvantages. First, from a normative perspective, if soft law instruments are effective, they can be criticized for their relative obscurity, since they can remove law-making from democratic oversight, such that provisions with distributive implications are not fully discussed within legislative or other government bodies.[37] Second, from the perspective of effectiveness, soft law instruments create little or no legal obligation and provide no binding third-party dispute-settlement to resolve disputes among the parties and fill in the details of incomplete contracts. Soft law instruments, depending on their level of precision, may also make it difficult to determine whether a state is acting in accordance with its commitments and thus create greater opportunities to evade

---

[35]Trubek, Cottrell and Nance (2006, p. 75).
[36]Brunnee and Toope (1997).
[37]See Klabbers (1998), Levit (2008).

responsibility.[38] For example, the OECD created a Financial Action Task Force (FATF) of financial experts which issued guidelines which limit sovereignty costs because of their soft law nature. Some commentators, however, have found that the task force guidelines have been largely ineffective in leading to policy change.[39] Similarly, at the 1992 Rio Summit, the parties only agreed to a non-binding set of principles and an Agenda 21 to create a "comprehensive plan of action," contrary to the demands of environmental non-governmental organizations (NGOs) for a hard law treaty. Skeptics question the effectiveness of these soft law instruments. They contend that much of international law, when it lacks teeth, can be simply symbolic, constituting a form of junk law.[40]

It would nonetheless be a mistake, in our view, to view hard law instruments as always preferable to soft law instruments from the standpoint of effectiveness, even though states may sometimes use soft law instruments only to paper over differences. As Kal Raustiala points out, we must distinguish between the concepts of compliance (as with hard law obligations) and effectiveness.[41] He writes, "compliance as a concept draws no causal linkage between a rule and behavior, but simply identifies a conformity between the rule and behavior. To speak of effectiveness is to speak directly of causality: to claim that a rule is 'effective' is to claim that it led to certain behavior or outcomes, which may or may not meet the legal standard of compliance."[42] In terms of the law-in-action, we are less concerned with formal compliance, which may mean little if the obligations reflect no policy change, than with effectiveness, in terms of attaining policy goals. Advocates of soft law

---

[38] Abbott and Snidal (2000, p. 446).

[39] Simmons (2000, pp. 244–263). Cf. Rocha Machado (2009).

[40] Cf Edelman (1964); Goldsmith and Posner (2005); Raustiala (2005); and Susskind and Ozawa (1992).

[41] Raustiala (2000, p. 398); Raustiala and Slaughter (2002). On the "depth" of cooperation, i.e. cooperative agreements that require a greater change in state behavior relative to the status quo, see Downs, Rocke and Barsoom (1996).

[42] Raustiala (2000, p. 398).

as an alternative contend that soft law can be more effective in practice than many formally binding treaties.

In sum, hard and soft law instruments offer different advantages for different contexts involving a range of factors that actors consider. For these reasons, a growing number of scholars in law and political science have advocated a pragmatic approach, selecting alternative hard and soft law approaches depending on the characteristics of the issue and the negotiating and institutional context in question. Scholars have noted, in particular, how hard and soft law instruments may be effectively combined to lead to greater cooperation. Yet as Abbott and Snidal write, while "soft law sometimes [is] designed as a way-station to harder legalization, ... often it is preferable on its own terms" as an alternative.[43]

2.3. Hard and soft law interaction as complements

Although the respective costs and benefits of hard and soft law remain a subject of contention, legal and political science scholars have moved increasingly towards a view that hard and soft international law can build upon each other as complementary tools for international problem-solving. These scholars contend that hard and soft law mechanisms can build upon each other in two predominant ways: (1) non-binding soft law can lead the way to binding hard law, and (2) binding hard law can subsequently be elaborated through soft law instruments. For example, a leading US international law casebook introduces the concept of soft law in terms of how "soft law instruments are consciously used to generate support for the promulgation of treaties or to help generate customary international law norms [i.e., binding hard law]," and how "treaties and state practice give rise to soft law that supplements and advances treaty and customary norms."[44] Scholars thus take a pragmatic policy-oriented approach to show how hard and soft law instruments provide not only alternative tools for cooperation, but also serve as complements of each other in dynamic processes of

---

[43]Abbott and Snidal (2000, p. 423).
[44]Dunoff et al. (2006, p. 95).

legalization, leading to greater international [regulatory] cooperation and coordination over time.[45]

These scholars' views regarding hard and soft law complements can be divided into three camps: (1) positivist legal scholars who find that soft law is inferior to hard law but should not be discarded because it can potentially lead to hard law; (2) rationalist scholars with a political economy orientation who view soft law as a complement to hard law which serves state interests in many contexts, including because the hard law option is not available; and (3) constructivist scholars who view soft law as a complement to hard law which may be desirable in itself by facilitating dialogic and experimentalist transnational and domestic processes which transform norms, understandings and perceptions of state interests.

Positivist legal scholars find that soft law is inferior to hard law because it does not correspond to the ideal type of law.[46] That is, soft law lacks formally binding obligations which are interpreted and enforced by courts, and it thus fails to generate jurisprudence over time. For this reason, these scholars view soft law as a second-best alternative to hard law, either as a way-station on the way to hard law, or as a fall-back when hard law approaches fail.[47] Kirton and Trebilcock, for example, in a study of the use of soft and hard law in global trade, environment and social governance, find "strong support for the familiar feeling that soft law is a second-best substitute for a first-best hard law, being created when and because the relevant hard law does not exist and the intergovernmental negotiations to produce it have failed."[48] Sindico likewise writes, "[s]oft law, and voluntary standards in particular, are a stage in the creation of international legal norms. It is as a pioneer of hard law that soft law finds its *raison d'être* in the normative challenge for sustainable global governance."[49] The implication is that soft law otherwise has no *raison d'être*. Sindico, for example, views

---

[45] For an example, see Shelton (2000); Chinkin (1989, p. 853).
[46] See e.g. Klabbers (1996).
[47] See Weil 1983; Klabbers (1998).
[48] Kirton and Trebilcock (2004, p. 24).
[49] Sindico (2006, p. 846).

the corporate social responsibility (CSR) movement in terms of "the beginning of a step towards comprehensive hard law in this field,"[50] as opposed to a flexible, adaptive process which is valuable in itself.

These scholars often view soft law solely in terms of its *relationship* to a hard law ideal. In her valuable introduction to a special volume on soft law organized by the American Society of International Law (ASIL), for example, Dinah Shelton categorizes soft law in the following five ways, each of which is linked to positivist conceptions of hard law:

(i) Elaborative soft law, that is principles that provide guidance to the interpretation, elaboration, or application of hard law [i.e. soft law which *builds from* hard law]...

(ii) Emergent hard law, that is principles that are first formulated in non-binding form with the possibility, or even aspiration, of negotiating a subsequent treaty, or harden into binding custom through the development of state practice and *opinio juris* [i.e. soft law which *builds to* hard law]...

(iii) Soft law as evidence of the existence of hard obligations [i.e. soft law which *builds to* hard customary international law].

(iv) Parallel soft and hard law, that is similar provisions articulated in both hard and soft forms allowing the soft version to act as a fall-back provision.

(v) Soft law as a source of legal obligation, through acquiescence and estoppel, perhaps against the original intentions of the parties.[51]

Reinicke and Witte likewise stress, in their cross-cutting overview in the same volume, how soft law agreements "can and often do represent the first important element in an evolutionary process that shapes legal relationships among and between multiple actors, facilitating and ultimately enhancing the effectiveness and efficiency of transnational

---

[50] Sindico (2006, p. 836).

[51] Shelton (2000, pp. 30-31) (while putting forth this categorization, Shelton admits that it "is problematic in that it defines soft law in terms of its distinction from hard law, and not in its own terms"). Shelton's fourth category has also been referred to as co-regulation: a regulatory regime premised on both mandatory government regulation and voluntary self-regulation or regulatory measures with both binding and non-binding elements. See e.g., Gordon (1999).

policy-making."[52] Similarly, John Kirton and Michael Trebilcock conclude that "at best, it [soft law], is a complement."[53]

Abbott and Snidal, in contrast, taking a rational institutionalist political economy approach, are agnostic as to whether hard or soft law is preferable because they focus on varying state interests in different contexts. Sometimes states prefer hard law and sometimes soft law to advance their joint policy aims. In their work on the "pathways to cooperation," Abbott and Snidal nonetheless define three pathways of which two explicitly involve the progressive hardening of law. The three pathways are: the use of a framework convention which subsequently deepens in the precision of its coverage; the use of a plurilateral agreement which subsequently broadens in its membership; and the use of a soft law instrument which subsequently leads to binding legal commitments. They note how these three pathways can be "blended" and "sequenced," once more resulting in a mutually reinforcing, evolutionary interaction between hard and soft law mechanisms.[54]

Finally, constructivist-oriented scholars likewise focus on how hard and soft law are used as complements. Trubek and his coauthors, for example, contend that soft law instruments can help to generate knowledge (as through the use of benchmarking, peer review, and exchange of good practices), develop shared ideas, build trust, and, if desirable, establish "non-binding standards that can eventually harden into binding rules once uncertainties are reduced and a higher degree of consensus ensues."[55] Braithwaite and Drahos point both to the importance of using framework conventions and soft law as a first step which "can, over time be more detailed through rule-making."[56] They contend that neither hard nor soft law provisions should necessarily be privileged because states and non-state actors need flexibility to address situations that involve uncertainty and require experimentation. Janet Levit, working in a legal pluralist framework, finds that international

---

[52] Reinicke and Witte (2000, p. 76).
[53] Kirton and Trebilcock (2004, p. 27).
[54] Abbott and Snidal (2000, p. 80).
[55] Trubek, Cottrell and Nance (2006, p. 32).
[56] Braithwaite and Drahos (2000, pp. 261–262).

soft law instruments generate normativity that affects both subsequent hard law enactments and judicial decisions.[57] Some scholars working in an experimentalist "new governance" tradition go further, arguing that soft law approaches should generally be privileged to promote responsive governance.[58]

3. Theorizing International Hard and Soft Law Interaction: Power, Distributive Conflict and Regime Complexes

The existing literature on hard and soft law typically takes as its starting assumption the possibility of joint gains from cooperation among states, and proceeds to explore the advantages and disadvantages, the choice, and the effectiveness of hard and soft law approaches to international cooperation. We agree that the prospect of joint gains is an important prerequisite for international cooperation, and we have seen in Section 2 that such prospects continue to exist for international policy cooperation.

Nevertheless, we cannot fully understand our central question — the *interaction* of hard and soft law — without considering the ways in which power, distributional conflict, and regime complexes affect how hard and soft law regimes interact, and whether they will do so productively. Indeed, we argue below that the harmonious, complementary, mutually reinforcing interaction of hard and soft law relies on a hitherto unspecified set of scope conditions, including most importantly in particular a low level of distributional conflict among the players. These conditions may hold in certain areas, we maintain, but there are good theoretical and empirical reasons to believe that variation in distributive conflict will spur hard and soft law regimes to interact in different ways, sometimes as alternatives, sometimes as complements and sometimes as antagonists.

In this section, therefore, we lay out our theoretical argument about the reasons why, and the conditions under which, we expect hard

---

[57]Levit (2008, pp. 132–141).
[58]See e.g., Simon (2006) and Sabel and Simon (2006).

and soft law to interact as antagonists. The analysis is in three parts. First, reflecting the transatlantic theme of this volume, we examine the sources of United States and European Union power in international regulatory affairs, arguing that both market size and institutional characteristics have made the US and the EU the leading, and roughly equal, powers in global as well as bilateral regulatory cooperation (Sec. 3.1). Next, we argue that international regulatory cooperation, and indeed international cooperation more broadly, is frequently characterized by intense distributional conflict, in which actors like the US and the EU may have sharply differing preferences over regulatory outcomes, with each side attempting to export its own regulatory model and force the costs of adjustment onto others (Sec. 3.2). Finally, we examine the problems of "regime complexes" and legal fragmentation in international regulation, arguing that states with divergent preferences will have strong incentives to engage in forum-shopping and "strategic inconsistency," using competing legal fora to press their substantive preferences (Sec. 3.3). Sections 4 and 5 will then build on this analysis, making the argument that under conditions of distributive conflict and regime complexes, hard and soft law can interact not as alternatives or complements, but as mutually undermining antagonists.

3.1. *The EU, the US, and power in international regulatory governance*

The United States and European Union collectively represent over 50% of global production, and over 40% in terms of purchasing power parity.[59] In 2006, EU gross domestic product was slightly larger than the United States', but not by a significant extent. Because of the size of their markets, where the US and EU agree on a common regulatory policy, they are well-positioned to promote it globally. For example, as Germain contends in the area of financial regulation, the size of the

---

[59] See World Bank, at *http://siteresources.worldbank.org/DATASTATISTICS/ Resources/GDP.pdf*, and *http://siteresources.worldbank.org/DATASTATISTICS/ Resources/GDP.pdf* (EU GDP at 27.2% of world GDP in 2006, and at 20.6% in PPP terms; and US GDP at 24.6% of world GDP in 2006, and at 20% in PPP terms).

international markets handled in New York, London and a few other major cities "empower their respective state authorities" to be leaders in global regulation.[60] Where they disagree, there is often deadlock, reflecting the equal size of their economies and markets. With the rise of the economies of China, India, Brazil and other developing countries, the US and EU have a long-term interest in exercising global regulatory leadership now in order to lock their preferences into international law and institutions, but conflicts between them may inhibit their ability to do so.

The US and EU have launched a series of initiatives to promote transatlantic collaboration in global governance which we have assessed in our earlier work. The creation of the New Transatlantic Agenda (NTA) and the Transatlantic Economic Partnership (TEP) during the 1990s were premised on the idea of joint gains from transatlantic economic integration and in particular from joint regulatory cooperation across a wide range of issue-areas.[61] Alongside the traditional processes of trade negotiation and trade dispute resolution, the transatlantic partners forged new mechanisms for cooperation among economic regulators in areas ranging from competition policy to data privacy, the environment, and food safety.[62] Among the goals of the NTA was to promote US and EU joint leadership in global economic governance. These goals have been reasserted during the second term of the George W. Bush administration, in particular with the creation, in 2007, of a Transatlantic Economic Council designed to lend high-level impetus to new and continuing efforts at transatlantic economic cooperation in various issue-areas.[63]

---

[60] Germain (1997, p. 163).

[61] Pollack and Shaffer (2001).

[62] Bermann, Herdegen and Lindstreth (2001); Pollack and Shaffer (2001).

[63] See Framework for Advancing Transatlantic Economic Integration between the United States of America and the European Union, April 30, 2007, US Dept of State Press Release (establishing a Transatlantic Economic Council), available at http://www.state.gov/p/eur/rls/prsrl/84004.htm. The two sides created "a framework for advancing transatlantic economic integration," prioritizing cooperation for the protection of intellectual property, the assurance of secure trade, the reconciliation and accommodation of accounting standards, the support of innovation, and

Although market size generally explains the growing role of the EU as a global actor in economic and regulatory fields, US and EU bargaining power can also be affected by each side's *institutional* characteristics. Where policy-making is reserved to a sub-federal level in the United States or a sub-EU level in the European Union, then the US or EU respectively will be in a weaker bargaining situation at the international level. The United States over time has more frequently been a global leader in regulatory domains because it has had greater institutional power at the federal level, combined with its great market power. However, in many regulatory areas, the US has fragmented authority over regulatory standard-setting, leaving it to US states within the federal context or to private associations. As Walter Mattli and Tim Büthe write, "When standardization becomes an increasingly international process, the organizational characteristics of the European standardization system make for a more felicitous match between the national and international institutions than the characteristics of the largely anarchic American system."[64] They conclude, "[t]he process of aggregating technical preferences and projecting consensus standards to a higher level is considerably more difficult in the decentralized and uncoordinated standards system of the US, where the nominal national representative for international standardization is a weak and contested institution."[65]

As greater policy-making powers have been delegated within Europe to EU institutions over time, the EU has increased its negotiating clout internationally. Because of the size of the EU's internal market, once the EU member states harmonize regulatory policies at the EU level and develop corresponding EU-level regulatory institutions, the EU is well-positioned to exercise economic clout as a global actor. To give an example, Elliot Posner addresses how the establishment of the EU's regulatory competence and its extraterritorial

---

the removal of barriers to investment. *Id.* A central objective of the new initiative is to facilitate joint US and EU global leadership in international trade and regulatory governance.

[64] Mattli and Büthe (2003, p. 27).

[65] Mattli and Büthe (2003, p. 27).

reach are key explanations for the EU's increased authority over financial services regulation.[66] Institutional developments in the EU have affected powerful US firms who, in turn, motivated the US Securities and Exchange Commission to work with EU authorities to accommodate and recognize EU standards in a number of areas. This development occurred following an extended period of benign (or malign) US neglect of European approaches to financial services regulation. As the EU assumes greater institutional power in Europe, it should also be able to exercise greater authority in international governance. In other words, the EU enhances its international authority both by widening (enhancing its market power through increasing EU membership) and by deepening (enhancing its institutional power through expanding the scope of EU authority to more policy areas).

Finally, the US and EU exercise considerable authority globally because of the regulatory expertise they have developed domestically. In their study of thirteen areas of global business regulation, John Braithwaite and Peter Drahos conclude that "the fact that US and EU law are modeled more than others is not only because of their economic hegemony and the fact that weaker economies want to meet their terms for admission to the clubs they dominate. In the case of the US in particular, modeling is underwritten by the sheer depth of regulatory expertise Washington agencies can offer."[67] They find that the US played a leading role in twelve of the thirteen areas they studied (all but for international labour regulation) and the EU played a leading role in nine of these areas.[68] Overall, they find that "the US is the biggest demander of new regulatory agreements as well as the strongest resister of regimes other states want."[69] However, "the EC [European Community] is more important because of the way it dominates the US in agenda-setting in a few arenas — prescription drugs, food, automobile safety — and is nearly an equal partner to the

---

[66] Posner (2005).
[67] Braithwaite and Drahos (2000, p. 542).
[68] *Id.*, at 476–477 (see chart).
[69] *Id.*, at 478.

US in agenda-setting for other regimes."[70] As a result, they find that while "most global regulatory agendas are set by the US; if the EC vetoes those agendas, they go nowhere."[71]

In sum, effective cooperation between the world's two economic powers offers the promise of joint gains for both sides and more effective global leadership on regulatory matters. Yet a careful cross-sectoral analysis of transatlantic economic relations demonstrates that their cooperation varies significantly by issue area, limiting the two sides' ability to exercise joint leadership in global governance.[72] This variation reflects the distributive implications of the governance alternatives respectively favored by the US and EU. It is to these distributive issues that we now turn.

3.2. The challenge of distributive conflict

Despite the general promise of regimes in fostering international cooperation to achieve joint gains, international relations scholars have identified a number of potential obstacles to successful regime-based cooperation.[73] We focus in this chapter on two such impediments: the problems of distributive conflict (discussed in this section) and of fragmented regime complexes (discussed in Sec. 3.3). Distributive conflicts, we note immediately, need not arise from narrow economic

---

[70] *Id.*, at 485.

[71] *Id.*, at 485.

[72] Andrews *et al.* (2005).

[73] The realist literature, for example, has emphasized the dual challenges of (1) cheating and (2) relative gains as the primary obstacles to successful cooperation, focusing on concerns over national security and the balance of power. See Grieco (1988), Baldwin (1993), and Hasenclaver *et al.* (1997, pp. 113–135). Subsequent work by neoliberal institutionalists, however, has demonstrated the ability of international regimes to mitigate concerns about cheating, while relative gains emerges in a careful analysis as a minor impediment to cooperation which operates only under certain restrictive conditions; see e.g. Powell (1991); Snidal (1991); Baldwin (1993); Hasenclaver *et al.* (1997, pp. 125–134). We therefore focus on two other impediments to international cooperation — distributive conflict and regime complexes — which are both consistent with realist *and* institutionalist analyses, and particularly relevant for our question of the interaction of hard and soft law.

or protectionist motives on the part of states, but can and do reflect different configurations of interests, institutional procedures and ideological and cultural perspectives at the national level — in other words, different interests, institutions and ideas — which in turn shape the regulatory preferences of states at the international level.[74]

International law theorists, taking from regime theory in international relations, often point to the Prisoner's Dilemma (PD) game in assessing the role of international law. To give one leading example, Andrew Guzman in his impressive book *How International Law Works*, writes, "It is in the context of [the prisoner's dilemma] game that the theory is applied throughout most of this book."[75] The distributive challenge to regime theory calls into question the appropriateness of the Prisoner's Dilemma game as the proper model for most instances of international cooperation because it fails to capture the potential for distributive conflicts among the participants. In the classic PD model, states are assumed to have a common interest in reaching a cooperative outcome, and the primary impediment to successful cooperation is the fear that other states will cheat on their agreements. In PD models of international relations, these problems are typically addressed by creating mechanisms for the monitoring of state behavior and the sanctioning of states that violate the terms of the agreement — i.e., international law. If PD is an accurate description of the situation facing states, then international regimes and international hard and soft law should indeed facilitate cooperation by monitoring compliance and (in the case of hard law dispute-settlement bodies) by providing for enforcement.

However, the Prisoner's Dilemma game deemphasizes another important obstacle to successful cooperation, namely conflicts among states with *different interests* over the *distribution* of the costs and benefits of cooperation.[76] That is to say, when states cooperate in

---

[74]For a broader discussion, see Pollack and Shaffer (2009, Chapter 2).

[75]See e.g., Guzman (2008, p. 25).

[76]The distributive conflict to which we are referring here relates, not to the problem of relative gains, but to the distribution of *absolute* gains from cooperation among two or more states. For a range of views on the challenge of distributive conflict in international

international politics, they do not simply choose between "cooperation" and "defection," the binary choices available in PD games, but rather they choose specific *terms* of cooperation, such as the specific level of various tariffs in a trade regime, or the precise levels of greenhouse gas emissions in an environmental regime, and so on. As James Morrow notes, "There is only one way to cooperate in prisoners' dilemma; there are many ways to cooperate in the real-world."[77] In game-theoretic terms, there may be multiple equilibria — multiple possible agreements that both sides prefer to the status quo — and states face the challenge of choosing among these many possible agreements.

Different terms of cooperation can have different distributive implications, affecting states' calculation of costs and benefits, both economically and politically. In an international trade agreement, for example, one side may prefer to drastically reduce tariffs on industrial goods, while another may place a stronger emphasis on reducing agricultural tariffs or agricultural subsidies. In this view, states face not only the challenge of monitoring and enforcing compliance with a trade agreement, as in the PD model, but also of deciding on the terms of cooperation. Yet PD models, with their binary choice of cooperation or defection and their emphasis on Pareto-improving outcomes, fail to capture these elements of international cooperation.

We therefore offer three specific, overlapping arguments that are most relevant to international regulatory cooperation and the use of hard and soft law instruments toward that end.

First, regime theory, with its emphasis on PD and collective-action models, has under-emphasized both distributive conflict and the role of state power in determining the outcome of regulatory conflicts. This, in turn, has affected international law scholarship, much of which has welcomed regime theory for its validation of international law's role. In international politics, as Stephen Krasner argues, efforts at cooperation often take the form of a Battle of the Sexes game, in which different

---

cooperation, see Krasner (1991), Morrow (1994), Fearon (1998), Gruber (2000), Koremenos *et al.* (2001), Mattli and Büthe (2003), and Drezner (2007).

[77] Morrow (1994, p. 395).

states have clear preferences for different international standards.[78] Even if all states benefit from a common standard, raising the prospect of joint gains, the distribution of those gains depends on the specific standard chosen, and the primary question is whether and how states can secure cooperation on their preferred terms.

Put differently, Krasner argues, the most important question is not whether to move toward the "Pareto frontier" of mutually beneficial cooperation, but *which point* on the Pareto frontier will be chosen. Under such circumstances, he suggests, outcomes are determined primarily by the use of state power, which may be employed in one of three ways: (1) to determine who may play the game (regime membership); (2) to dictate the rules of the game (for our purposes, whether through hard or soft law), including the possibility of a single state moving first and imposing a *de facto* standard on others; and (3) to employ issue-linkages, including through the application of threats and promises in related issue-areas, to change the payoff matrix for other states and induce those states to accept one's preferred standards.[79] Krasner views such coordination regimes as stable and self-enforcing, yet this self-enforcing nature of the regime should not obscure the fact that the regime produces winners (who secure cooperation on terms closer to their preferences) and losers (forced to cooperate on terms favorable to others), and that state power plays a key role in determining the shape of the regime and the standards adopted under the regime.

We should, therefore, expect the outcome of a Battle of the Sexes game to be determined in large part by powerful states, with weaker

---

[78] In the Battle of the Sexes game, both states agree on the least preferable outcome or outcomes to be avoided, and both agree to coordinate their behavior to avoid such an outcome, but each one prefers a specific (equilibrium) outcome. The canonical example, from which the Battle game takes its name, is one in which two players (say, a husband and wife) agree that they want to take a vacation together, but disagree on the destination (he prefers the mountains, she the beach). In such a game, the primary challenge is not the threat of cheating (since both players prefer *some* joint vacation to being alone), but rather of deciding which of two possible equilibrium outcomes (the mountains or the beach) will be selected. Krasner (1991, p. 339); Stein (1982, p. 314).

[79] Krasner (1991, p. 340).

players being excluded from negotiations, or forced to accept a *fait accompli*, or induced to accept powerful states' terms through threats and promises in related issue-areas. In the global regulatory context, therefore, we would expect the United States and the European Union to play dominant roles in bargaining, with smaller countries being placed in a difficult situation when the US and the EU agree, as well as when they clash. When the US and EU agree, smaller countries will be under considerable pressure to adapt to US and EU standards. When the US and EU disagree, smaller countries may have a greater range of choices, on the one hand, but they may face considerable countervailing pressures on the other, caught between the US-EU conflict.

Second, distributive conflict is not unique to Battle of the Sexes games, but emerges as a generic and nearly ubiquitous feature of all international cooperation. By contrast with the approach of situation-structuralists in international relations theory who distinguish among different types of game contexts,[80] James Fearon has argued in a landmark article that it is misleading to attempt to characterize international cooperation over any given issue as *either* a Prisoners' Dilemma *or* a Battle game. Rather, Fearon maintains,

> ...understanding strategic problems of international cooperation as having a common strategic structure is more accurate and perhaps more theoretically fruitful. Empirically, there are always many possible ways to arrange an arms, trade, financial or environmental treaty, and before states can cooperate to enforce an agreement they must bargain to decide which one to implement. Thus, regardless of the substantive domain, problems of international cooperation involve first a bargaining problem (akin to the various coordination games that have been studied) and next an enforcement problem (akin to a Prisoners' Dilemma game).[81]

---

[80] For good overviews of the situation-structural approach, see e.g. Snidal (1985); Oye (1986); Martin (1992); and Hasenclaver *et al.* (1997). For a critique of the approach, see Fearon (1998, pp. 272–275). For a pioneering application to international law, see Goldsmith and Posner (2005), and the critiques in Guzman (2006), and Hathaway and Lavinbuk (2006).

[81] Fearon (1998, p. 270).

More specifically, Fearon models international cooperation as a two-stage game in which states first agree on the terms of cooperation, and then establish any monitoring and sanctioning provisions necessary for enforcement. Linking these two stages into a single game provides useful insights into the significant challenges of successful international cooperation. For example, a long "shadow of the future" can lessen problems of enforcement, by reassuring the players that the game is an iterated one and that compliance will be rewarded and noncompliance punished over the long haul. By the same token, however, a long shadow of the future can *exacerbate* distributional conflicts: if states know that the rules and standards they adopt will bind them and their successors for many years to come, they will have a greater incentive to bargain hard and to hold out for their preferred standard, knowing that it can shape the patterns of gains and losses well into the future.[82] In this view, enforceable, hard law agreements may increase the shadow of the future and hence make bargaining more difficult, whereas soft law instruments may make enforcement more problematic but alleviate distributional conflicts in bargaining over the precise terms.

Third, the setting of international regulatory standards is particularly prone to distributive conflicts, and international standard-setting can and should be theorized as a coordination game that often creates incentives for parties to engage in strategic bargaining. Some standard-setting negotiations may take the form of a "pure coordination" game, in which the various participants are entirely indifferent among the possible standards to be adopted.[83] Indeed, the constructivist or "world society" literature depicts international standard-setting as an essentially technocratic and deliberative process in which calculations of interest and power recede into the background.[84] However, as Walter Mattli and Tim Büthe have argued convincingly, almost any potential international standard is likely to have varying distributive implications for states and firms, and so we can expect actors to attempt to "export" their domestic standards to the international level, minimizing their

---

[82]Fearon (1998, pp. 270–271).
[83]Stein (1982).
[84]Loya and Boli (1999).

adaptation costs, while their trading partners and competitors are forced to adapt and adjust to a new and different standard.[85] Negotiating environmental, health and safety standards where they have significant trade implications, for example, can be particularly difficult because of the distributional stakes.[86]

3.3. *The challenge of fragmented regime conflicts*

Thus far, we have argued that the making of international regulations, both hard and soft, is likely to be characterized by sharp distributive conflict, with outcomes being decided in large part by dominant economic powers such as the US and the EU. This distributive conflict, we now argue, may take a distinctive form in issue-areas that are characterized by a proliferation of hard and soft law rules and regimes. Preliminary formulations of the concept of international regimes identified regimes by specific issue-areas.[87] Yet an increasing number of real-world problems do not fall neatly within the jurisdiction of a single regime, but rather lie at the intersection of multiple regimes. These overlapping regimes result in a *regime complex*, which Kal Raustiala and David Victor have defined as: "an array of partially overlapping and nonhierarchical institutions governing a particular issue-area." As they state,

> Regime complexes are marked by the existence of several legal agreements that are created and maintained in distinct fora with participation of different sets of actors. The rules in these elemental regimes functionally overlap, yet there is no agreed upon hierarchy for resolving conflicts between rules. Disaggregated decision making in the international legal system means that agreements reached in one forum do not automatically extend to, or clearly trump, agreements developed in other forums.[88]

---

[85] Mattli and Büthe (2003, pp. 10–11).
[86] Bernauer and Sattler (2006, pp. 8–9).
[87] Krasner (1983, p. 1).
[88] Raustiala and Victor (2004, p. 279). For important related work, see Helfer (2004), Alter and Meunier (2006).

Decision-making in these regime complexes is characterized by several distinctive features, of which we emphasize three in terms of their implications for hard and soft law interaction.

First, negotiations in a given regime will not begin with a blank slate but will typically demonstrate "path dependence," taking into account developments in related international regimes, and, in particular for our purposes, the WTO-trade regime. Second, individual states, responding to domestic political contexts and seeking to advance their interests, will engage in "forum-shopping," selecting particular regimes that are most likely to support their preferred outcomes. More specifically, states will select regimes based on characteristics such as their membership (e.g., bilateral, restricted or universal), voting rules (e.g., one-state-one-vote vs. weighted voting, and consensus vs. majority voting), institutional characteristics (e.g., presence or absence of dispute-settlement procedures), substantive focus (e.g., trade finance, environment or food safety), and predominant functional representation (e.g., by trade, finance, environment or agricultural ministries), each of which might be expected to influence substantive outcomes in more or less predictable ways.[89]

Third, the dense array of institutions in a given regime complex will create legal inconsistencies among them. States will respond to these inconsistencies with efforts either to demarcate clear boundaries among various regimes, or to assert the primacy or hierarchy of one regime over the others, in reflection of a state's substantive preferences. States may engage in "strategic inconsistency," attempting through one regime to create conflict or inconsistency in another in the hopes of shifting the understanding or actual adaptation of the rules in that other regime in a particular direction. Powerful states are likely to be particularly adept at such strategies.[90]

The political science analysis of overlapping regimes is complemented by a growing legal literature about the "pluralism" and

---

[89]For an excellent discussion of forum-shopping in international relations, see Jupille and Snidal (2006).
[90]Benvenisti and Downs (2007); Drezner (2007).

"fragmentation" of international law.[91] In 2000, for example, the International Law Commission (ILC) included the topic "Risks ensuing from the fragmentation of international law" into its work program, and in 2002 it created a Study Group to make recommendations concerning the topic, renamed "Fragmentation of international law: difficulties arising from the diversification and expansion of international law."[92] For many international lawyers, the result of such fragmentation is legal uncertainty and potential conflict between international legal regimes.[93] As the 2006 ILC report states:

> [W]hat once appeared to be governed by "general international law" has become the field of operation for such specialist systems as "trade law," "human rights law," "environmental law," "law of the sea," "European law"... each possessing their own principles and institutions. The problem, as lawyers have seen it, is that such specialized law-making and institution-building tends to take place with relative ignorance of legislative and institutional activities in the adjoining fields and of the general principles and practices of international law. The result is conflicts between rules or rule-systems, deviating institutional practices and, possibly, the loss of an overall perspective on the law.[94]

Scholars disagree regarding the causes of such fragmentation and whether fragmentation is positive or negative for international law, but they largely concur on its development.[95] Many legal scholars view this development as a manifestation of the rise of a global legal pluralism, which refers to "the presence in a social field of more than one legal

---

[91] See e.g., International Law Commission (2006); and Berman (2007).
[92] International Law Commission (2006).
[93] See e.g., Delmas-Marty (1998, p. 104); Dupuy (1999); Koskenniemi and Leinmo (2002); and Roberts (2004). On the WTO and public international law, see Marceau (2001); and Pauwelyn (2003).
[94] International Law Commission (ILC) (2006, p. 9).
[95] Compare, on the one hand, Charney (1996) and Koskenniemi and Leinmo (2002) (both contending that a positive development), and on the other, Benvenisti and Downs (2007) and Dupuy (1999) (contending that problematic).

order."[96] As a theory or analytic framework, legal pluralism differs from much of regime theory in that it challenges monist conceptions of the state and of state interests, and rather emphasizes the inter-action between distinct normative orders — state and non-state — while deemphasizing the role of formal texts. In this sense, legal plu-ralism has a "radically heterogeneous" conception of law and social order, taking a post-modernist, constructivist orientation that focuses on social diversity and informality more than on formal rules and hier-archic authority.[97]

Although legal pluralism and theories of regime complexes have quite different starting points, in particular regarding their concep-tions of the role of states, they both raise the question of how legal regimes interact and potentially constrain one another where there is no central authority. As Roderick Macdonald writes from a legal plu-ralist perspective, "[d]ifferent legal regimes are in constant interaction, mutually influencing the emergence of each other's rules, processes and institutions."[98] These regimes are not "self-contained,"[99] in a way that some positivist legal commentators fear, but rather exercise normative pressure on each other, as we will demonstrate below. Lines of com-munication between regimes exist, but, crucially, there is no hierarchy imposing a particular discipline. We are interested in the *interaction* of "harder" and "softer" forms of international law within a regime com-plex, which calls into question much of the previous theorizing about them.

4.   Hard and Soft Law Interaction as Antagonists

Having discussed the significance of distributive conflict and regime complexes for international cooperation in general, we are now ready to

---

[96]Griffiths (1986).
[97]See Macdonald (1998, pp. 76, 80); Fisher-Lescano and Teubner (2004, pp. 1004–07); and Levit (2008).
[98]Macdonald (1998, p. 77).
[99]Simma (1985).

return to the issue of how hard and soft law interact in the international realm. We contend that careful scrutiny of the interaction of hard and soft law instruments within a fragmented international law system demonstrates that they are not necessarily mutually supportive, but also can counteract and undermine each other under certain conditions. More precisely, individual states may deliberately use soft law instruments to undermine hard law rules to which they object, or vice versa, creating an antagonistic relationship between these legal instruments. The scope conditions for such behavior, we argue, are determined by the two factors discussed in the previous section, namely distributive conflict and regime complexes. Where distributive conflict is low, we have argued, states are likely to utilize hard and soft law instruments selectively, adopting each type of instrument for its relative strengths, and utilizing those instruments in a complementary fashion, i.e., with soft law provisions either supplementing existing hard law or leading the way to new hard law in an evolutionary process. In situations of intense distributive conflict, however, the content of international norms and rules are fundamentally contested by states, which therefore have an incentive to use soft law to undermine hard law provisions to which they object, and vice versa. Put differently, distributive conflict provides an incentive for states to contest, undermine, and possibly replace legal provisions — hard and soft — to which they object.

Within a single international regime, states are likely to enjoy limited opportunities to contest and undermine existing legal provisions, particularly if the new provisions are enacted under a stable membership and institutional rules. In a fragmented regime complex, however, the prospects for antagonistic interaction of hard and soft law increase dramatically. Even in the absence of sharp distributive conflict among states, different regimes are likely to be characterized by different memberships, decision rules, and substantive foci, creating tensions and inconsistencies among both hard and soft international norms and rules. These problems of coordination, however, are likely to be magnified substantially insofar as states engage in distributive conflict over the content of international regulations. In such instances, we may expect states to engage in the full range of forum-shopping strategies discussed in the literature on regime complexes and international law fragmentation, using hard or soft law provisions in favored regimes to counter or undermine legal developments in neighboring regimes. Put differently, if distributive conflicts provide states with an *incentive* to use hard and soft law instruments strategically, the existence of international regime complexes increases their *opportunities* to do so.

Our argument is summarized in Table 1, which illustrates our expectations about the interaction of hard and soft law under different combinations of distributive conflict and regime complexes. Where distributive conflict is low and regimes can be easily isolated, as in the upper left-hand cell, states have little incentive to undermine existing law, and hard and soft law are likely to interact and evolve in complementary ways, reflecting the existing literature. In the lower left-hand cell, we imagine a world in which distributive conflict is again low, but regime complexes coexist with no hierarchical structure, such as when

Table 1: Distributive conflict, regime complexes, and the interaction of hard and soft law.

	Dist. Conflict Low	Dist. Conflict High
Single, isolated regime	Complementary interaction of hard and soft law, as per existing literature.	Possible antagonistic interaction of hard and soft law within the regime, although opportunities limited by invariant memberships, rules, and substantive content of regime.
Regime complex	Possible complementary interaction of hard and soft law, although differing memberships, rules and substantive foci may render coordination difficult even in the absence of major distributive conflicts.	Likely antagonistic interaction of hard and soft law between regimes with different decision-making rules, memberships and substantive foci.

an issue area comprises multiple functional domains. Here, we would not expect states to actively contest or undermine existing legal provisions, but we would anticipate some coordination problems among regimes with different memberships, decision rules, and substantive foci.

Compare these two outcomes to those in the right-hand column, where distributive conflict is high. Where states engage in distributive conflict within a single, isolated regime, as in the upper-right cell, states will have an incentive to undermine existing legal provisions, but their opportunities for doing so will be limited, in particular because most international organizations operate by consensus decision-making so that any state benefiting from existing law could block adoption of countervailing legal instruments.[100] In fact, however, we would expect this scenario to be relatively rare, for the simple reason that distributive conflict among states provides a strong incentive for states that are dissatisfied with a given regime to press for the creation or development of new regimes to compete with or undermine existing regimes, particularly insofar as the existing regime is resistant to change. Put differently, the choice to create new regimes is, at least in part, *endogenous* to the presence of distributive conflict, which would tend to push outcomes from the upper right-hand cell to the lower right-hand cell, where distributive conflicts are present and multiple regimes overlap in a single issue-area. In such cases, we argue, states enjoy both an incentive and an opportunity to act strategically, by forum-shopping, favoring some regimes over others, and using hard and soft law instruments to advocate their preferred norms and rules and undermine those to which they are opposed.

In such settings, we can imagine multiple combinations of overlapping and competing hard and soft law regimes asserting jurisdiction over a given issue. For a state that is certain of its interests and intent on

---

[100] However, where there are different bodies operating within a single organization, it is possible for hard and soft law to act as antagonists. For example, UN General Assembly resolutions could be purposefully adopted to counter existing hard law, whether the hard law is created by the UN Security Council, the International Court of Justice or another public international law tribunal.

undermining an existing regime, for example, new hard law provisions would most likely be preferable, *ceteris paribus*, and we find some examples of states establishing such conflicting hard law regimes below. In practice, however, states often choose instruments of a relatively softer law nature to counter existing hard law, as our examples will show. We can imagine several reasons for such a choice. One explanation may be that states do not wish to counter existing hard law directly for systemic reasons, but rather prefer to soften it indirectly, such as through affecting the interpretation of the existing hard law, and thus its precision and clarity. Thus, even when states choose a formally hard law instrument, the instrument may be soft along the dimension of delegation in order to avoid two judicial bodies pronouncing on a single issue in distinct regimes. Another explanation may be that the existing hard law is of a broad scope of coverage, such as the rules of the World Trade Organization, so that states do not wish to undermine the overall system, but merely affect the operation of some legal provisions within the existing regime. Another explanation may be, from a constructivist perspective, that the existing hard law exercises some normative pull so that states find it difficult to find a sufficient number of allied states to enter into a new hard law instrument that directly counters the existing one. Finally, it may be that some (revisionist) states, dissatisfied with existing regimes, do indeed press for conflicting hard law provisions, but are unable to secure the agreement of other (status quo) parties on such provisions, and fall-back on soft law agreements as a second-best alternative.

Regardless of the specific combinations of hard and soft law provisions, our central point is that, in the presence of distributive conflict and fragmented regime complexes, the interaction of hard and soft law is likely to be not complementary but antagonistic, with the strengths of each regime being undermined through such interaction. In such a setting, we contend, soft law provisions are likely to be "hardened," losing many of the purported advantages of soft law such as experimentation and flexibility as a result of their link to hard law regimes. Hard law provisions, by contrast, may be "softened," as states, international courts and tribunals are increasingly forced to weigh the black-letter provisions of one regime against the competing normative provisions of neighboring regimes. This scenario, moreover, is more than simply a theoretical possibility: if distributive conflict over the terms of cooperation is ubiquitous, as we have argued above, and if a given issue is subject to multiple regimes in the ever-thickening web of international norms, rules, and institutions, then we may expect hard and soft law to interact antagonistically across a broad range of issues in international politics. To illustrate this argument empirically, we begin in this section with the case of agricultural biotechnology, an area of international regulation that has been subject to both distributional conflict and a well-developed regime complex, before moving on in Section 5 to articulate additional hypotheses and examine a range of additional empirical cases.

As we have demonstrated at length elsewhere, the US and EU have taken sharply divergent approaches to the regulation of agricultural biotechnology.[101] Simplifying only slightly, the United States has, since the 1980s, adopted a set of regulations that treated genetically modified (GM) foods as largely equivalent to their conventional counterparts, which contributed in turn to the early adoption of agricultural biotechnology by US firms and farmers. In the European Union, by contrast, regulators and publics have taken a far more cautious approach to genetically modified organisms (GMOs), treating genetically modified foods and crops as different from their conventional counterparts, and adopting increasingly strict and complex regulatory procedures for their approval and marketing. Unlike in the United States, GM foods and crops face considerable regulatory hurdles in the EU, including requirements for mandatory pre-approval of all GM products, as well as provisions on the mandatory labeling and traceability of all GM products, which have made it difficult and sometimes impossible for US farmers to export genetically modified foods to markets in Europe. They also face greater social resistance, with activists campaigning against GM foods and ripping up GM crops from fields, and public opinion far more mobilized over GM foods than in the United States. Reflecting this "regulatory polarization," US and EU negotiators have

---

[101] The analysis in this section draws in part on our book, Pollack and Shaffer (2009).

demonstrated sharply divergent preferences over global GMO regulation, with each side consistently seeking to export its own approach to the global level. The level of distributive conflict in this area is, therefore, high.

This transatlantic dispute over GMO regulation, moreover, has played out against the backdrop of a regime complex comprising both soft law regimes, including the non-binding guidelines and recommendations issued by the OECD and Codex Alimentarius Commission (Codex), alongside regimes having more hard law characteristics, such as the Cartagena Biosafety Protocol and the World Trade Organization, the latter of which combines relatively detailed, legally binding rules with a particularly strong system of third-party dispute-settlement to interpret and enforce them. In this setting, both the US and the EU have attempted to export their different approaches to various international regimes, engaging in "forum-shopping" to find particularly hospitable regimes, and producing awkward compromises within, as well as inconsistencies among, various international regimes. In the process, soft and hard law mechanisms have not interacted in a complementary and progressive manner, as theorized in the existing literature, but rather served to constrain and undercut each other. More flexible soft law regimes like the Codex Alimentarius Commission have been "hardened" by concerns over the implications of their decisions in the hard law WTO regime, while the hard law WTO Agreement on Sanitary and Phytosanitary Standards (SPS Agreement) has been "softened," being made more flexible and less predictable as the WTO judicial process has sought means to avoid deciding the substantive issues in dispute.

Let us explain how this has worked in some detail. The existing WTO regime favors the US position that any import restrictions of genetically modified (GM) products must be based on a scientific risk assessment, even if the regulatory restrictions apply equally to domestically produced and imported products. From the perspective of the EU, the 1992 Convention on Biodiversity (CBD), one of a series of framework agreements adopted at the 1992 Conference on Environment and Development at Rio de Janeiro, Brazil, offered a promising alternative forum for the regulation of GM products. In particular, it offered a forum within which the EU could press for an international environmental agreement supporting its precautionary approach to biotech regulation. Thanks to EU entrepreneurship, countries adopted a new Biosafety Protocol to the CBD in September 2003, which had been ratified by over 140 parties by early 2008.

The United States attempted to block adoption of the Protocol but was unsuccessful. The US nonetheless actively participated in the negotiations, including over the drafting of a provision governing the relationship of the Biosafety Protocol to the WTO agreements. The US demanded a "savings clause" to preserve WTO rights because otherwise there would be an argument under international law that conflicting provisions in a treaty signed last in time prevail over those in a prior treaty (known as *lex posteriori*).[102] The US obtained such a clause, but it failed to obtain a clear reservation of its WTO rights.[103] Rather, references to other "international agreements" were only made in the Protocol's preamble, and these references are in tension with each other. The preamble provides that "this Protocol shall not be interpreted as implying a change in the rights and obligations of a Party under any existing international agreements." The next phrase, however, states that "the above recital is not intended to subordinate this Protocol to other international agreements." As an EU representative stated, the two clauses effectively "cancel each other out," leaving the legal relationship between the two regimes unclear and allowing both sides to claim a partial victory.[104] The EU, therefore, could point to the Biosafety Protocol as evidence of an international consensus (involving over 140 parties). It could (and did) modify its existing legislation to comply with its international commitments under the Biosafety Protocol, pointing to these international obligations in its defense against the United States' WTO challenge to the EU's biotech regime in 2003. From a legal positivist perspective, the Biosafety Protocol is a form of "hard" law as its rules are binding on the parties to it, but it is "softer"

---

[102] Safrin (2002, p. 613–14).
[103] For useful overviews of the Biosafety Protocol and its relation to the SPS Agreement, see Safrin (2002), and Winham (2003).
[104] Inside US Trade (2000).

than the WTO regime along a hard-soft law continuum, since third-party dispute-settlement is not central to its operation.

Overall, the EU has found a more favorable forum in the Biosafety Protocol to fashion international rules and norms that contain its "fingerprints," coinciding with and supporting its regulatory approach to agricultural biotechnology. In particular, the Protocol has created new rules providing for the application of the precautionary principle in national decision-making, and the requirement of labeling of Living Modified Organisms (LMOs) in conformity with an importing country's requirements. In addition, discussion continues regarding risk assessment and risk management principles, including the taking into account of "socio-economic considerations" in regulatory approvals, as well as liability rules. In this way, the Protocol serves as a counterweight to the WTO SPS Agreement's narrower focus on science-based justifications for SPS measures affecting trade.

Both the US and EU also attempted to export their policies to a third organization, the Codex Alimentarius Commission, an intergovernmental body established in 1962 by the UN Food and Agriculture Organization (FAO) and the World Health Organization (WHO) to facilitate international trade in food through the adoption of international food-safety standards, which consisted of 178 members by early 2008. Traditionally the US and EU have driven Codex agendas and still do so to a large extent. Each works to find allies for its own positions.

Codex traditionally represented a form of soft law, since the standards were not binding and, by definition, there was no need for a dispute-settlement system to enforce them.[105] The process for producing Codex standards involves committees of experts which are established to deliberate over the appropriate standards. A designated Codex committee elaborates a draft standard or guideline subject to comments by member governments and interested international organizations. Once the process is completed, standards are approved by the full Codex Alimentarius Commission, which meets once every two years.

---

[105] Once countries adopted them, however, this "soft" law clearly could have real legal effects.

Overall, Codex became a sort of gentleman's club — or epistemic community — of food specialists, with many designated by industry, based on the following characteristics:

(1) the position of Codex as relatively isolated from international hard law and politics, (2) the voluntary nature of Codex activities and output, (3) agreed-upon norms, which restrained members from both obstructing the process of elaborating new Codex standards and from letting trade considerations override all other considerations, and (4) lack of sanctions in situations where [standards are] not followed.[106]

Those attending Codex meetings were (and the majority remain) food safety experts, often with technical scientific backgrounds from national administrations and industry.[107] Although only governments can vote, the process has often been driven by industry, which seeks to reduce compliance costs resulting from multiple national regulations.

The situation of the Codex, however, changed considerably with the creation of the WTO and the adoption of the SPS Agreement in 1995. Under the WTO's SPS Agreement, implementation of a Codex standard creates a presumption of compliance with "harder" WTO law provisions, subject to binding dispute-settlement. More precisely, article 3.1 of the SPS Agreement provides that WTO members shall base their food-safety standards on international standards, guidelines and recommendations (specifying those of Codex), subject to certain exceptions. Article 3.2 further states that a member's conformity with these international standards shall be presumed to comply with WTO law. These SPS provisions have significantly increased the significance of Codex standards, providing a significant impetus to harmonization activities, but also "hardening" Codex decision-making by providing US and EU negotiators with an incentive both to export and to protect their respective regulatory standards.

---

[106]Veggeland and Borgen (2005, p. 684).

[107]See e.g., Millstone and van Zwanenberg (2002). Put another way, in the words of an FDA official, Codex was a "backwater," as exciting as "watching the paint dry or the grass grow." Shaffer telephone interview Jan. 29, 2008.

The effect of Codex standards became clear in the US-EU trade dispute over the EU's ban on beef produced with growth hormones. In 1995, at the first Codex session following the creation of the WTO, the United States strategically "forced a vote and the adoption of Codex standards" covering five bovine growth hormones, winning the vote by a 33–29 margin, with seven abstentions.[108] It was hardly a consensus decision, but it was enough to establish a "voluntary" international Codex standard under the organization's voting rules. Shortly afterwards, the US initiated its WTO complaint against the EU, contending that the EU's ban was not "based" on an international (Codex) standard as required by the SPS Agreement.

Since then, the United States and European countries have placed increasing importance on the negotiation of new regulatory principles and standards within Codex, since these principles and standards may be invoked (and already have been invoked) in the decisions of WTO panels and of the Appellate Body. As a European Commission representative before Codex concludes, "In the past, if we disagreed with Codex standards or Code of Practice, we could ignore it and take our own legislation. Now we can't."[109] In response, states began sending more than food experts and food agency officials to Codex meetings, complementing them with "delegates from the diplomatic services and ministries of trade, industry, finance, and foreign affairs." In an empirical study, Veggeland and Borden note an increase of such representatives to the Codex Committee on General Principles from 10 in 1992, to 32 in 2000, and to 41 in 2001.[110]

The Codex process has encountered particularly severe difficulties in addressing issues that implicate risk management policy over transgenic varieties. Three Codex sub-groups have addressed them: the Committee on General Principles (regarding the use of the precautionary principle and "other legitimate factors" besides science in risk management); the Committee on Labeling (regarding the labeling of GM

---

[108]Victor (2004, p. 899); and Charnovitz (1997, p. 1786).
[109]Quoted in Veggeland and Borgen (2005, p. 683).
[110]Veggeland and Borgen (2005, p. 689).

foods); and the Committee on Food Import and Export Inspection and Certification Systems (regarding the issue of traceability). Here, we find arduous negotiations between the US and EU, each of which put forward distinctive and sharply opposed proposals for international standards and guidelines on issues that could have a direct bearing on the application of the SPS Agreement to national regulatory measures, and in particular in the WTO biotech case that the US initiated in 2003, resulting in deadlock in the soft law Codex regime.[111]

The results of these negotiations in the purportedly soft law Codex forum have not produced consensus. Like the paragraphs of the Cartagena Protocol dealing with the relation between Cartagena and WTO law, much of these Codex texts simply paper over rather than settle the differences among the parties, potentially delegating clarification of these issues, if at all, to the WTO dispute-settlement system. Rather than hard law and soft law working in coordination toward genuine "problem-solving," the hard law of the WTO has constrained and to some extent "hardened" what was supposed to be a flexible, "voluntary" process for harmonized rule-making and guidance to facilitate trade in agricultural products. Strategic bargaining in defense of trade interests has often replaced technical discussions. As Victor writes, we are often now more likely to see "dueling experts," reflecting US adversarial legalism, than "independent expert panels" working collaboratively to "synthesize complex technical information."[112] As Veggeland and Borgen add, we now see a "replication of WTO coalition[s] and positioning pattern[s] in the Codex."[113] An organization in which decision-making was formerly based primarily on a "logic of arguing" based on deliberation has been transformed to one more frequently based on a "logic of consequentiality" based on bargaining.

The United States was concerned with the spread of regulation in other countries restricting the growth and sale of GM products, which

---

[111]For a detailed analysis of the negotiations over these provisions, see e.g., Poli (2003), and Pollack and Shaffer (2009, Chapter 4).
[112]Victor (2004, p. 933).
[113]Veggeland and Borgen (2005, p. 698).

was spurred and legitimated by the Biosafety Protocol. In response, the United States finally brought a WTO complaint against EU regulatory measures in 2003, which the US hoped would have significant implications for other countries' practices. After considerable delay, the WTO dispute-settlement panel finally issued its decision in September 2006. The underlying conflict over the conflicting US and EU regulatory approaches, however, arguably affected the panel's decision. The impact of the panel's decision would be felt outside the trade regime, in both domestic law and politics and in the international regimes regulating other aspects of agricultural biotechnology. As a result, we contend, the WTO hard law dispute-settlement system adopted a cautious approach in its interpretation and application of the SPS Agreement, providing less clarity as to members' SPS commitments, arguably reducing their credibility. The linkage of the agricultural biotechnology issue to other substantive regimes, we argue, helped to "soften" the effect of WTO hard law, which lost several of the defining characteristics of hard law in practice. We find that the SPS Agreement was effectively made less binding in practice in this case, for reasons that we now explain.

Even though the panel's decision weighed in at over one thousand pages of text, the panel expressly avoided examining many crucial issues, most particularly the questions "whether biotech products in general are safe or not" and "whether the biotech products at issue in this dispute are 'like' their conventional counterparts." The panel did find in favor of the United States, but largely on procedural and not substantive grounds, with less hard law substantive bite. As a result, the substantive outcome and application of SPS rules remain unclear. As regards measures adopted at the EU level, the panel only found that the EU had engaged in "undue delay" in its approval process. The panel found that because of this delay, the EU had never taken an actual "SPS measure." On these grounds, the panel did not examine the EU's actions under the SPS Agreement's substantive provisions. It thus avoided determining whether the EU had violated its obligation to base a decision on a risk assessment, whether any assessments showed greater risks of GM varieties than for conventional plant varieties, whether the EU was consistent in its application of food safety regulations, and whether the EU could adopt regulations that are less trade restrictive while accomplishing its safety objectives. Regarding safeguards enacted by EU member states, in contrast, the panel found that all of them were "SPS measures" that violated the EU's substantive obligations under article 5.1 of the SPS Agreement because they were "not based on a risk assessment." However, the panel only reached this conclusion by looking to risk assessments already conducted at the EU level, finding that the member-state bans were inconsistent with the EU's internal risk assessment findings.

Even though the WTO biotech panel found that the Biosafety Protocol's provisions did not apply because the United States is not a party to the Protocol, panelists can implicitly take the Protocol into account. They can do so through their appreciation of the political stakes of alternative interpretations of WTO rules (from a rationalist perspective), and through the Protocol's impact on the framing and broader social understanding of the issues (from a constructivist one). The existence of the Protocol can affect the interpretation of WTO legal provisions and the appreciation of the underlying facts of the case to which WTO law is applied. Moreover, it is simply not in the interest of the WTO as an organization to ignore the content of an international environmental agreement, especially one having over 140 parties. In the context of agricultural biotechnology regulation, the CBD's Biosafety Protocol has created normative pressure for a WTO panel not to be too demanding on the risk assessment requirement.

WTO judges, both panelists and the members of the Appellate Body, have some independent agency. They are not only interpreters and appliers of WTO legal provisions. The pattern of their jurisprudence suggests that they also assume a mediating role. The WTO Appellate Body and judicial panels at times have an incentive to write opinions that are slightly ambiguous, leading to different interpretations as to how they can be implemented. In this way, they can shape their decisions, especially in hard cases, to facilitate amicable settlement, and thereby uphold the WTO legal system from normative challenge.

In doing so, however, they render the WTO's hard law text less clear, and thus less binding in practice. For example, through finding that neither the EU general nor product specific moratoria were "SPS measures," the panel left a WTO decision over the crucial substantive issue of whether EU-level decision-making was based on a scientific risk assessment for another day. As regards the member state safeguard measures, the panel found that they were inconsistent with the EU's substantive WTO commitments to base SPS measures on a risk assessment, but did so by relying on risk assessments conducted by the EU itself. The panel even indicated a means for the EU to comply with SPS requirements, including for member state safeguards, in a manner that would enhance EU discretion.[114] The panel decision was not unique to the GMO case. As we have discussed elsewhere, even before the panel's GMO decision, the jurisprudence of the Appellate Body indicated a willingness to provide significant discretion to domestic regulators regarding SPS measures.[115]

Under the panel's reasoning, only once the EU actually makes a decision which results in an "SPS measure" regarding a GM variety may a complainant bring a substantive claim. In such case, the complainant would have to restart the process from scratch. A panel would have to be formed and experts consulted. The actual delay in the panel making a decision on the substance of EU decision-making will thus be much longer than the three and half years that the case formally took (not to count subsequent procedures regarding the EU's implementation of the ruling), if indeed a new claim is ever filed. The panel thereby effectively parried deciding on the substance of EU decision-making. The panel's delay can be viewed in socio-legal terms. The panel was not anxious to make a substantive decision on EU procedures regarding

---

[114]The panel stated that "if there are factors which affect scientists' level of confidence in a risk assessment they have carried out, a Member may in principle take this into account." It declared that "there may conceivably be cases where a Member which follows a precautionary approach, and which confronts a risk assessment that identifies uncertainties or constraints, would be justified" in adopting a stricter SPS measure than another member responding to the same risk assessment. The panel repeated this same analysis verbatim in assessing whether a member state safeguard could be found to meet the requirements under 5.7 for provisional measures. See Panel Report, at Sections 7.3065 & 7.3244–7.3245.

[115]Pollack and Shaffer (2009, chapter 4).

the politically controversial issue of GMOs, resulting in a softening of the binding nature of the WTO commitments in question.[116]

In sum, the intense politicization of the issue, and the entrenchment of two sharply divergent regulatory systems governing the world's two largest economies meant that the various multilateral negotiations on agricultural biotechnology resembled a Battle of the Sexes game, in which each side sought common international standards *on its own terms.* These various regimes have interacted, but the result has been some "hardening" of the soft law regimes like Codex, and to some "softening" (and more flexibility and less predictability) of the hard law WTO dispute-settlement system. The Codex has lost some of its traditional advantages as a soft law regime, growing more contentious, more difficult, and less deliberative over time because states are concerned about how its decisions can be used in the hard law WTO dispute-settlement system. By contrast, the quintessential hard law regime of the WTO dispute-settlement system has been softened somewhat, as panelists and Appellate Body members need to take into account not only political pressures from the member states, but also the growing overlaps, tensions, and conflicts between the WTO legal order and the provisions — both hard and soft — of neighboring international regimes.

5. Hypotheses as to the Interaction of Hard and Soft Law Instruments

As we have now shown, although hard and soft law mechanisms can complement each other, they do not necessarily interact in a complementary, mutually reinforcing manner. We advance three hypotheses as to how these tools operate in international governance. In each case, we refer to policy examples. We offer these arguments as conjectures subject to further testing.

---

[116]For a detailed, step-by-step analysis of the decision, see Shaffer (2008).

1. *Where the US and EU agree on a regulatory approach, we are more likely to see hard and soft law work as complements in an evolutionary manner.*

Because of US and EU collective market power, where the US and EU agree on a policy, it is much easier for them to promote it globally. As Richard Steinberg writes regarding the Uruguay Round of trade negotiations, for example, "[f]rom the time the transatlantic powers agreed to [a common] approach in 1990, they definitively dominated the agenda-setting process, that is, the formulation and drafting of texts that would be difficult to amend."[117]

We have seen many examples of this process.[118] One side may initially be the primary entrepreneur behind the international regulatory initiative, eventually bringing the other side on board. The US has often taken the lead in initiatives that have resulted in successful international regulatory cooperation, from international agreements to protect the ozone layer to the anti-bribery convention to the Uruguay Round of trade negotiations. In both the ozone protection and anti-bribery cases, the initial instruments were of a soft law nature, and hard law agreements were reached once EU members were convinced of the benefits of a hard law approach. Yet with the increased institutionalization and harmonization of European regulation at the EU level, the EU may likewise play an increasingly important entrepreneurial role in global governance.[119] Generally speaking, the success of international endeavors, from the International Organization of Securities Commissions (IOSCO), to the Basel Committee, to the export credit soft law arrangement, depends on the cooperation of the US and the EU or its

---

[117]Steinberg (2002). See also Drezner (2007), arguing that US/EU agreement is both a necessary and sufficient condition for global regulatory cooperation.

[118]Braithwaite and Drahos cite the United States' successful use of forum-shifting in the global regulation of intellectual property and telecommunications to the WTO, respectively from WIPO and the ITU, as well as competition policy, away from UNCTAD. They also cite the EU's successful "initiative of establishing the international Conference on Harmonization as an alternative forum to WHO" for the regulation of pharmaceutical drugs. Braithwaite and Drahos (2000, p. 566–568).

[119]Elliot Posner makes this argument regarding financial services. See Posner (2005).

members.[120] Indeed, we suggest that much of the existing literature on the complementary interaction of hard and soft law exhibits selection bias by drawing disproportionately from cases in which the US and EU agree on the aims and terms of regulation because there are no, or only minimal, distributive conflicts between them.

2. *Where the US and EU disagree on a regulatory approach, i.e., where there are distributive conflicts between them, we are more likely to see hard and soft law work in opposition to each other, especially where the issue in question is governed by multiple, overlapping regimes. Given the fragmented nature of the international system, the US and EU will attempt to advance their interests in those regimes — both hard and soft law — that they find to be most favorable to their respective positions.*

Given the relatively equal economic power of the US and EU, where the two sides disagree on a policy position, they are relatively well-positioned to use their market power to offset each other's efforts to export their own regulatory practices to the international level. In these struggles, they look for allies to advance their aims, whether in an existing forum or a new one. In many cases, the result of US–EU conflict will be either international instruments containing general language that does not take a position either way or competing international hard or soft law instruments. For example, competition law is an area where the US and EU often have convergent policies and the sides have collaborated in a soft law International Competition Network in promoting competition law globally. However, the US and EU disagree regarding the appropriate policies toward dominant firms, reflected in their different approaches to Microsoft's policies. As a result, the International Competition Network working group efforts on single firm dominance have resulted in recommendations that are at a high degree of generality because of disagreements between the US and Europe on these issues.[121]

---

[120] See Levit (2008); Raustiala (2002); and Zaring (2005).
[121] See also Kovacic (2008). We also thank Professor Spencer Waller for his email of June 8, 2008 on this point.

We have shown how the US and EU have attempted to export their policy approaches in the area of agriculture biotechnology to different international regimes. Although the US formally won the WTO case, it has often appeared that the EU has been winning the struggle on the ground, since most countries signed the new Biosafety Protocol and have begun to implement domestic legislation to restrict the import and production of GM products, and to create stringent labeling requirements. However, the US has actively provided technical assistance around the world to develop local constituencies for the promotion of agricultural biotech. The US has been somewhat successful as plantings have rapidly risen in the largest developing countries, and in particular in China, India, Brazil and Argentina.[122] A number of these countries are members of the Biosafety Protocol. Efforts under the Protocol to adopt more stringent labeling requirements have run into obstacles in the last years, as agricultural ministries have realized the potential impact of these requirements on agricultural trade.[123] In the case of voluntary soft law-making in Codex, the US–EU conflict regarding risk management policies has given rise to hard bargaining resulting either in no agreement or, where some agreement is reached, in general compromise language that papers over the US–EU differences.

We posit that the tension among international regimes will generally apply in trade and social policy issues where the US and EU take divergent positions, and that the WTO will lie at the center of inter-regime conflicts given its broad scope of coverage and its implications because of its hard law dispute-settlement system.[124] We provide a second example here. The US and EU have long taken different positions regarding the regulation of trade in cultural products, and in particular, films and other media. This issue was particularly contentious during the Uruguay Round in which the EU pushed for an express "cultural exception," while the US pressed for the liberalization of national policies.[125] Neither side was fully successful. The 1995 WTO

---

[122] James (2006).
[123] Pollack and Shaffer (2009, chapter 4).
[124] See also Kelly (2006).
[125] Graber (2006). See also Voon (2006).

General Agreement on Trade in Services (GATS) provides that countries are not bound to open their markets to audiovisual services unless they make express commitments. Although the US failed to obtain any EU commitments to open its market to audiovisual services under the GATS, the US set up a framework for future negotiations that could lead to such liberalization, and it was able to obtain commitments from some WTO members.[126]

The EU then turned to a more favorable forum to advance its interests, the United Nations Educational Scientific and Cultural Organization (UNESCO). In 2000, the Council of Europe adopted a declaration on cultural diversity. This European declaration helped to pave the way, in 2001, for UNESCO's adoption of a Universal Declaration on Cultural Diversity, a soft law instrument. UNESCO then turned to the drafting of a binding convention, the Convention on the Protection and Promotion of the Diversity of Cultural Expressions, which 148 countries signed in October 2005. Only two countries opposed it, the United States and Israel. The United States "vehemently opposed" the convention throughout the negotiations, maintaining that it was protectionist and inappropriately implicated UNESCO in trade policy.[127] The convention went into effect in March 2007.

Although the convention is formally binding, its core provisions are defensive. As Christophe Beat Graber writes, "the principal role of the [Convention] will be to act as a counterpart to the WTO whenever conflicts between trade and culture arise."[128] Article 1(g) of the convention, for example, provides that one of its objectives is "to give recognition to the distinctive nature of cultural activities, goods and services as vehicles of identity, values and meaning" — as opposed to having value only in economic terms. Article 5 of the convention then affirms the sovereign right of the parties "to formulate and implement their cultural polices and to adopt measures to protect and promote the diversity of cultural expressions and to strengthen international

---

[126] Graber (2006, p. 554).
[127] Graber (2006, pp. 560, 565).
[128] Graber (2006, p. 565).

cooperation to achieve [such] purposes." Article 6 provides that each party "may adopt measures aimed at protecting and promoting the diversity of cultural expressions within its territory," including "financial assistance" and other "regulatory measures." Article 8 goes further, maintaining that, "Parties may take all appropriate measures to protect and preserve cultural expressions in situations [where cultural expressions are] in need of urgent safeguarding."

Much of the rest of the convention is of a soft law nature. In contrast to its recognition of parties' *rights*, the convention only creates soft law *obligations*, such as for parties to further public awareness of cultural diversity's importance (article 10), to acknowledge civil society's role (article 11) and to generally exercise their "best efforts" to implement the convention through cultural policy measures.[129] The convention provides for dispute-settlement, but it too is of a soft law nature, relying on negotiation, mediation and conciliation.[130] The conciliation system, moreover, is non-binding, and parties may also opt out of it.

A key issue thus became the relationship of the convention to other international treaties, and particularly the WTO agreements. The convention provides another example of strategic ambiguity in this respect. Article 20 of the convention states that, "without subordinating this convention to any other treaty," the parties "shall foster mutual supportiveness" with other treaties and "take into account the relevant provisions" of the convention "when interpreting and applying ... other treaties" and "when entering into other international obligations." At the same time, the article provides that "nothing in this Convention shall be interpreted as modifying rights and obligations of the Parties under any other treaties to which they are parties."

Article 20's focus on the fostering of "mutual supportiveness" among treaty regimes can be read as an attempt to soften WTO rules to accommodate the convention's norms. The EU and other parties to the convention can now refer to an international convention that

---

[129] Graber (2006, p. 564).
[130] Article 25 of the Convention.

expressly notes their sovereign rights under international law to take measures, including trade measures, to protect their cultural diversity. As the number of countries ratifying the convention grows, the convention, together with the 2001 UNESCO Universal Declaration, could be viewed as emerging customary international law which applies to all nations except those non-signatories who persistently object to it.[131]

The UNESCO convention could thus have an impact on future WTO negotiations and on future WTO cases involving cultural products, even where they involve a WTO member that is not a party to it. The UNESCO convention can be used, in particular, to attempt to constrain WTO jurisprudence so that WTO panels interpret WTO rules in a manner that treads lightly in this area, with the result that the application of WTO agreements to cultural products will be softened. Article XX(f) of the General Agreement on Tariffs and Trade (GATT) 1994, for example, creates an exception to GATT obligations where a measure is "imposed for the protection of national treasures of artistic, historic or archaeological value," and Article XX(a) does the same for measures "to protect public morals." The interpretation of these or other GATT provisions could be influenced by the UNESCO convention, creating greater uncertainty as to the extent of WTO commitments as regards cultural products.

In sum, in this case as in the case of agricultural biotechnology regulation, the potential link between the UNESCO cultural regime and the WTO trade regime, together with the stark distributive differences between the US and the EU, have led to a "hardening" of bargaining over the UNESCO convention, and could, in time, produce a softening of WTO jurisprudence in this area.

3. *Even where the US and EU agree on a regulatory approach, smaller states can use hard and soft law strategies to attempt to thwart US and EU aims, again choosing regimes more favorable to their positions in a fragmented international system. However, the US and EU have significant advantages because of their market power and resources.*

---

[131] By May 1, 2008, 81 countries had become members of the convention.

The US and EU are not the only actors that can engage in strategies of deliberate countering of one hard or soft law instrument through activities in a separate regime resulting in distinct hard and soft law instruments. International law can also have distributional implications for developing countries, with intellectual property law being a prime example.[132] In their article on regime complexes, Raustiala and Victor show how the US and EU leveraged market power in trade negotiations under the Uruguay Round to create new rules under the Agreement on Trade-Related Aspects of Intellectual Property Rights (TRIPS) which were closely modeled on US or EU law, requiring the recognition of intellectual property rights in plant varieties. Developing countries responded by attempting to reframe intellectual property protection in light of environmental and development goals under the 1992 Convention on Biodiversity. Their efforts led to a 2002 Treaty on Plant Genetic Resources (PGR), which partly undercuts TRIPS rules.[133]

Laurence Helfer has also explored how developing countries "engage in regime shifting," adopting "the tools of soft lawmaking."[134] In doing so, they often work with non-governmental groups who serve as allies to help generate counter norms that are development-oriented.[135] Helfer shows how developing countries have attempted to counter the creation of hard intellectual property rights under the TRIPS Agreement and bilateral TRIPS-plus agreements through forum-shifting tactics involving the CBD, World Intellectual Property Organization (WIPO) and the World Health Organization (WHO). They have attempted to do so regarding an array of issues involving biodiversity, plant genetic resources for food and agriculture, public health, and human rights. They aim to generate "new principles, norms and rules of intellectual property" within these institutions which "are more closely aligned with these countries' interests."[136] For example, the Conference of the Parties to the

[132] Maskus (2000).
[133] Raustiala and Victor (2004, pp. 301–302).
[134] Helfer (2004, pp. 17, 32).
[135] Helfer (2004, pp. 32, 53–54).
[136] Helfer (2004, p. 6).

CBD has created workshops, established working groups and developed guidelines to address the issues of indigenous knowledge and the sharing of benefits from the use of genetic resources.[137] Concurrent efforts within the FAO gave rise to the 2002 Treaty on Plant Genetic Resources (PGR) which recognizes "farmers rights," "sovereign rights" over plant genetic resources, and equitable "sharing of the benefits arising from commercialization." This treaty constitutes hard law in that it is formally binding, although it is much weaker than the TRIPS Agreement in its dispute-settlement provisions. Once again, countries have engaged in strategic ambiguity in defining the PGR Treaty's relation to the TRIPS Agreement.

Eyal Benvenisti and George Downs nonetheless question the efficacy of these strategies.[138] They contend that powerful countries are best able to make use of fragmented international regimes through forum-shopping strategies to shape international law over time. They find that fragmented regime complexes increase the transaction costs for participants, favoring those with greater resources. They argue that "creating institutions along narrow functionalist lines ... limits the opportunities that weaker states have to build cross-issue coalitions that could potentially increase their bargaining power and influence."[139] The counter-regimes mentioned by Helfer, for example, are soft law regimes compared to the TRIPS Agreement, and weaker states have adopted tactics that are primarily reactive in these soft law venues. Benvenisti and Downs note, in particular, how "serial bilateralism is being used with increasing frequency by powerful states to shape the evolution of norms in areas such as intellectual property protection and drug pricing where they have vital interests at stake and where their position on issues is far different from those of the vast majority of states."[140] These bilateral agreements constitute hard law along all three dimensions defined by Abbot and Snidal. Benvenisti and Downs find a similar process in the negotiation of investment

---

[137] Helfer (2004, pp. 32–34).

[138] Benvenisti and Downs (2007). See also Drezner (2007).

[139] Benvenisti and Downs (2007, p. 595).

[140] Benvenisti and Downs (2007, p. 611).

protections through bilateral investment treaties.[141] The earlier failure of developing countries to create a "new international economic order" in the 1970s, including through the United Nations Conference on Trade and Development as a rival institution to the GATT, suggests that there are severe limits to weaker countries' use of this option.[142]

6. Conclusions

Taken together, our hypotheses suggest that hard and soft law *may* interact in a complementary and evolutionary fashion, as predicted in the canonical literature, but *only under certain conditions*. Specifically, where the US and the EU, as the dominant players in global regulation, agree on the aims and terms of regulation, soft and hard law may complement each other in the ways discussed by Abbott and Snidal, Shelton, and others, so as to promote greater regulatory cooperation. However, in the absence of such an agreement, or in the presence of distributive conflict between the US and the EU and third countries, we can predict, and indeed we have seen in several concrete instances, that states will strategically use different hard and soft law regimes to advance their respective aims in the international arena. In these cases, hard and soft law regimes may be placed in active opposition to each other, with soft law regimes taking on the "hard bargaining" characteristics of hard law regimes, while the terms of hard law regimes may become increasingly flexible, uncertain and "soft," insofar as policy-makers and adjudicators tread softly in deciding cases with implications in neighboring regimes.

---

[141] Benvenisti and Downs (2007, pp. 611–612). See also Guzman (1998).

[142] Krasner (1985). Braithwaite and Drahos (2000, p. 565) come to a similar conclusion, writing: "Clearly, very few actors in the context of global regulation have the capacity to run strategies of forum-shifting.... Forum-shifting is a strategy that only the powerful and well-resourced can use." Yet they also concede that, "in some way weaker players are better off in a world where there are multiple fora capable of dealing with similar agendas," thus providing smaller states with a slightly increased ability to resist US and EU efforts to set global standards.

None of our analysis is to suggest that either hard or soft law is inherently flawed or not worth pursuing. Where the scope conditions are right, hard and soft law *can* interact productively, as discussed above. Furthermore, even where particular issues are characterized by distributive conflicts and fragmented international regimes, both hard and soft law regimes can play a positive role in encouraging cooperation, provided that our expectations of these regimes remain realistic. Even in these situations, while regimes can be expected to lose some of their traditional law advantages — such as flexibility and deliberative, technocratic decision-making in soft law regimes and legal certainty in hard law regimes — they nevertheless offer useful fora in which states may *bargain* over the adoption of international standards and attempt to address their implications. More generally, multilateral regimes, while subject to distributive conflicts and to forum-shopping and inconsistency across regimes, can still provide their traditional functions of lowering the transaction costs of negotiations, providing a common vocabulary for the parties, clarifying at least some of the mutual understandings and obligations of the parties, and contributing to regulatory capacity building in less-developed countries.[143]

In addition, we suggest, tensions and even conflicts among hard and soft international law regimes should not necessarily be lamented. The tensions we observe simply reflect underlying differences among states and state constituencies, and in particular among powerful ones, in a diverse, pluralist world. In such a context, overlapping, fragmented regimes can also provide a service to each other, signaling states and international decision-makers to tread softly in applying their particular rules, taking account of developments in other spheres of international law and politics.[144] For example, they can prompt internal responses within the WTO regime to preserve its own political legitimacy. In the context of agricultural biotechnology regulation, the CBD's Biosafety Protocol has provided a counter-voice which can protect the WTO system from the WTO dispute-settlement system's relative insularity

---

[143] See e.g., the environmental regime case studies in Haas, Keohane and Levy (1993).
[144] For a related concept of "dialectical review" involving the interaction of international and national courts, see Ahdieh (2004).

from global politics. These agreements, we contend, will interact, and over time, they can operate recursively. In doing so, they can help stabilize conflict and reduce the likelihood of trade wars. They can also facilitate states' mutual accommodation of regulatory difference at least to a greater extent than in the absence of such institutions.

Ultimately, we contend, the relationship between international hard law and soft law instruments cannot be characterized in a universal or invariant fashion. Rather, we have argued, the interaction of hard and soft law depends in the first instance on the broader context of international cooperation, including the respective power of the key players, the degree of distributive conflict among them, and the constellation and character of regimes within a given regime complex. The canonical, complementary and evolutionary relationship between hard and soft law is not a myth, we maintain, but that relationship holds only under a set of scope conditions, including broad agreement between the US and the EU on the aims and terms of international law. Where these conditions fail to hold, the interaction between hard and soft law can be far more adversarial than the canonical literature suggests. Understanding the varied interactions of hard and soft law in a wider set of cases, we believe, represents the next major challenge in this field of study.

References

Abbott, Kenneth W., Robert O. Keohane, Andrew Moravcsik, Anne-Marie Slaughter and Duncan Snidal (2000). "The Concept of Legalization," *International Organization*, Vol. 54, No. 3, pp. 17–35.

Abbott, Kenneth W. and Duncan Snidal (2000). "Hard and Soft Law in International Governance," *International Organization*, Vol. 54, No. 3, pp. 421–456.

Abbott, Kenneth W. and Duncan Snidal (2004). "Pathways to Cooperation," in *The Impact of International Law on International Cooperation: Theoretical Perspectives*, Eyal Benvenisti and Moshe Hirsch, (eds.), New York: Cambridge University Press. pp. 50–84.

Ahdieh, Robert (2004). "Between Dialogue and Decree: International Review of National Courts," *New York University Law Review*, Vol. 79, pp. 2029–2163.

Alter, Karen J. and Sophie Meunier (2006). "Nested and Overlapping Regimes in the Transatlantic Banana Trade Dispute," *Journal of European Public Policy*, Vol. 13, No. 3, pp. 362–82.

Andrews, David M., Mark A. Pollack, Gregory C. Shaffer and Helen Wallace (eds.) (2005). *The Future of Transatlantic Economic Relations: Continuity Amid Discord*. European University Institute, Florence, Italy.

Baldwin, David A. (ed.) (1993). *Neorealism and Neoliberalism: The Contemporary Debate*. New York: Columbia University Press.

Benvenisti, Eyal and George W. Downs (2007). "The Empire's New Clothes: Political Economy and the Fragmentation of International Law," *Stanford Law Review*, Vol. 60. Available at SSRN: http://ssrn.com/abstract=976930, accessed on 3 January 2008.

Berman, Paul (2007). "Global Legal Pluralism," *Southern California Law Review*, Vol. 80, pp. 1155–1237.

Bermann, George A., Matthias Herdegen, Peter Lindseth (2000). *Transatlantic Regulatory Cooperation: Legal Problems and Political Aspects*. Oxford: Oxford University Press.

Bernauer, Thomas and Thomas Sattler (2006). "Dispute-Escalation in the WTO: Are Conflicts over Environment, Health and Safety Regulation Riskier?" Center for Comparative and International Studies Working Paper, Zurich, No. 21.

Braithwaite, John and Peter Drahos (2000). *Global Business Regulation*. New York: Cambridge University Press.

Brunnee, Jutta and Stephen J. Toope (1997). "Environmental Security and Freshwater Resources: Ecosystem Regime Building," *American Journal of International Law*, Vol. 91, pp. 26–59.

Charney, Jonathan I. (1996). "The Implications of Expanding International Dispute-Settlement Systems: The 1982 Convention on the Law of the Sea," *American Journal of International Law*, Vol. 90, pp. 69–75.

Charnovitz, Steve (1997). The World Trade Organization, Meat Hormones and Food Safety, 14 Int'l Trade Rep. (BNA), No. 41, 1781 (Oct. 15, 1997).

Chayes, Abraham and Antonia Handler Chayes (1993). "On Compliance," *International Organization*, Vol. 47, No. 2, pp. 175–205.

Chinkin, Christine (1989). "The Challenge of Soft Law: Development and Change in International Law." *International and Comparative Law Quarterly*, Vol. 38, pp. 851–55.

Delmas-Marty, M. (1998). *Trois défis pour un droit mondial*. Paris: Seuil.

Downs, George W. David M. Rocke and Peter N. Barsoom (1996). "Is the Good News About Compliance Good News About Cooperation?" *International Organization*, Vol. 50, No. 3, pp. 379–406.

Drezner, Daniel W. (2007). *All Politics is Global: Explaining International Regulatory Regimes*. Princeton University Press.

Dunoff, Jeffrey, Steven Ratner and David Wippman (2006). *International Law: Norms, Actors, Process: A Problem-Oriented Approach*, 2nd edition. Aspen Law and Business Publishers.

Dupuy, Pierre-Marie (1999). "The Danger of Fragmentation or Unification of the International Legal System and the International Court of Justice," *NYU Journal of International Law and Politics*, Vol. 31, pp. 791–808.

Edelman, Murray (1964). *The Symbolic Uses of Politics*. Illinois: University of Illinois Press.

Evenett, Simon and Robert Stern (2010). "Condemned to Cooperate," in *Systemic Implications of Transatlantic Regulatory Cooperation and Competition*, Simon Evenett and Robert Stern (eds.). Singapore: World Scientific.

Fearon, James (1998). "Bargaining, Enforcement, and International Cooperation," *International Organization*, Vol. 52, No. 2, pp. 269–305.

Finnemore, Martha and Stephen J. Toope (2001). "Alternatives to 'Legalization': Richer Views of Law and Politics," *International Organization*, Vol. 55, No. 3, pp. 743–758.

Fisher-Lescano, Andreas and Gunter Teubner (2004). "Regime Collisions: The Vain Search for Legal Unity in the Fragmentation of Global Law, *Michigan Journal of International Law*, Vol. 25, pp. 999–1046.

Franck, Thomas M. (1990). *The Power of Legitimacy Among Nations*. New York: Oxford University Press.

Germain, Randall (1997). The International Organization of Credit. New York: Cambridge University Press.

Goldsmith, Jack and Eric Posner (2005). *The Limits of International Law*. New York: Oxford University Press.

Goodrich, Peter (2000). "Law-Induced Anxiety: Legalists, Anti-Lawyers and the Boredom of Legality," *Social and Legal Studies*, Vol. 9, pp. 143–163.

Gordon, Kathryn (1999). "Rules for the Global Economy: Synergies between Voluntary and Binding Approaches", *OECD Working Paper on International Investment*, Vol. 3.

Graber, C., (2006). "The New UNESCO Convention on Cultural Diversity: A Counterbalance to the WTO?" *Journal of International Economic Law*, Vol. 9, No. 3, pp. 553–574.

Grieco, Joseph (1988). "Anarchy and the Limits of Cooperation," *International Organization*, Vol. 42, No. 3, pp. 485–507.

Griffiths, John (1986). "What is Legal Pluralism?" *Journal of Legal Pluralism and Unofficial Law*, Vol. 24, pp. 1–55.

Gruber, Lloyd (2000). *Ruling the World: Power Politics and the Rise of Supranational Institutions*. New Jersey: Princeton University Press.

Guzman, Andrew (1998). "Why LDCs Sign Treaties That Hurt Them: Explaining the Popularity of Bilateral Investment Treaties" *Virginia Journal of International Law*, Vol. 38, pp. 639–688.

Guzman, Andrew (2005). "The Design of International Agreements," *The European Journal of International Law*, Vol. 16, No. 4, pp. 579–612.

Guzman, Andrew (2006). "The Promise of International Law," *Virginia Law Review*, Vol. 92, No. 3, pp. 533–564.

Guzman, Andrew (2008). *How International Law Works: A Rational Choice Theory*. Oxford University Press.

Haas, Peter M., Robert O. Keohane and Marc A. Levy (eds.) (1993). *Institutions for the Earth: Sources of Effective International Environmental Protection*. MIT Press.

Hasenclaver, Andreas, Peter Mayer and Volker Rittberger (1997). *Theories of International Regimes*. New York: Cambridge University Press.

Hathaway, Oona and Ariel N. Lavinbuk (2006). "Rationalism and Revisionism in International Law," (Book Review), *Harvard Law Review*, Vol. 119, No. 5, pp. 1404–1443.

Held, David, *et al.* (1999). *Global Transformations: Politics, Economics and Culture*. Stanford: Stanford University Press.

Helfer, Lawrence (2004). "Regime Shifting: The TRIPS Agreement and New Dynamics of Intellectual Property Lawmaking," *Yale Journal of International Law*, Vol. 29, pp. 1–83.

Hillgenberg, Hartmut (1999). "A Fresh Look at Soft Law", *European Journal of International Law*, Vol. 10, pp. 499–515.

Inside US Trade (2000). "Democracy, Science and Free Trade: Risk Regulation on Trial at the World Trade Organization," *Michigan Law Review*, Vol. 98, p. 2330.

International Law Commission (2006). *Fragmentation of International Law: Difficulties Arising from the Diversification and Expansion of International Law*, para. 8, U.N. Doc. A/CN.4/L/682 (Apr. 13, 2006) (finalized by Martti Koskenniemi).

James, Clive (2006). ISAAA Brief 35, Executive Summary, Global Status of Commercialized Biotech/GM Crops: 2006, http://www.isaaa.org/Resources/Publications/briefs/35/executivesummary/default.html, accessed on 8 January 2008.

Jupille, Joseph and Duncan Snidal (2006). The Choice of International Institutions: Cooperation, Alternatives and Strategies," unpublished paper, http://sobek.colorado.edu/~jupille/research/20060707-Jupille-Snidal.pdf, accessed on 15 January 2008.

Kelly, Claire (2006). "Power, Linkage and Accommodation: The WTO As An International Actor And Its Influence On Other Actors And Regimes," *Berkeley Journal of International Law*, Vol. 24, pp. 79–128.

Kirton, John J. and Michael J. Trebilcock (2004). "Introduction" in John J. Kirton and Michael J. Trebilcock (eds.). *Hard Choice, Soft Law: Voluntary Standards in Global Trade, Environment and Social Governance*, pp. 3–29. Ashgate Publishing, Ltd.

Klabbers, Jan (1996). "The Redundancy of Soft Law," *Nordic Journal of International Law*, Vol. 65, pp. 167–182.

Klabbers, Jan (1998). The Undesirability of Soft Law," *Nordic Journal of International Law*, Vol. 67, pp. 381–391.

Koh, Harold (1998). "The 1998 Frankel Lecture: Bringing International Law Home," *Houston Law Review*, Vol. 35, pp. 623-81.

Koskenniemi, Martti and Päivi Leinmo (2002). "Fragmentation of International Law. Postmodern Anxieties?" *Leiden Journal of International Law*, Vol. 15, No. 3, pp. 553–579.

Koremenos, Barbara, Charles Lipson and Duncan Snidal (2001). "The Rational Design of International Institutions," *International Organization*, Vol. 55, No. 4, pp. 761–800.

Kovacic, William E. (2008). "Competition Policy in the European Union and the United States: Convergence or Divergence?" Bates White Fifth Annual Antitrust Conference Washington, D.C. June 2, 2008, available at http://www.ftc.gov/speeches/kovacic/080602bateswhite.pdf.

Krasner, Stephen D. (ed.) (1983). *International Regimes.* Ithaca: Cornell University Press.

Krasner, Stephen D. (1985). *Structural Conflict: The Third World Against Global Liberalism.* Berkeley: University of California Press.

Krasner, Stephen D. (1991). "Global Communications and National Power: Life on the Pareto Frontier," *World Politics*, Vol. 43, No. 3, pp. 336–356.

Levit, Jane (2008). "Bottom-Up Lawmaking Through a Pluralist Lens: The ICC Banking Commission and the Transnational Regulation of Letters of Credit," *Emory Law Journal*, Vol. 57, pp. 101–120.

Lipson, Charles (1991). "Why Are Some International Agreements Informal?" *International Organization*, Vol. 45, No. 4, pp. 495–538.

Loya, Thomas and John Boli (1999). "Standardization in the World Polity: Technical Rationality over Power," in *Constructing World Culture: International Nongovernmental Organizations Since 1875*, John Boli and George Thomas (eds.). Stanford: Stanford University Press. pp. 169–197.

Macdonald, Roderick A. (1998). "Metaphors of Multiplicity: Civil Society, Regimes and Legal Pluralism," *Arizona Journal of International and Comparative Law*, Vol. 15, No. 1, pp. 69–91.

Marceau, Gabrielle (2001). "Conflicts of Norms and Conflicts of Jurisdictions: The Relationship between the WTO Agreement and MEAs and Other Treaties," *Journal of World Trade*, Vol. 35, No. 6, pp. 1081–1131.

Martin, Lisa (1992). *Coercive Cooperation.* Princeton: Princeton University Press.

Maskus, Keith E. (2000). *Intellectual Property Rights in the Global Economy.* Washington, DC: Institute for International Economics.

Mattli, Walter and Tim Büthe (2003). "Setting International Standards," *World Politics*, Vol. 56, No. 1, pp. 1–42.

Millstone, Erik and Patrick van Zwanenberg (2002). "The Evolution of Food Safety Policy-making Institutions in the UK, EU and Codex Alimentarius," *Soc Pol. and Admin*, Vol. 36, No. 6, pp. 593–609.

Morrow, James (1994). "The Forms of International Cooperation," *International Organization*, Vol. 48, No. 3, pp. 387–423.

Oye, Kenneth (ed.) (1986). *Cooperation under Anarchy.* Princeton: Princeton University Press.

Pauwelyn, Joost (2003). "The Role of Public International Law in the WTO: How Far Can We Go?" *American Journal of International Law*, Vol. 95, pp. 535–578.

Poli, Sara (2003). "Setting Out International Food Standards: Euro-American Conflicts within the Codex Alimentarius Commission," in *Risk Regulation in the European Union: Between Enlargement and Internationalization*, Giandomenico Majone (ed.). Florence: European University Institute. pp. 125–147.

Pollack, Mark A. and Gregory C. Shaffer (eds.) (2001). *Transatlantic Governance in the Global Economy.* Lanham, MD: Rowman and Littlefield.

Pollack, Mark A. and Gregory C. Shaffer (2009). *When Cooperation Fails: The International Law and Politics of Genetically Modified Foods.* Oxford: Oxford University Press.

Posner, Elliot (2005). "Market Power Without a Single Market: The New Transatlantic Relations in Financial Services," in *The Future of Transatlantic Economic Relations,*

David M. Andrews *et al.* (eds.). Florence: Robert Schuman Centre for Advanced Studies.

Powell, Robert (1991). "The Problem of Absolute and Relative Gains in International Relations Theory," *American Political Science Review*, Vol. 85, pp. 1303–20.

Raustiala, Kal (2000). "Compliance and Effectiveness in International Regulatory Cooperation," *Case Western Reserve Journal of International Law*, Vol. 32, pp. 387, 398.

Raustiala, Kal. (2002). "The Architecture of International Cooperation: Transgovernmental Networks and the Future of International Law," *Virginia Journal of International Law*, Vol. 43, No. 1, pp. 1–92.

Raustiala, Kal (2005). "Form and Substance in International Agreements," *American Journal of International Law*, Vol. 95, pp. 581–614.

Raustiala, Kal. and Anne-Marie Slaughter (2002). "International Law, International Relations, and Compliance," in *Handbook of International Relations*, Walter Carlsnaes, Thomas Risse and Beth A. Simmons (eds.). New York: SAGE Publications, 2002. pp. 538–558.

Raustiala, Kal and David G. Victor (1998). "Conclusions," in David G. Victor, Kal Raustiala and Eugene B. Skolnikoff, *The Implementation and Effectiveness of International Environmental Commitments: Theory and Practice*. Cambridge: MIT Press. pp. 659–707.

Raustiala, Kal and David G. Victor (2004). "The Regime Complex for Plant Genetic Resources," *International Organization*, Vol. 58, No. 2, pp. 277–309.

Reinicke, Wolfgang and Jan Martin Witte (2000). "Interdependence, Globalization and Sovereignty: The Role of Non-binding International Legal Accords," in *Commitment and Compliance*, Dinah Shelton (ed.). New York: Oxford University Press.

Report from the Commission to the Council and the European Parliament on the Implementation of EC No. 1829/2003 of the European Parliament and of the Council on Genetically Modified Food and Feed, COM (2006) 626 final (Oct. 25, 2006).

Roberts, Simon (2004). "After Government: On Representing Law without the State," *Modern Law Review*, Vol. 68, No. 1, pp. 1–24.

Robilant, Anna (2005). "A Genealogy of Soft Law", *American Journal of Comparative Law*, Summer.

Rocha Machado, Maira (2009). "Financial Regulation and International Criminal Policy: The Anti-Money Laundering System in Brazil and Argentina," working paper.

Ruggie, John Gerard (1998). "What Makes the World Hang Together? Neo-utilitarianism and the Social Constructivist Challenge," *International Organization*, Vol. 52, No. 4, pp. 855–885.

Sabel, Charles and William Simon (2006). "Epilogue: Accountability without Sovereignty," in *Law and New Governance in the EU and the US*, Gráinne de Búrca and Joanne Scott (eds.). Oxford: Hart Publishing. pp. 395–411.

Safrin, Sabrina (2002). "Treaties in Collision? The Biosafety Protocol and the World Trade Organization Agreements," *American Journal of International Law*, Vol. 96, No. 3, pp. 606–628.

Scott, Joanne and Gráinne de Búrca (2006). *Law and New Governance in the EU and the US*. Oxford, Hart Publishing.

Shaffer, Gregory (2009). "A Structural Theory of WTO Dispute-Settlement: Why Institutional Choice Lies at the Center of the GMO Case," *NYU Journal of International Law and Politics*, Vol. 41, No. 1, pp. 1–101.

Shelton, Dinah (2000). *Commitment and Compliance: The Role of Non-Binding Norms in the International Legal System*. New York: Oxford University Press.

Simma, Bruno (1985). "Self-Contained Regimes," *Netherlands Yearbook of International Law*, Vol. 16, pp. 111–120.

Simmons, Beth (2000). "International Efforts Against Money Laundering." In *Commitment and Compliance*, Dinah Shelton (ed.). New York: Oxford University Press.

Simon, William (2006). "Toyota Jurisprudence: Legal Theory and Rolling Rule Regimes," in *Law and New Governance in the EU and the US*, Gráinne de Búrca and Joanne Scott (eds.).

Sindico, Francesco (2006). "Soft Law and the Elusive Quest for Sustainable Global Governance," *Leiden Journal of International Law*, Vol. 19, No. 3, pp. 829–846.

Snidal, Duncan (1985). "Coordination Versus Prisoner's Dilemma: Implications for International Cooperation and Regimes," *American Political Science Review*, Vol. 79, No. 4, pp. 923–942.

Snidal, Duncan (1991). "International Cooperation Among Relative Gains Maximizers," *International Studies Quarterly*, Vol. 35, No. 4, pp. 387–402.

Snyder, Francis (1993). "The Effectiveness of European Community Law: Institutions, Processes, Tools and Techniques," *The Modern Law Review*, Vol. 56, No. 1, pp. 19–54.

Stein, Arthur (1982). "Coordination and Collaboration: Regimes in an Anarchic World," *International Organization*, Vol. 36, No. 2, pp. 399–324.

Steinberg, Richard H. (2002). "In the Shadow of Law or Power? Consensus-Based Bargaining and Outcomes in the GATT/WTO", *International Organization*, Vol. 56, No. 2, pp. 339–374.

Susskind, Lawrence and Connie Ozawa (1992), "Negotiating More Effective International Environmental Agreements," in The International Politics of the Environment: Actors, Interests, and Institutions, Andrew Hurrell and Benedict Kingsbury (eds.). Oxford: Clarendon Press.

Trubek, David M., Patrick Cottrell and Mark Nance (2006). "Soft Law, Hard Law and European Integration: Toward a Theory of Hybridity," in, *New Governance and Constitutionalism in Europe and the US*. Joanne Scott and Gráinne de Búrca (eds.). Oxford: Hart Publishing Ltd., pp. 65–94.

Veggeland, Frode and Svein Ole Borgen (2005). "Negotiating International Food Standards: The World Trade Organization's Impact on the *Codex Alimentarius* Commission," *Governance*, Vol. 18, No. 4, pp. 675–708.

Victor, David G. (2004). "The Sanitary and Phytosanitary Agreement of the World Trade Organization: An Assessment After Five Years," *New York University Journal of International Law and Politics*, Vol. 32, No. 4, pp. 865–937.

Voon, Tania (2006). "UNESO and WTO. A Clash of Cultures?" *International and Comparative Law Quarterly*, Vol. 55, No. 3, pp. 635–651.

Weil, Prosper (1983). "Towards Relative Normativity in International Law?" *American Journal of International Law*, Vol. 77, pp. 413–442.

Winham, Gilbert (2003). "International Regime Conflict in Trade and Environment: The Biosafety Protocol and the WTO," *World Trade Review*, Vol. 2, No. 2, pp. 131–155.

World Bank, at *http://siteresources.worldbank.org/DATASTATISTICS/Resources/GDP.pdf,* and *http://siteresources.worldbank.org/DATASTATISTICS/Resources/GDP.pdf.*

Zaring, David T. (2005). "Informal Procedure, Hard and Soft, in International Administration," *Chicago Journal of International Law*, Vol. 5, pp. 547–603.

Chapter 5

EU–US Regulatory Cooperation and Developing Country Trade*

Bernard M. Hoekman
World Bank and CEPR
Bhoekman@worldbank.org

Alessandro Nicita
UNCTAD
alessandro.nicita@unctad.org

The trade policy literature has for many years emphasized the impact and importance of non-tariff measures (NTMs). Policymakers recognize that regulatory policies may impose excessive (needless) costs on firms, and the importance of removing impediments to competition on product markets, including service markets (finance, transport, distribution, etc.). Recent research on trade and development has emphasized the impact on trade costs of administrative red tape and entry barriers, driven in part by the emergence of new datasets such as the World Bank's "Doing Business."

From a domestic welfare perspective the challenge for governments is to identify the most appropriate regulatory instruments to achieve a specific objective. In the trade negotiation context, NTMs

*A preliminary version of this paper was presented at the conference "Systemic Implications of Transatlantic Regulatory Cooperation and Competition," Ford School of Public Policy, University of Michigan May 8-9, 2008. We are grateful to Alan Deardorff, Simon Evenett and Keith Maskus for helpful suggestions. The views expressed are personal and should not be attributed to the World Bank or UNCTAD.

and regulatory regimes and instruments that raise trade costs have been on the agenda for many years because they can impede the ability of foreign firms to contest a market — either precluding this altogether or significantly raising the costs of doing so. Whether a policy instrument that impedes market access is efficient or not in attaining domestic objectives is not necessarily of interest to exporters to the market concerned — what matters to them is market access. But for regulators and domestic policymakers the impacts on foreign firms are likely to be of secondary importance at best — their concern will be (should be) on the efficacy and efficiency of the regulatory instruments they have (want to) put in place. From the perspective of achieving regulatory objectives, nationality often will (and should) not matter. But even if regulation applies to all sources of supply, it can still have the effect of segmenting markets and reducing competition.

One result of this well known tension is that efforts to pursue "deep integration" on domestic and regulatory policy (behind-the-border) have become an increasingly important feature of trade agreements. Such efforts span many aspects of product and market regulation, including product standards, government procurement, investment, competition policy, labor, and environmental policies, and protection of intellectual property and other intangible as well as tangible assets. The trade impeding effect of regulatory policies can be especially important for services industries. International efforts to address the market-segmenting effects of domestic regulation — where the objective is not (primarily) to discriminate against foreign or among foreign suppliers of a good or service — takes various forms, including deregulation (removal of policies), mutual recognition and harmonization. All have implications for domestic welfare as well as trade, and a major challenge for developing countries is to determine when mutual recognition or harmonization is in their interest, both in terms of improving access to partner country markets and in terms of domestic welfare (the functioning of local markets).

The focus of this volume is on EU–US transatlantic regulatory policy cooperation/competition. Cooperation, in particular insofar as it leads to greater mutual recognition or harmonization of regulatory regimes across the Atlantic, can have significant implications for developing countries. The same is true more generally of international efforts to agree to common standards in specific regulatory areas. What will eventually emerge from the EU–US effort is unknown at this point. More is known however about the extent to which subsets of "regulatory" policies currently differ across countries. These differences allow something to be said about the scope for greater convergence of policies and its potential effects.

In this paper we characterize the status quo that prevails in various trade-related policy areas affecting market access and trade costs and assess the potential implications of greater convergence. We do not deal with subjects such as intellectual property rights or GMOs, in large part because there are significant disagreements in the literature regarding the sign and magnitude of the consequences for welfare of developing countries of adopting "OECD" standards in these areas — indeed, there are fundamental disagreements between the EU and the US on the appropriate policy towards biotechnology. Instead, we limit attention to traditional border barriers such as tariffs and NTMs, as well as the sources of domestic trade costs on which there is a consensus in the literature regarding the effect on trade of undertaking reforms that lower such costs.

The analysis is by no means comprehensive as available data on sources of trade costs is not comprehensive. Nonetheless, the discussion will hopefully shed some light on the potential effects of further convergence by developing countries to the norms and policies that prevail in higher income countries in the areas covered. In practice, of course, the effects of adopting specific (harmonized) regulatory standards or of the EU and US agreeing to adopt common norms must be analyzed on a case-by-case, country-by-country basis.[1] But such

---

[1]For example, an increasing body of evidence has shown that a "one size fits all" approach — including international "best practice" norms — may not be appropriate. For example, burdensome regulatory requirements for banks relating to documentation, collateral, and money laundering ("know your customer" type requirements) restrict access to credit for small enterprises and the rural poor, while not affecting large firms or the urban rich much. A fear of being blacklisted generates a chilling effect on the incentives for banks to explore or propose less burdensome alternatives to regulatory requirements. Barth, Caprio and Levine (2006), in a comprehensive cross-country

analysis must wait until more is known regarding what emerges from the transatlantic initiative.

The plan of the paper is as follows. Section 1 summarizes the current pattern of tariff protection and the aggregate of all NTMs captured in the UNCTAD database (TRAINS/WITS). Section 2 summarizes the market access implications for groups of countries. Section 3 discusses some of the components of the aggregate NTM measure, as well as regulatory policies not included in the NTM database — in particular, services policies and domestic trade transactions costs. Section 4 summarizes some of the recent research that assesses the impact of international regulatory convergence on developing countries, as well as the potential impact of reducing domestic trade and logistics costs. In Section 5 we develop an argument in favor of convergence between the EU and the US in an area that is not highlighted as part of the agenda for transatlantic cooperation: doing more to develop and jointly provide technical and financial assistance that targets the sources of trade costs and assists developing countries to improve the policy environment for services activities. Section 6 concludes.

1.   Trade Policies

Ad valorem tariffs are the most widely used policy instruments to restrict trade, with specific duties — taxes that are levied on units (kilograms, liters, alcohol content, etc.) rather than on import values — often being used for agricultural products. Statutory tariffs may be complemented by ad-hoc surcharges, surtaxes, and safeguards on a temporary basis, e.g., to cover budget deficits or to protect specific domestic industries.

The use of non-tariff measures (NTMs) has been increasing both in terms of products covered and the number of countries utilizing them.

---

assessment of the impact of the Basel Committee's influential approach to bank regulation, conclude that there is no evidence that any single set of "best practice" regulatory norms — including the Basel capital adequacy standards — is appropriate for promoting well-functioning banks. The same is true for IFRS accounting standards (Mattoo and Payton, 2007).

NTMs include quantitative restrictions, technical product regulations, anti-dumping and countervailing measures and discretionary licensing. Although some of these measures, such as product standards, are not necessarily protectionist in intent — indeed, often they will not be — they all affect the cost of trading and thus affect trade volumes. NTMs are more prevalent in high and middle income countries which tend to have lower ad valorem average tariffs (Figure 1).

What follows uses two indices of trade restrictiveness: the tariff trade restrictiveness index (TTRI) and the overall trade restrictiveness index (OTRI) (Kee, Nicita and Olarreaga, 2009; World Bank and IMF, 2008). Both the TTRI and the OTRI represent a measure of the uniform tariff equivalent of observed trade policies on a country's imports; they represent the ad valorem tariff that would be needed to generate the observed level of trade. The difference between the TTRI and OTRI is that the OTRI includes the effect of both tariff and NTMs, while the TTRI captures only tariffs.[2] These indices are superior to

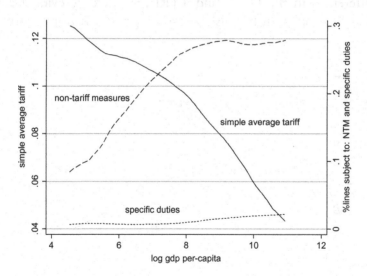

Figure 1: Use of tariffs, specific duties and NTMs (% of HS6digit lines).

---

[2]The inclusion of NTM in the OTRI is made possible by the estimation of the ad valorem tariff equivalents of non-tariff measures (Kee, Nicita and Olarreaga, 2009).

commonly used indicators such as average tariffs or NTM frequency measures as they take into account the elasticity of import demand with respect to prices: in calculating these indices greater weight is given to products for which demand is more responsive to changes in prices (so that smaller movements in prices produce larger shifts in imports).

The prevailing average TTRI and OTRI across countries is illustrated in Figures 2 and 3. Trade policies are generally more restrictive in developing countries than in high income countries, reflecting both lower tariffs in the latter and the fact that imports mostly comprise manufactures, which face relatively low barriers. Agricultural trade is much more restricted than manufacturing, both in terms of the TTRI and the OTRI, especially in high income countries. This reflects both higher tariffs and greater use of NTMs in agricultural trade. A comparison of Figures 2 and 3 reveals that NTMs contribute substantially to the overall trade restrictiveness of applied policies, especially in agriculture.

Differences in the OTRI and TTRI are not only evident across levels of development, but also across geographic regions (Table 1).

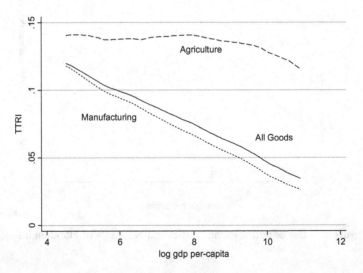

Figure 2: TTRI and GDP per-capita, 2006 (polynomial locally-weighted regression).

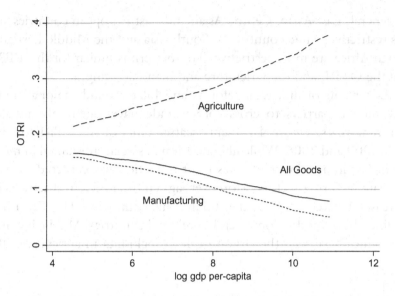

Figure 3: OTRI and GDP per-capita, 2006 (polynomial locally-weighted regression).

Table 1: OTRI and TTRI by developing country region.

Region (dev. countries only)	Total Trade	Agriculture	Manufacturing
East Asia	**11.3%**	**26.6%**	**10.4%**
	5.0%	*8.7%*	*4.8%*
Europe and Central Asia	**10.1%**	**25.9%**	**9.0%**
	4.5%	*10.3%*	*4.0%*
Latin America	**15.0%**	**28.1%**	**13.8%**
	5.4%	*6.6%*	*5.3%*
Middle East and N Africa.	**21.6%**	**32.3%**	**19.4%**
	11.9%	*12.1%*	*11.8%*
South Asia	**19.5%**	**46.4%**	**18.2%**
	14.0%	*31.4%*	*13.2%*
Sub-Saharan Africa	**14.4%**	**24.9%**	**12.9%**
	8.4%	*13.8%*	*7.6%*

Source: Own calculations.

In general, East Asian, Central Asian and East European countries are less restrictive, while countries in South Asia and the Middle East and North Africa are more restrictive. This pattern is similar for the TTRI and the OTRI, and for agriculture and manufacturing.

As a result of unilateral reforms and bilateral and regional trade agreements, barriers to cross-border trade have fallen substantially in recent years. Figure 4 presents scatter plots of the TTRI for the years 2000 and 2006. While liberalization has been substantial in most countries, in a number of cases tariff reduction has centered mainly on manufacturing sectors. Moreover, agricultural trade restrictiveness increased between 2000 and 2006 in some countries.[3] The TTRI has declined both for developing and developed countries. Middle income economies have seen the largest decline, including in agriculture. By

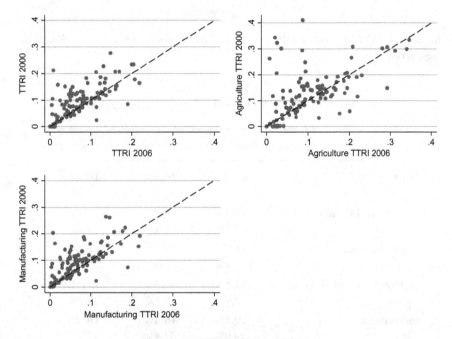

Figure 4:   TTRI 2000 and 2006.

---

[3]As NTM data has not been updated recently, the change in the OTRI is not reported.

region, countries in East Asia and Latin America (sub-Saharan Africa) have reduced tariffs the most (least).

2. Market Access

The effect of trade policies on exporters' access to markets differs across trading partners and geographic regions. The average restrictiveness that exporters face in a particular market depends not just on tariffs and NTMs but on the composition of exports and the extent and incidence of preferential tariffs. Table 2 reports the level of restrictiveness from a market access perspective, using both the TTRI and the OTRI. These market access versions of the indicators measure the restrictiveness of policies confronting exporters from in each geographic region and country group. Upper middle income countries generally enjoy better market access in both developing and developed countries. This is largely due to the composition of exports from these countries, which are skewed toward manufacturing. Low income countries face more restrictive market access conditions because their exports are more biased toward agriculture.

Across developing country regions, South Asia faces the most restrictive market access, due to export composition (agriculture, textiles and apparel) and because it has relatively limited preferential access. Sub-Saharan countries have the best market access, especially in high income countries, reflecting again export composition (commodities, plantation agriculture) and low or zero tariffs in many high income countries.

Comparing the MA-TTRI and the MA-OTRI suggests that NTMs are generally more important in restricting trade than tariffs: their measured ad valorem equivalent is much higher than existing tariffs. Standards, licensing and similar instruments typically affect all products entering a market regardless of their origin, so that the impact of NTMs is generally similar across trading partners. Tariffs, conversely, are generally negotiated on a bilateral basis, thus giving some trading partners a substantial advantage in market access. With the increase in reciprocal and nonreciprocal preferential agreements, almost all trade flows today are affected by some sort of tariff preference. This is particularly

Table 2:   Market access TTRI and OTRI.

Importing Countries	High Income	Upper Middle Income	Lower Middle Income	Low Income	East Asia	E. Europe Cent. Asia	Latin America	Mid. East N. Africa	South Asia	Sub-Saharan Africa
					Exporting Countries					
High Income	**6.3**	**5.7**	**7.9**	**9.1**	**8.3**	**5.1**	**7.0**	**4.3**	**10.4**	**4.4**
	2.4	*1.2*	*2.5*	*2.4*	*2.6*	*1.1*	*1.5*	*0.8*	*3.1*	*0.7*
QUAD*	**6.3**	**5.2**	**8.6**	**10.6**	**8.9**	**5.2**	**6.9**	**4.4**	**13.6**	**4.5**
	2.1	*0.9*	*2.5*	*2.5*	*2.7*	*0.8*	*1.2*	*0.5*	*3.3*	*0.5*
Upper Middle	**15.6**	**11.8**	**15.8**	**14.7**	**19.2**	**10.2**	**13.6**	**6.0**	**14.3**	**5.9**
	5.6	*3.8*	*5.6*	*5.7*	*7.2*	*4.4*	*2.6*	*2.5*	*6.6*	*3.5*
Lower Middle	**12.4**	**11.1**	**12.9**	**9.4**	**13.6**	**11.2**	**12.6**	**6.7**	**9.9**	**4.0**
	7.1	*4.8*	*6.7*	*5.1*	*6.6*	*6.2*	*5.1*	*2.8*	*6.2*	*2.7*
Low Income	**18.2**	**14.3**	**19.5**	**25.4**	**22.2**	**17.7**	**15.9**	**16.3**	**16.2**	**16.3**
	10.9	*8.1*	*12.2*	*12.9*	*13.8*	*6.2*	*9.0*	*10.0*	*10.4*	*12.2*

*QUAD countries are Canada, the European Union, Japan and USA.
Source: Own calculations. MA-OTRI in bold; MA-TTRI in italics

true for high income countries, where market access is subject to an increasing number of such agreements. The proliferation of preferential trade arrangements makes it important to properly measure the preferential margins confronting countries.

3. Non-tariff Measures

The foregoing discussion of the trade restrictiveness of policies illustrates that NTMs are a major source of barriers to trade but that tariffs also remain important, especially in developing countries. The average magnitude of NTMs clearly suggests that measures to reduce their trade-impeding effects could have high payoffs. How to achieve this is an important practical question. Many of the NTMs that are captured by the UNCTAD database are explicitly discriminatory, but many are not. This is the case in particular for product standards and technical regulations. These often serve to promote important public policy objectives such as consumer protection, or public health and safety. However, they can also impose costs on manufacturers due to the need to adapt products and production processes.

The use of standards has increased steadily. There is a vigorous debate in the literature whether a "standards-as-barriers" view of the world is the more accurate one, or whether it is more accurate to take a "standards-as-catalyst" perspective (Jaffee and Henson, 2004; Anders and Caswell, 2009). Standards and technical regulations can either facilitate or block trade. They can impose additional variable or fixed costs on exporters to the extent that it is necessary to alter production processes to adapt products for export. Moreover, certification requirements to demonstrate compliance can raise trade costs. Standards can also reduce trade costs for firms when produced to international norms for multiple markets. On the other hand, standards can also reduce trade costs for firms when produced to international norms for multiple markets.

The net impact of product standards on trade will depend on the relative magnitude of these effects. The empirical evidence is limited in this area, primarily due to the cost and complexities associated with collecting reliable data and constructing indicators on standards in different sectors across countries. Disdier, Fontagné and Mimouni (2009), using WTO technical barriers to trade (TBT) and Sanitary and phyto-Sanitary Measures (SPS) notifications, find that standards have negative trade impacts, in particular for exports from developing countries to OECD countries. Otsuki, Wilson, and Sewadeh (2001a, b), Peterson and Orden (2007) and Wilson, Mann and Otsuki (2004) are examples of papers that come to the same conclusion. Wilson and Otsuki (2003) use firm level data on standards and find that in Sub-Saharan Africa, firms invest on average 7.6% of sales in order to comply with foreign standards. Their data also show that experiences differ greatly from one firm or country to another: the range of investment costs reported by firms runs from close to zero to over 100% of annual sales. For firms in countries such as Kenya and Uganda average investment compliance costs as a share of sales can approach 10%, while the average in other regions rarely exceeds 4%. Case studies focusing on the costs and benefits of health and safety standards come to similar conclusions: the costs are often nontrivial. Maskus, Otsuki and Wilson (2005) find that a 1% increase in investment to meet compliance costs raises variable (per unit) production costs by between 0.06 and 0.13% — a small amount, but statistically significant. But the lump-sum fixed costs of compliance are non-trivial: averaging US$ 425,000 per firm in their sample, or about 4.7% of value added.

Those taking a standards-as-catalyst view stress that the overall gains from making the associated investments can be significant (Jafee and Henson, 2004). Moenius (2004) concludes that country-specific standards tend to promote trade in manufactures, whereas they have a negative impact on trade in homogeneous products such as commodities and agricultural products. This finding is consistent with the interpretation that higher information costs in manufactures can be mitigated with harmonized standards. Anders and Caswell (2009) study the effect of a 1997 introduction of a mandatory Hazard Analysis Critical Control Point (HACCP) standard for seafood by the United States. They concluded that this had a negative overall effect on exporters to the US, with developed country exporters as a group gaining and developing country exporters losing. However, when they focused the analysis at the country level, per-capita income level of the exporter was not statistically significant: what mattered was scale. The leading seafood exporters gained market share after the HACCP was mandated; while most of the smaller exporters faced losses or stagnant sales. This phenomenon is also stressed by Maskus and Wilson (2001) and Jafee and Henson (2004): tighter standards result in a shakeout of the industry. More efficient suppliers benefit and less efficient ones may be forced out of the market altogether.

Maertens and Swinnen (2009) note that an assessment of the effects of (tighter) standards needs to go beyond a focus on firm-level impacts. In the case of Senegal they show that tougher EU standards were accompanied by an *increase* in exports, and that this led to rising rural incomes and poverty reduction. The standards had an impact on market structure, inducing a shift from smallholder contract farming to integrated estate production. This in turn changed the channels through which poor households benefited from expanding trade opportunities: through labor markets (wage income) instead of product markets (profits and prices of output sold).

Finally, there are also spillovers associated with specific standards or decisions to tighten standards. Debaere (2005) has shown how a shift in EU policy to zero tolerance of antibiotics had a major adverse effect on Thai exports of shrimp to the EU, much of which was diverted to the US market, which resulted in the launch of a series of US anti-dumping actions — not just against Thailand but also other exporters such as Vietnam. Peterson and Orden (2005) also conclude that raising US standards on poultry has had trade deflection effects.

3.1. *Other sources of trade costs*

The NTMs included in the indicators discussed above are only a subset of the policies that result in impediments to trade. Internal and international trade costs may be of equal if not greater importance in reducing volumes of trade. While some of these costs can be measured — such as shipping costs — many trade costs reflect the domestic economic environment: the legal and regulatory framework, the efficiency of infrastructure services and related regulation, customs clearance procedures, administrative red tape, etc. For OECD countries there is a substantial amount of information on the extent of product market regulation compiled by the OECD secretariat (e.g., Nicoletti and Scarpetta, 2003), but this type of data is not available for developing countries. What is available for a large number of developing countries is information on the performance of logistics services and on the internal costs associated with shipping goods from the factory gate to the port, and from ports to retail outlets. The first is captured by the Logistics Performance Index (World Bank 2007) and complementary indicators of trade facilitation (Helble, Shepherd and Wilson, 2007); the second by the *Doing Business* database (World Bank, 2008). All of these indicators capture dimensions of prevailing regulatory regimes that affect trade.

The *Doing Business* "cost of trading" indicator measures the fees associated with completing the procedures to export or import a 20-foot container in US dollars (Figures 5 and 6). These include costs

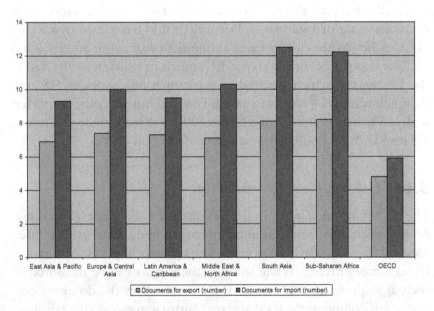

Figure 5: Number of export and import procedures.

Source: Doing Business.

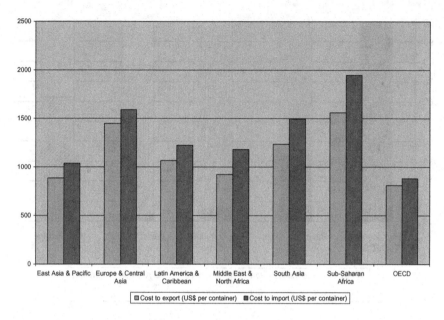

Figure 6: The cost of export and import procedures (US$).

Source: Doing Business.

for documents, administrative fees for customs clearance and technical control, terminal handling charges and inland transport. The cost measure does not include tariffs or trade taxes. Only official costs are recorded. The *Doing Business* "cost of trading" is part of the *Doing Business* trading across borders indicators which compiles the number of documents, the cost and the time necessary for procedural requirements for exporting and importing a standardized cargo of goods by ocean transport. Local freight forwarders, shipping lines, customs brokers and port officials provide information on required documents and cost as well as the time to complete each procedure. The methodology, surveys and data are available at http://www.doingbusiness.org.

Based on a worldwide survey of global freight forwarders and express carriers and data on the performance of key components of the logistics chain, the *Logistics Performance Index* (LPI) assesses seven factors: efficiency of the clearance process by customs and other border agencies; quality of transport and information technology

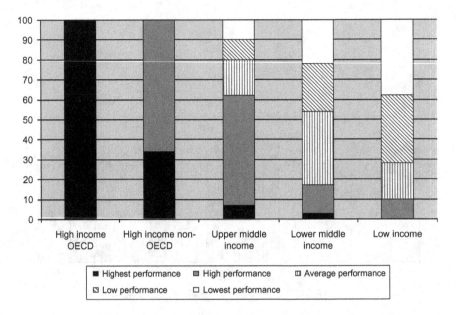

Figure 7:   Trade logistics performance — income group.

Source: LPI.

infrastructure for logistics; ease and affordability of arranging international shipments; competence of the local logistics industry; ability to
track and trace international shipments; domestic logistics costs; and
timeliness of shipments in reaching destination. Figure 7 summarizes
the distribution of the LPI within each income country group.

Table 3 reports the average of these indices by income country
groups. Developing countries not surprisingly have lower scores on the
LPI and higher trade costs. Although the LPI score does not register
large differences between low income and middle income countries,
this is due in part to the fact that Table 3 spans only a subset of the LPI
(efficiency of customs and the ease of international shipment). Import
costs are much higher than export costs in low income countries, while
in high income these costs are more similar. Thus, for low income
countries the import "tax equivalent" associated with the regulatory
regime is higher than the export tax equivalent.

Table 3:   Measures of domestic trade costs (averages by country group).

	High Income	Middle Income	Low Income
LPI (score)	3.9	3.0	2.8
Doing Business (DB) import (US$)	813.6	1024.2	1212.0
DB export (US$)	774.4	867.2	949.3

3.2.   *Services policies*

As is well known, services trade and investment is not restricted by tariffs and similar policy instruments applied at the border. Instead, trade is affected by a plethora of regulatory policies, which may or may not be discriminatory. Little is known about the balance of discrimination vs. nondiscrimination, or about the overall impact of policies that reduce competition and/or raise costs for firms. Two different approaches have been taken in the literature to assess the magnitude of barriers to trade in services. The first involves collection of information on applied policies, converting these into coverage/frequency indicators and using the resulting indices as explanatory variables in a statistical analysis to explain observed measures of prices or costs. The second approach is to rely on indirect methods such as calculation of price-cost margins by sector across countries or gravity regressions to estimate what trade flows "should be" and obtain an estimate of the "tariff equivalent" of policies from the difference between estimated and observed flows.

A major problem impeding the latter type of approach is that bilateral data on services trade flows are not available for most countries. Francois, Hoekman and Wörz (2008) developed a methodology that allows aggregate trade and FDI data to be used to infer what the value of trade "should" be, using a gravity model framework in which a measure of the overall multilateral resistance to trade is estimated. The approach uses a CES aggregator over domestic and imported services to estimate import demand for services (total and by sector) as a function of total demand, the import expenditure share, a measure of economic distance from sources of service supply (the GDP-weighted distance to a hypothetical centre of the world), and policy-based trade costs. Income (GDP per-capita) and population are used to control for the first and second variables (for demand linked to level of development and size of given national economies).[4] This setup allows a measure to be derived of the general openness of a country to trade in services.[5]

Averaged individual country-specific coefficients by income groups suggest that average "protection" in the service sector is around 20% of delivered service prices for low and middle income countries, as compared to 12% for high income countries (assuming a substitution elasticity of 3.6, the default value used in many CGE models). "Protection" is considerably higher in the transport sector — in the 30+ % range — and lower in non-producer related service categories such as travel services.[6]

An ongoing World Bank research project is compiling information on the policies that presumably underpin these estimates of service market openness. The focus of this project is on the extent to which

---

[4] On the assumption that level of development and size — reflecting economic structure — are correlated with country specific tastes and preferences as well as technologies employed to provide services, these variables also implicitly control for differences in preferences and technologies.

[5] Using a pooled sample of 178 countries over 10 years (1994–2004) from the IMF's Balance of Payments database, service imports are first regressed on GDP per-capita, population, and distance to a hypothetical centre of the world (an index of "centrality"). The residuals that are obtained are then regressed on country dummies so as to allow for different strategies for pooling sectors to estimate openness. Working with a panel of countries over time where data are pooled across different service sectors addresses the problem affecting cross-section gravity regressions that by definition all estimated barriers sum up to zero.

[6] For the subset of OECD countries, Francois, Hoekman and Wörz (2008) also control for the impact of regulatory policies as documented in the OECD's product market regulation database. Inclusion of these measures of policy does not significantly affect the openness estimates for OECD countries.

policies discriminate against foreign services providers. To date surveys have been implemented in 24 OECD countries and 32 developing countries, covering five key sectors: financial services, telecommunications, retail distribution, transportation, and professional services.[7] The survey focuses primarily on policy barriers to cross border trade in services and commercial presence or FDI. Survey results to date are summarized in Figure 8.[8]

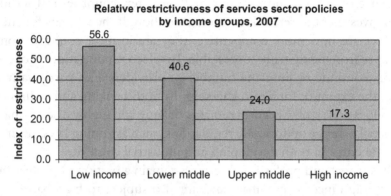

Figure 8:   Restrictiveness of services trade policies, 2007.

Source: Gootiz and Mattoo (2008).

---

[7] The sectors are further disaggregated into banking (retail and merchant), insurance (life, non-life, and reinsurance), road transport, railway shipping, maritime shipping and auxiliary services, air transport (freight and passengers), accounting, auditing, and legal services.

[8] Results of the survey are summarized in an index of restrictiveness. For each sector and mode of supply the openness of policy towards foreign suppliers is mapped on a 5-point scale ranging from 0 (for no restrictions) to 1 (highly restricted), with three intermediate levels of restrictiveness (0.25, 0.50 and 0.75). Sectoral results are aggregated across modes of supply using weights that reflect judgments of the relative importance of the different modes for a sector, and scaled up by a factor of 100. For example, mode 4 (temporary movement of suppliers) is important for professional services, but not for telecommunications, where mode 3 is the dominant mode of contesting a market. All indices are scaled up by a factor of 100. Sectoral restrictiveness indices are aggregated using sectoral GDP shares as weights. The country income group indices are derived using GDP weights for the countries in the sample.

The survey reveals that developing countries have significantly liberalized a range of service sectors over the last couple of decades, but in some areas protection persists. In fact, the overall pattern of policies across sectors is increasingly similar in developing and industrial countries. In telecommunications, public monopolies seem in most countries a relic of history, with at least some measure of competition introduced in both mobile and fixed services. In banking too, domination by state-owned banks has given way to increased openness to the presence of foreign and private banks. Very few countries restrict foreign investment in retail. However, even though the markets for these services are now more competitive, they are in most countries some distance from being truly contestable. In telecommunications, governments continue to limit the number of providers and, particularly in Asia, the extent of foreign ownership. In both banking and insurance, the allocation of new licenses remains opaque and highly discretionary. In retail, a range of domestic regulations, such as zoning laws, severely impede entry in both developing and industrial countries.

Transport and professional services remain a bastion of protectionism in high income countries and are also subject to high barriers in developing countries (Figure 9). In maritime transport, even though

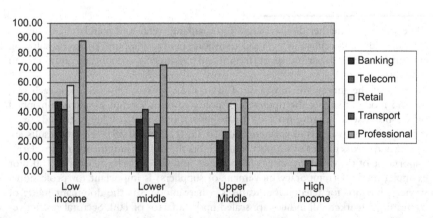

Figure 9:   Services trade restrictiveness indices by sector.

Source: Gootiz and Mattoo (2008).

international shipping is quite open today, entry into cabotage and aux-iliary services such as cargo handling is restricted in many countries. In air transport, restrictions on foreign investment co-exist with limi-tations on cabotage and cross-border trade — though conditions for freight transport are much more liberal than those for passenger trans-port. In professional services, even though there is increased scope for international trade through electronic means, in which many develop-ing countries are also beginning to participate, there remain restrictions on foreign presence. In general, accounting and the practice of inter-national law tend to be more open than auditing and the practice of domestic law. The restrictions on foreign investment are far less strin-gent than the restrictions on the presence of foreign professionals.

4. Reducing Regulatory Differences and Associated Cost Differentials

The impact of the procedures and costs that are captured by the Doing Business database and LPI indicators on trade performance of the countries concerned is significant. Djankov, Freund, and Pham (2010) find that each additional day a product is delayed prior to shipping cuts trade by at least 1%. Moreover, a day's delay reduces a country's relative exports of time-sensitive to time-insensitive agricultural goods by 6%. Sadikov (2007), using the Doing Business data, finds that each extra signature exporters have to collect before a shipment can take place reduces export volumes by 4.2%. Excessive bureaucracy in trade has an even larger impact on exports of differentiated products — each signature reduces exports of differentiated products by 8.4%.

The relative importance of trade has been expanding in recent years as tariffs have been reduced. Berthelon and Freund (2008) show that notwithstanding important improvements in logistics and transport technologies, the effect of distance on trade has not changed much over the last 20 years. Tariffs have fallen faster than technological change has reduced trade costs, so that the latter continue to play a large role in driving world trade. Analysis based on the Doing Business database, among other sources, suggests that developing country exporters, on average, are more affected than traders in developed countries by

(1) costs associated with frequent reloading of goods, (2) port congestion, (3) complicated customs-clearance procedures, (4) lack of transparency of administrative requirements, (5) limited use of automation, and (5) the uncertainty about the enforceability of legal and property rights (Portugal-Perez and Wilson, 2008).

The policy agenda that is associated with reducing the types of costs that are picked up by DB and LPI are almost all domestic: they require actions by the relevant governments. However, this does not imply there is no scope to use international cooperation or convergence strategies — in many of the policy areas concerned, adoption of "good practices" and regulatory principles and approaches that have been used in other countries could do much to improve matters. This suggests that this is an area where development cooperation — and more specifically, joint action by the EU and the US — could have high payoffs. We return to this topic below.

As discussed above, standards are an important element underpinning the NTMs that are put in place by countries. This is a policy area where cooperation and convergence can have a direct payoff as well. It differs from the domestic trade cost agenda in that actions by the EU and US can help reduce costs for developing countries. Thus, harmonization of standards (and the specific national rules related to testing, certification, and accreditation) can help lower trade costs through lower production costs for products sold in multiple markets.

Harmonization benefits could be enhanced insofar as the transatlantic initiative results in greater common EU–US standards, by creating a larger market where the same standards apply or partner norms are accepted as equivalent. If, as a result, fixed costs of compliance can be spread over more sales, third countries will benefit from convergence. Baldwin (2000) notes that cooperation on standards will have fewer adverse effects — if any — on third parties than would arise from the preferential removal of tariffs. Insiders may benefit from lower costs as a result of mutual recognition or the adoption of common standards, but this is also likely to benefit outsiders.

Chen and Mattoo (2008) investigate whether EU harmonization of technical regulations help or hinder third countries, focusing on Harmonization Directives issued by the European Commission that lay down common, mandatory regulations that apply in all EU Member States for specific sectors. Chen and Mattoo find that these directives increase trade between EU countries but not necessarily with the rest of the world. Harmonization of standards may actually reduce the exports of excluded countries, especially in markets that have raised the stringency of standards. Among excluded countries, developing countries may be the worst sufferers since their firms are likely to be less well-equipped to comply with stricter standards.

Czubala, Shepherd, and Wilson (2007) focus on voluntary standards promulgated by the European Committee for Standardization, using a database on EU standards for textiles and clothing to examine the impact of EU standards on African exports of textiles and clothing. Their analysis shows that (non-harmonized) EU standards tend to hold back African exports. Their findings are consistent with the idea that capacity constraints in Africa can make it difficult for firms to adapt products to meet multiple standards. By contrast, in instances where the EU has adopted the standards developed by the ISO, there is a much weaker negative impact on African exports to the EU.

Shepherd (2007) analyzes the impacts of harmonization on the range of products exported by a country's trading partners. Market specific fixed costs of exporting are used to model product standards. Numerical simulations show that international harmonization can promote penetration of new markets in third countries (i.e., those that do not harmonize) provided that compliance costs do not increase too much as a result of harmonization. Using the same database as Czubala *et al.* (2007), Shepherd finds that more product standards tend to reduce partner country export variety, while international harmonization acts weakly in the opposite direction. A 10% increase in the number of EU standards is associated with a 6% decline in the range of product varieties (tariff lines) exported by the EU's trading partners. A similar increase in the proportion of EU standards that are internationally harmonized produces a small but significant effect (0.2%) in the opposite direction. The data suggest that the strength of this harmonization effect may be up to 50% greater for low income countries, which is consistent with the existence of constraints to product or process adaptation in developing countries.

Harmonization to facilitate trade has been pursued most intensively by the EU. The European experience suggests that this is unlikely to be a productive strategy as agreement is very difficult to obtain under a consensus rule. Mutual recognition, under which countries agree to recognize (accept as equivalent) each others' standards and conformity assessment procedures, proved to be a more effective approach. Mutual recognition agreements (MRAs) are a cooperative mechanism through which the transaction costs associated with conformity assessment systems to establish compliance with standards can be reduced. MRAs may require some degree of harmonization of either standards or test procedures, especially in areas where mandatory standards or regulations apply, to ensure that the underlying norms satisfy basic minimum standards.

The 1998 EU–US Mutual Recognition Agreements for Conformity Assessment aims at achieving agreement that product test results, inspections, and certifications performed by independent entities would be accepted in both markets. It covers such sectors as telecommunications terminal equipment, electromagnetic compatibility, electrical safety, recreational craft, medical devices and pharmaceutical Good Manufacturing Practices. Significant differences in European and US testing and certification systems made the MRA difficult to negotiate. The European system relies less on self-declaration of conformity by enterprises than the US system, and more on mandatory third-party testing and certification. Under the EU's global approach to conformity assessment, only recognized testing, certification, and marking institutions are able to issue certification marks. Another obstacle concerned the extent to which certification and inspection agencies of one country are willing and legally permitted to devolve authority for testing and inspection to the other country's regulators. It was eventually agreed that the EU would accept that the US Federal Drug Administration (FDA) was an independent agency that could not be overruled. Since the legal and mandatory product requirements of the importing party must be fulfilled, the MRA does not call for any harmonization of product or conformity assessment requirements. Each country maintains its own legislation and regulatory requirements and remains free to set its health, safety and environmental protection levels it deems necessary (subject to WTO rules).

Mutual recognition proved a powerful tool for increasing competition in European market. What about effects on excluded countries? Chen and Mattoo (2008) find that MRAs of conformity assessment promote the trade of *both* covered and excluded countries. As both Baldwin (2000) and Chen and Mattoo (2008) note, the impact on third parties of MRAs depends on whether "restrictive rules of origin" apply, i.e., whether the goods must be produced in the territory of a party to a MRA, and whether a harmonized norm is accepted as being identical in an importing country. Some MRAs impose restrictive origin rules — e.g., agreements between the EU and Australia and New Zealand. This implies that non-members cannot benefit from the MRA by having their goods tested in MRA countries.

The extant research on product standards suggests that efforts to reduce multiplicity in standards through regional or international harmonization may help reduce overall costs for developing countries. Financial or capacity constraints might make it difficult for developing country exporters to pursue a harmonization strategy. Moreover, the norms may be inappropriate for the circumstances prevailing in the developing country. Even if developing countries adopt European, American or international (e.g., ISO) standards, significant institutional strengthening is likely to be required for partner countries to be willing to accept "home country supervision."

The potential for recognition to reduce transaction costs and increase real income can be significant. The EU requires third-party testing, certification or quality system registration for certain regulated sectors by organizations certified to the Commission by the member states as technically competent. The requirement that these assessments be undertaken by EU-certified bodies raises the costs of testing and certification to non-EU manufacturers in many sectors and was a prime motivation for EU–US MRA negotiations in the 1990s. A major question for developing countries is whether mutual recognition is a viable option to pursue. The process relies heavily on mutual trust in the competence and ability of the institutions responsible for enforcing

mandatory standards and a willingness to be flexible in setting minimum standards. Much also depends not just on capacity to enforce
norms in developing countries but on efforts on the part of the EU
and the US to work with these countries and demonstrate flexibility
and a willingness to both assist and accept differences in systems and
approaches.

4.1. *Trade costs vs. border barriers: Gravity simulations*

Hoekman and Nicita (2008) use a gravity model framework to assess
the impacts of differences in trade costs and regulatory policies on
merchandise trade flows. In a nutshell, the gravity model predicts bilateral trade flows based on the economic sizes of and distance between
two countries. Country specific trade costs are captured by country
fixed effects or multilateral resistance terms. The literature has recently
focused more on quantifying domestic costs of trading. These additional trade costs have been generally measured by the inclusion of
specific variables (generally a measure of infrastructures such as roads,
railways, phone lines, etc.). In general, the literature supports the
hypothesis that domestic trade costs and business environment are significant determinants of the volume of trade between countries.

   In addition to the TTRI and the NTM component of the OTRI (the
difference between the OTRI and the TTRI), Hoekman and Nicita
(2008) use the indicators of domestic trade and logistics costs discussed
above. Their results suggest that traditional trade policies (tariffs and
NTMs) as well as domestic trade costs are statistically significant determinants of trade volumes. More specifically, they quantify a one point
reduction in the LPI score in an increase of trade volumes by about
50%, both in terms of exports and imports. Similar results are found
for internal trade costs as captured by the Doing Business indicators. A
10% reduction in the cost associated with importing (exporting) would
increase imports (exports) by about 4.8% (4.7%).

   To assess the relative magnitudes of internal trade costs and the
trade-impeding effect of trade policies, Table 4 reports the predicted
effect on trade if low income countries were to converge to a set of

Table 4:   Effects of convergence by low income countries to middle income average.

Indicator/Policy Area	Increase in Imports	Increase in Exports
LPI Score	15.2%	14.6%
Doing Business, cost of trading	7.4%	4.1%
TTRI for low income countries reduced to 5%	5.7%	
OTRI for low income countries reduced to 10%	8.4%	

policies that would generate the observed average levels of the various indicators in middle income countries (as reported in Table 4 above). These results are compared with the average effect of an increase of 1 percentage point in relative preferential access to global markets (not just the OECD) and with a reduction in the TTRI and OTRI to 5% and 10%, respectively.

The predicted increases in trade volumes of low income countries of this convergence experiment are substantial. The largest increases in trade are associated with actions to improve the logistics (as measured by the LPI). Improving performance on the Doing Business measure of internal trade costs has an impact that is similar to what could be obtained by further traditional trade policy reform — reducing the TTRI or bringing down the restrictiveness of NTMs.

4.2.   *Services*

The effect of services policies are not considered in the empirical literature for the simple reason that the requisite data do not exist. Reducing the barriers that are documented in Gootiz and Mattoo (2008) would undoubtedly have beneficial effects. Liberalizing access to service markets (enhancing contestability) will reduce what Konan and Maskus (2006) call the cartel effect — the markup of price over marginal cost that incumbents are able to charge due to restricted entry; and attenuate what they call the cost inefficiency effect — the fact that in an environment with limited competition, the marginal costs of incumbents are likely to be higher than if entry was open. These effects can have significant impacts on all sectors and households in an economy.

There is an emerging body of econometric evidence that policy reforms to increase competition in services industries, including through international liberalization, can help boost growth prospects and enhance welfare. Mattoo, Rathindran and Subramanian (2006) find that countries that fully liberalized the telecommunications and financial services sectors grew, on average, about 1.5 percentage points faster than other countries. Eschenbach and Hoekman (2006) find that financial and infrastructure services policy reforms had an important, statistically significant positive impact on per-capita growth of transition economies during the 1990–2004 period. Country-specific analyses have found a positive relationship between services liberalization, services sector performance and total factor productivity growth at the level of firms that use the services concerned relatively intensively. These studies tend to find that FDI in services is an important mechanism through which new techniques are diffused to host countries.[9] The policy implication is that liberalization — increasing the contestability of services markets — can have large payoffs. However, as has been discussed extensively in the literature, the Doha Round is making very little progress in fostering such reform.

5. Policy Implications

The focus of trade and investment policy debate and international cooperation is more and more on regulatory policies and their effects. The focus in this paper has been on the subset of such policies that

---

[9]For example, in firm-level analyses of the Czech Republic, a set of African economies and India, Arnold, Javorcik and Mattoo (2006) and Arnold, Mattoo and Narciso (2008) find a positive relationship between services liberalization, FDI in services and the TFP performance of domestic firms that use services. The presence of services FDI is the most robust variable affecting TFP in user firms.

directly affect trade costs, including traditional trade policies. The latter continue to be important in developing countries as well as for some sectors in high income countries (agriculture in particular). This raises the question of which set of policies is more important as a trade impediment.

In general terms, recent research suggests that trade policies are a less important source of impediments to trade than are administrative and regulatory policies. The impact of reducing the costs associated with policies that increase transactions costs at- and behind-the-border will have a greater payoff than further reductions in tariffs and NTMs. This supports a policy focus on reducing the internal costs of trade. A key question for policymakers is of course how performance can be improved. More specifically in terms of the theme of this conference, the question is to what extent can adoption of international regulatory norms ("good practices") help achieve the desired reductions in trade costs, and what would this cost. These are questions that require issue- and country-specific analysis.

That said, it is also clear that there are still large gains from trade to be had from traditional trade liberalization. Moreover, the rationale underlying regulatory policies is generally different from that motivating the use of trade policy (explicit discrimination against foreign products). Removal of such discrimination is in principle much easier than improving regulatory practice and administrative procedures that raise the costs of trade. The results of recent papers such as Djankov, Freund and Pham (2010), Francois and Manchin (2007) and Hoekman and Nicita (2008) suggest that focusing attention on the policies that underpin the logistics and trade facilitation indices will have a bigger impact than actions to reduce the costs of the procedures that are captured by the Doing Business "cost of trading" variable. While suggestive, it should be stressed that it is not more than that and further work is needed to "unpack" these findings. There is significant overlap between some of the indicators measuring trade costs, and none of the empirical literature considers the relative impacts of services policies. A more detailed analysis of the "policy inputs" underlying the various indicators is also needed in order to be able to discuss and assess what might be done through the vehicle of convergence to international regulatory norms in these areas as opposed to investment in hardware and infrastructure.

Improved regulation — ranging from pro-competitive regulation of network-based transport and communication services to the efficient enforcement of product standards — is a critical input into lower trade and transactions costs. Development assistance that focuses on improving domestic regulation and attaining regulatory objectives could do much to remedy the status quo. Both the EU and the US have supported the call for an increase in "aid for trade" that has been made in recent years, most recently at the 2005 Hong Kong WTO ministerial.[10] Trade facilitation and improving the quality and cost of ancillary services requires more than technical assistance to help countries make market access commitments in trade agreements. It must extend to assistance for regulatory strengthening and resources to strengthen services-related infrastructure. To benefit from trade opportunities, many developing countries need to bolster the competitiveness of their firms and farmers by lowering the cost of, and increase access to, services such as transport, finance, and communications. This in turn requires a mix of policy reforms — including liberalization — as well as investments in infrastructure, training, and institutional strengthening.

A joint effort by the EU and the US to revitalize the Doha Round and move forward on reducing tariffs (and thus the TTRI), services liberalization and trade facilitation agendas, complemented by more assistance to improve regulatory policies and lower the trade-restricting effects of NTMs would be the best type of cooperation between the EU and the US from the perspective of developing countries. If Doha were to prove to be the first multilateral trade negotiation to fail, enhanced cooperation between the EU and the US on the policy areas discussed in this paper could have substantial positive payoffs for developing countries, constituting a development-supportive "plan B." Even if Doha can be brought to closure, this "plan B" is important: it focuses on an agenda that will unambiguously generate significant benefits for developing country firms and households.

---

[10] See Prowse (2006) for an in-depth discussion of aid for trade issues and options.

6. Concluding Remarks

The 2007 Framework for Advancing Transatlantic Economic Integration puts great emphasis on regulatory convergence as an objective. Although well worth pursuing, making concrete progress towards convergence and/or mutual recognition will not be easy. The internal EU experience illustrates that this is a difficult process that will take substantial time and require concerted attention from policymakers. A joint effort by the EU and US to cooperate in moving the multilateral liberalization agenda forward could generate not just larger benefits in terms of improved access to markets for EU and US firms, but also produce benefits for developing countries. Targeting increased "aid for trade" to the trade facilitation and services regulatory reform agenda in developing economies would help to build and maintain support for liberalization and open markets, not just in developing countries but, as importantly, in the EU and the US.

References

Anders, Sven and Julie A. Caswell (2009). "Standards as Barriers Versus Standards as Catalysts: Assessing the Impact of HCAAP Implementation on U.S. Seafood Imports," *American Journal of Agricultural Economics*, Vol. 91, No. 2, pp. 310–321.

Arnold, Jens Matthias, Beata Javorcik and Aaditya Mattoo (2006). "The Productivity Effects of Services Liberalization: Evidence from the Czech Republic," World Bank Policy Research Working Paper 4109.

Arnold, Jens Matthias, Aaditya Mattoo and Gaia Narciso (2008). "Services Inputs and Firm Productivity in Sub-Saharan Africa: Evidence from Firm-Level Data," *Journal of African Economies*, Vol. 17, No. 4, pp. 578–599.

Baldwin, Richard (2000). Regulatory Protectionism, Developing Nations and A Two-Tier World Trade System, CEPR Discussion Paper No. 2574.

Barth, James, Gerard Caprio and Ross Levine (2006). *Rethinking Bank Regulation: Till Angels Govern*, Cambridge and New York: Cambridge University Press.

Berthelon, Matias and Caroline Freund (2008). "On the Conservation of Distance in International Trade," *Journal of International Economics*, Vol. 75, No. 2, pp. 310–320.

Chen, Maggie Xiaoyang and Aaditya Mattoo (2008). "Regionalism in Standards: Good or Bad for Trade?" *Canadian Journal of Economics*, Vol. 41, No. 3, pp. 838–863.

Czubala, Witold, Ben Shepherd and John S. Wilson (2007). "Help or Hindrance? The Impact of Harmonized Standards on African Exports," *Journal of African Economies*, Vol. 18, No. 5, pp. 711–744.

Debaere, Peter (2005). "Small Fish, Big Issues: The Effect of Trade Policy on the Global Shrimp Market," CEPR Discussion Paper No. 5254.

Disdier, Anne-Célia, Lionel Fontagné and Mondher Mimouni (2009). "The Impact of Regulations on Agricultural Trade: Evidence from SPS and TBT Agreements," *American Journal of Agricultural Economies*, Vol. 90, No. 2, pp. 336–350.

Djankov, Simeon, Caroline Freund and Cong Pham (2010). "Trading on Time," *Review of Economies and Statistics*, Vol. 92, No. 1, pp. 166–173.

Eschenbach, Felix and Bernard Hoekman (2006). "Services Policy Reform and Economic Growth in Transition Economies, 1990–2004," *Review of World Economics*, Vol. 142, No. 4, pp. 746–764.

Francois, Joseph, Bernard Hoekman and Julia Wörz (2008). "Does Gravity Apply to Intangibles? Trade and FDI in Services," mimeo.

Francois, Joseph and Miriam Manchin (2007). "Institutions, Infrastructure, and Trade," Policy Research Working Paper No. 4152, The World Bank.

Gootiz, Batshur and Aaditya Mattoo (2008). "Restrictions on Services Trade and FDI in Developing Countries," World Bank, mimeo.

Helble, Matthias, Ben Shepherd and John S. Wilson (2007). *Transparency and Trade Facilitation in the Asia Pacific: Estimating the Gains from Reform*, Washington, D.C.: The World Bank.

Hoekman Bernard and Alessandro Nicita (2008). "Trade Policy, Trade Costs and Developing Country Trade," Policy Research Working Paper Series 4797, The World Bank, Washington, DC.

Jaffee, Steve and Spenser Henson (2004). "Standards and Agro-Food Exports from Developing Countries: Rebalancing the Debate," Policy Research Working Paper 3348, The World Bank, Washington, DC.

Kee, Hiau Looi, Alessandro Nicita and Marcelo Olarreaga. 2009. "Estimating Trade Restrictiveness Indices," *The Economic Journal*, Vol. 119, No. 534, pp. 172–199.

Konan, Denise Eby and Keith E. Maskus (2006). "Quantifying the Impact of Services Liberalization in a Developing Country," *Journal of Development Economics*, Vol. 81, No. 1, pp. 142–162.

Maertens, Miet and Johan Swinnen (2009). "Trade, Standards, and Poverty: Evidence from Senegal," *World Development*, Vol. 37, No. 1, pp. 161–178.

Maskus, Keith E., Tsunehiro, Otsuki and John S. Wilson (2005). "The Cost of Compliance with Product Standards for Firms in Developing Countries: An Econometric Study," Policy Research Working Paper 3590, The World Bank, Washington, DC.

Maskus, Keith E. and John S. Wilson (2001). *Quantifying the Impact of Technical Barriers to Trade: Can It Be Done?* University of Michigan Press.

Mattoo, Aaditya and Lucy Payton (eds.) (2007). *Services Trade and Development: The Experience of Zambia*, Washington, D.C.: Palgrave and World Bank.

Mattoo, Aaditya, Randeep Rathindran and Arvind Subramanian (2006). "Measuring Services Trade Liberalization and its Impact on Economic Growth: An Illustration," *Journal of Economic Integration*, Vol. 21, pp. 64–98.

Moenius, Johannes (2004). "Information Versus Product Adaptation: The Role of Standards in Trade," International Business and Markets Research Center Working Paper, Northwestern University.

Nicoletti, Giuseppe and Stefano Scarpetta (2003). "Regulation, Productivity and Growth," *Economic Policy*, Vol. 36, pp. 9–72.

Otsuki, Tsunehiro, John S. Wilson and Mirvat Sewadeh (2001a). "Saving Two in a Billion: Quantifying the Trade Effect of European Food Safety Standards on African Exports," *Food Policy*, Vol. 26, pp. 495–514.

Otsuki, Tsunehiro, John S. Wilson and Mirvat Sewadeh (2001b). "What Price Precaution? European Harmonization of Aflatoxin Regulations and African Groundnut Exports," *European Review of Agricultural Economics*, Vol. 28, No. 3, pp. 263–284.

Peterson, Everett, and David Orden (2005). "Effects of Tariffs and Sanitary Barriers on High- and Low-Value Poultry Trade," *Journal of Agricultural and Resource Economics*, Vol. 30, No. 1, pp. 109–127.

Peterson, Everett, and David Orden (2007). "Avocado Pests and Avocado Trade," *American Journal of Agricultural Economics*, Vol. 90, No. 2, pp. 321–335.

Portugal-Perez, Alberto and John S. Wilson (2008). "Lowering Trade Costs for Development in Africa: A Summary Overview," mimeo.

Prowse, Susan (2006). "Aid for Trade: A Proposal for Increasing Support for Trade Adjustment and Integration," in Evenett, S. and B. Hoekman, (eds.), *Economic Development and Multilateral Trade Cooperation*, pp. 229–268, Washington, D.C.: Palgrave Macmillan and the World Bank.

Sadikov, Azim (2007). "Border and Behind-the-Border Trade Barriers and Country Exports," IMF Working Paper 07/292.

Shepherd, Ben (2007). "Product Standards, Harmonization, and Trade: Evidence from the Extensive Margin," World Bank Policy Research Working Paper No. 4390.

Wilson, John and Tsunehiro Otsuki (2004). "To Spray or not to Spray: Pesticides, Banana Exports, and Food Safety," *Food Policy*, Vol. 29, pp. 131–146.

Wilson, John S., Catherine Mann and Tsunehiro Otsuki (2003). "Trade Facilitation and Economic Development: A New Approach to Measuring the Impact," *World Bank Economic Review*, Vol. 17, No. 3, pp. 367–389.

World Bank (2007). *Connecting to Compete: Trade Logistics in the Local Economy*. Washington DC: World Bank.

World Bank (2008). *Doing Business Report 2008*. Washington DC: World Bank.

World Bank and IMF (2008). *Global Monitoring Report, 2008*. Washington DC: World Bank.

Chapter 6

Transatlantic Trade, the Automotive Sector: The Role of Regulation in a Global Industry, Where We Have Been and Where We Need to go, How Far Can EU–US Cooperation go Toward Achieving Regulatory Harmonization?

Vann H. Wilber

Alliance of Automobile Manufacturers
vwilber@autoalliance.org

Paul T. Eichbrecht

General Motors
paul.t.eichbrecht@gm.com

We review why we have widely disparate regulations between the two transatlantic markets and just how important harmonization of technical regulation is to the long term profitability of the automotive industry. We consider how harmonization efforts were focused in the past, what worked or did not work, and how the time is right now for a higher expectation for success. We look at the "model" for regulatory harmonization offered by the agreements administered by the United Nations Economic Commission for Europe (ECE) Working Party 29, assess the effectiveness of the Transatlantic Business Dialog of the mid-1990s, and identify new initiatives for regulatory reform such as "A Competitive Automotive Regulatory System for the 21st Century," December 12, 2005, and the "Framework for Advancing Transatlantic Economic Integration between the European Union and the United States of America," signed April 30, 2007.

We discuss how the industry is positioning itself to better engage in the development of global technical regulations and how this impacts the domestic agenda of both the European region and America. We also discuss the concept of a two-standards world and how best to assess the true cost/benefit of regulatory harmonization. Finally, we conclude with our vision for the future and what next steps are needed to achieve the objectives of globally harmonized technical regulation for the automobile industry.

1. Globalization

The automobile industry is an integral part of the global economy. Automotive trade represents roughly 10% of world trade, and much of the growth in demand for vehicles is coming from emerging economic markets, such as China, Russia, India and Brazil. In 2007, just 20 million of the 70 million motor vehicles produced world-wide were built in North America, and North America's share of total world vehicle production is expected to continue to fall. In Western Europe, vehicle sales are expected to be relatively flat, while sales continue to grow in Central and Eastern Europe as these economies grow. By 2016, mature automotive markets, such as the United States, Europe, and Japan, are expected to continue to be dominant markets due to their size but they are projected to account for less than half of the world's vehicles sales. The automotive sales share in emerging markets will continue to increase: by 2016, the top 11 emerging automotive markets are projected to grow to about 40% of global auto sales.

A growing automotive market is an indicator of increasing national economic growth and individual prosperity, as people around the world aspire to the social and economic benefits of personal mobility. Governments in developing countries recognize that the auto industry can be an important engine of economic growth and will encourage local production to gain the benefits of this relatively high skill, high wage, high multiplier, high technology, capital- and labor-intensive industry.

Most studies show a high correlation between Gross Domestic Product (GDP) and vehicle ownership: countries with high GDP per capita, such as the US, Australia, Canada and the UK, also have high rates of vehicle ownership; conversely, countries with lower levels of GDP per capita typically have lower rates of vehicle ownership. Economic status within regions also may include economies in various stages of development. For example, even in the European Union (EU), there are substantial differences between the relatively wealthy regional EU-10 economies and the new member states, where GDP per capita is less than the price of a new small car. As economies grow, they can expect to experience increasing demand for vehicles. Consumers in the emerging automotive markets benefit from increasing trade through greater product choice and lower cost.

In this highly competitive automotive marketplace, automakers offer vehicles to meet consumers' needs and demands. To accomplish this goal, automakers explore options to increase economies of scale in the vehicle development and production process and to expand global sourcing to obtain the optimum materials. All customers benefit from this increased trade through enhanced product choices at affordable prices.

2. Regulating a Global Industry

A motor vehicle is one of the most comprehensively regulated global products, covering various vehicle performance and operation attributes. Also, because of its size and importance to the economy, the automotive industry receives greater than average scrutiny on many other aspects of its operations. In considering regulations, the role of governments is to balance social and economic benefits with appropriate requirements for environmental and safety performance. Governments should also base regulations on sound science and economics and attempt to arrive at common solutions. It is important to note that we respect the sovereign right of countries to set standards through transparent and democratic processes.

In an economy, increasing rates of vehicle sales and expanding personal mobility tend to be accompanied by the development of a system of motor vehicle regulations that addresses "local" concerns about motor vehicle safety, environmental and energy performance. Historically, three markets — North America, the European Union, and Japan, which have accounted for the largest share of the world's passenger vehicle production and consumption, have also served as the primary centers for regulatory rulemaking in the world.

Disparate governments have different priorities based on local conditions, disposable income, etc. To the extent that different countries and different jurisdictions take different approaches to the task and outcomes of automotive regulation, potential exporters of motor vehicles are faced with an increasing array of divergent regulations that significantly increase vehicle development and production complexity, add development and product costs without measurable increases in consumer benefits, and can act as a significant barrier to automotive trade across economies. Over time, the US and Europe have developed very dissimilar systems for testing and certifying motor vehicle safety and environmental performance. For example, each has established numerous differing technical requirements for common vehicle safety objectives. Japan's system utilizes elements of both the US and European system, creating yet a third unique set of requirements. As the automotive markets in other countries have grown, their governments have started to create their own regulatory regimes. In many instances emerging economies are looking to existing regulations in other economies as a basis for their own local regulations, at least initially, and sometimes incorporating elements of the European or US systems. While drawing on the supposed best aspects of other systems may sound like an appealing approach, the end result has been a proliferation of new regulatory procedures and requirements that resemble neither the US nor Europe.

Since economies of scale are critical in the auto industry, there is a growing trend in automotive production to limit the number of locations any one model is produced and cross-shipped to the markets where there is demand. This approach has the advantage of reducing production costs — thereby improving vehicle affordability — and increasing product choice across more regions/countries. Unfortunately, this strategy can be seriously impeded by divergent national and regional regulatory requirements and test procedures.

Some of the products resulting from such a pattern of global production are called "world cars," because a common automotive brand name is used in multiple markets. However, in many cases, these are vehicles with common interchangeable components that may differ in appearance and performance, when produced or sold in different countries to meet differing local consumers' desires, uses, and affordability. In this way, specific automotive national identity can be maintained while the economies of multi-national production are achieved. Local consumers have the potential to benefit from products that are designed, tested, and offered in a global vehicle development system with minimal product development complexity across borders. However, governments must realize that differences in vehicle regulations impede this process and result in higher-cost production which ultimately means greater expense without vehicle benefits for the vehicle consumer.

Consider this recent example. One US-based Alliance of Automobile Manufacturers (Alliance)[1] member explored the possibility of exporting to Europe a model that had proven popular in the United States. However, that model's design was incompatible with a European restriction on exterior edge projection (the United States has no comparable standard). Thus, because marketing the product in Europe would have required major body retooling, this product never made it across the Atlantic. The same manufacturer then undertook to ensure that another model then on the drawing board would have maximum export capability built into its design. In order to sell this product in Europe, the manufacturer utilized 100 unique parts, incurred an additional US $42 million in design and development costs, had to undertake unique incremental testing of 33 vehicle systems, and involved

---

[1] The Alliance is a trade association or car and light truck manufacturers whose members are BMW Group, Chrysler LLC, Ford Motor Company, General Motors, Mazda, Mercedes-Benz USA, Mitsubishi, Porsche, Toyota, and Volkswagen, and serves as the leading advocacy group for the automobile industry on a range of public policy issues.

an additional 130 people in the program. Yet, the performance of the vehicle, in terms of safety and emissions, was unchanged. Sale of the product in additional markets beyond Europe would have required even further expenditure and complexity. Manufacturers face the same issues in reverse when considering selling a European-designed model in the United States.

Governments, therefore, should carefully analyze existing and proposed vehicle regulations to determine if the national objectives for which they are intended justify the added cost, and provide appropriate benefits while not encumbering the most efficient scale of production, which will allow their manufacturers to compete effectively in the global motor vehicle market. Conflicting and overlapping regulations impede that ability of manufacturers to export to other countries by adding cost and complexity and, in so doing; they hurt consumers. At a certain threshold, automakers must decide to offer fewer vehicle choices in certain markets. At a minimum, we would encourage countries to recognize the results of testing performed in another jurisdiction and to the greatest extent possible, harmonize test procedures (even if the required performance level remains different).

One way the US government can help is to take greater cognizance of foreign national and international standards and regulatory developments in its own work. The European Union (EU) is working toward a single internal market for its Member States. Working with the United Nations Economic Commission for Europe (ECE), through its Working Party 29 (World Forum on Harmonization of Vehicle Regulations — WP.29), the EU nations have recognized the value of regulatory harmonization and are adopting ECE regulations verbatim whenever possible.

Because intergovernmental efforts to harmonize regulations at a truly international (as opposed to regional) level have not always been pursued with adequate vigor, regulations established by the major vehicle-producing countries remain incompatible. There are many instances where nations' needs and objectives do not differ, yet their regulations do. Thus, regulations have inhibited international trade and citizens have gained no compensatory benefits of improved safety or environmental protection. Instead, they have sacrificed the economic gains that might have resulted from expanded international trade.

It is also important to understand that even while generally supporting regulatory harmonization, the auto industry recognizes that "one size fits all" regulatory solutions are not always practicable due to challenges from differing mixes of factors among jurisdictions such as roadway users, vehicle fleets, collision conditions, as well as varying environmental, political and demographic factors. In fact, the 1998 Global Agreement (discussed below) which was established to develop global technical regulations for motor vehicles, recognized the need for such regulatory flexibility in Article 1, paragraph 1.1.7 which reads as follows:

> To ensure that, where alternative levels of stringency are needed to facilitate the regulatory activities of certain countries, in particular developing countries, such needs are taken into consideration in developing and establishing global technical regulations.

Accordingly, we recognize there may be cases where harmonization may not be possible or desirable, but that should not undermine the determination to pursue harmonization in other cases.

3. Example of Disparity — Surrogates for Humans in Crash Testing

Regulatory disparities among jurisdictions often provide no measurable differences in safety benefits. For example, the basic measures of motor vehicle safety performance, especially human injury tolerances, are similar throughout the world. This is a reasonable argument for cooperative development and use of harmonized human test surrogates (test dummies). Accordingly, at least one harmonization objective should be a common "tool box," including common crash test dummies. The Hybrid III 50th percentile adult male frontal crash test dummy[2] (Figure 1a) is a successful example of a test device regulated

---

[2] Title 49 Code of Federal Regulations Part 572 Subpart E.

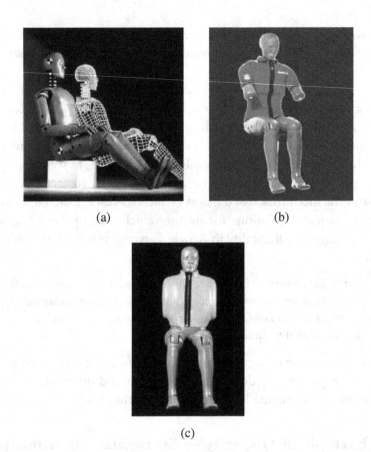

(a)   (b)

(c)

Figure 1:   (a) Hybrid III 50% tile Male – Frontal; (b) EuroSID 50% tile Male – Side; (c) SID 50% tile Male – Side.

and used commonly worldwide. In contrast, very different side impact crash test dummies with different injury measurement capabilities have been used in different regulatory jurisdictions; e.g., the EuroSID dummy for the EU and the SID dummy[3] for the US (Figures 1b and 1c, respectively). Harmonization of the regulated side impact crash test dummies continues to be an auto industry objective.

---

[3] Title 49 Code of Federal Regulations Part 572 Subpart F.

Dummy Portfolio

Rated & Regulated Crash Dummies
> Hybrid II 50th
> Hybrid III Family (50th, 5th, 95th, 3, 6)
> EUROSID (1, 2, 2re)
> SIDIIs
> DOT SID
> TNO-10
> P-Dummies (0, ,1.5, 3, 6, 10)
> Crabi 6,12,18

Non-regulated Crash Dummies (R&D)
> WorldSID 5th & 50th
> iDummy
> H3-10YO
> MAMA2B
> Aerospace Dummies
> OCATD
> BioRID
> RID3D
> Q Dummy (0, 1, 1.5, 3, 3s, 6)
> Pedestrian Dummy (50th, 5th, 95th)

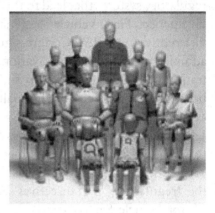

Dummy family

Figure 2: "Full family" crash test dummies.

The current "full family" of crash test dummies, regulated and unregulated, is shown in Figure 2.[4] Having multiple different crash test dummies of the same or similar size and purpose, all intended to measure the human response to crash injury, is a clear example of regulatory disharmony. In principle, regulations are intended to drive justifiable performance into motor vehicles based on benefits consistent with societal needs. Overall, the automotive industry worldwide has cooperatively demonstrated strong support for this principle. Evidence of that support, outlined below, is reflected in a long industry commitment to, and continuing cooperative efforts toward, regulatory harmonization. That commitment is one of the fundamental priorities of the Alliance: "To seek harmonization of global standards."

---

[4]Dummy information provided by First Technology Safety Systems.

4.   Comparison of US and EU Safety Regulations

Let us consider some of the differences between the US and European regulatory systems that lead to the very real consequences of regulatory divergence. First, vehicle safety standards themselves are established differently. In the US, Congress generally grants broad authority to an administrative agency, the National Highway Traffic Safety Administration (NHTSA), to develop and set actual regulations: "generally," because Congress also occasionally provides specific direction to the agency and, in the US system, legislation often drives regulation. In the US, for example, Congress passes "legislation" that requires an agency to initiate a safety study, possibly start rulemaking that may result in "regulation." In the EU, Parliament passes "legislation" that also is the "regulation." EU directives serve the same function as US Federal Motor Vehicle Safety Standards (FMVSS), which are set administratively in the US.

Not only is the process for setting standards different in the US and Europe, but the process for certifying conformity with their requirements is different as well. In Europe the test agencies conduct testing under the EU's "type approval" system. In the US, manufacturers are responsible for testing and meeting FMVSS (and also liable for recall and penalties if vehicles are later found not to meet any of the regulation's performance requirements).

Western European nations require vehicle manufacturers to demonstrate compliance with applicable regulations to authorities before the vehicle model represented can be offered for sale. Once "type approved," the manufacturer of the vehicle is free to market it throughout the European Union. Member countries that wish to challenge compliance of a vehicle model with applicable regulations must take the matter up with the government that certified the vehicle; it in turn works with the manufacturer to resolve the issue.

In contrast, in the US, vehicle manufacturers "self-certify" to Federal Motor Vehicle Safety Standards, which is to say that they declare, via a certification label placed on every vehicle, that the vehicle complies with all mandated safety requirements in effect at the time of manufacture and at that point the vehicle is introduced into the market.

Following their introduction, NHTSA regularly buys motor vehicles from dealerships and tests them for compliance as part of its enforcement efforts. If a non-compliance is found and verified, a recall is required (and may be ordered).[5] Additional fines or other punitive sanctions may also be applied.

5.   US–EU Market Competition and Manufacturer Cooperation

The automobile industry rapidly has evolved to collaborate across global economies. The United States (US)–European Union (EU) trade cooperation in automobiles has been part of that globalization. At the same time, automobile customer expectations for performance, safety, environmental responsibility, and more, have increased sharply around the world. Accordingly, the auto industry is faced with significant challenges to provide vehicles that serve many important, often competing, needs on a global basis. Although trade cooperation advances have been made, continued trade progress is impeded by the fact that automobile exporters still face an identifiable and burdensome inhibitor, namely, regulatory disharmony among jurisdictions. Governments continue to work to best meet their responsibilities to their constituents, while at the same time recognizing the challenges of regulating a global industry. At least for the auto industry, evidence of this can be seen in the following actions:

- 1965 — Canada and US establish conditional free trade under the "AutoPact"
- 1994 — NAFTA enters into force further liberalizing cross-border auto trade
- 1994 — Bogor Declaration is signed to facilitate trade in the APEC region

---

[5] Unless the inconsequential nature of the noncompliance can be established through a specific petition to and approval by the NHTSA.

- 1995 — The 1958 Agreement is amended for the first time in almost 40 years to allow broader participation of countries outside of Europe
- 1996 — Transatlantic Business Dialog Auto Sector Report
- 2000 — 1998 Agreement enters into force
- 2006 — CARS21 calls for "Better Regulation" including greater harmonization of regulatory standards with global standards
- 2008 — Enhanced Transatlantic Business Dialog focus on automotive industry

Consistent with the purpose of the conference — to assess the systematic, global implications of transatlantic regulatory cooperation and competition — it is clear for automobiles that bilateral US–EU regulatory activities have significant global implications.

6. EU–US Cooperation — The Transatlantic Business Dialogue

Much of the current automobile industry and government activity on motor vehicle global regulatory harmonization got underway in earnest with bilateral events in 1995 and 1996. The Transatlantic Business Dialogue (TABD), a forum comprised of US and European industry leaders, was initiated in 1995 by the US Department of Commerce, with assistance from the European Commission of the EU. It was conceived to encourage closer trade ties between the US and the EU, and to foster a more integrated transatlantic commercial marketplace. One of the TABD's primary outcomes[6] was recommendations concerning regulatory policy. Among the recommendations was the issuance of common standards of design, performance and/or controls in a number of industry sectors, including motor vehicles. Then US and EU Presidents Bill Clinton and Jacques Santer met at the December 1995 Madrid Summit to formally endorse the concept of harmonizing the myriad regulations facing business sectors on both sides of the Atlantic. Those recommendations were codified in a "Transatlantic

---

[6]From the November 1995 Seville Conference, and endorsed at the December 1995 Madrid Summit by US and European leaders.

Agenda" and "Action Plan" which included a call for regulatory harmonization; mutual recognition of regulatory certification procedures;
cooperation in the international standards-setting process; cooperative
development and implementation of regulations, and commitment to
a collaborative approach to the development of new testing and certification procedures.

6.1. *Transatlantic automotive industry conference on international regulatory harmonization*

In the context of the TABD, a broad cross-section of automobile industry representatives met at the April 1996 Transatlantic Automotive
Industry Conference on International Regulatory Harmonization in
Washington, DC. Representatives from US and European government
agencies participated as advisors. The purpose was to help advance
harmonization of motor vehicle safety and environmental regulations.
Table 1 summarizes the ten "First Principles" developed for, and agreed
at, the conference with the intention of initiating and stimulating dialog
toward regulatory harmonization among EU and US governments and
the auto industry. These principles reflected the auto industry thinking
at that time, and they are still appropriate today.

The April 1996 conference also provided specific industry recommendations for actions consistent with these principles.[7] Two key recommendations in this report were: greater cooperation and exchange
of information on regulatory and pre-regulatory research activities,
and a critical assessment of the "functional equivalence" of different
EU–US safety and environmental performance requirements.

7. International Harmonized Research Activities

At the May 1996 15th Enhanced Safety of Vehicles Conference in Australia, the US government (NHTSA) proposed and reached agreement
on an international harmonized research agenda (IHRA) for motor

---

[7]Transatlantic Automotive Industry Conference on International Regulatory
Harmonization — Working Papers on the Regulatory Process, Safety and Environment. Final Report — April 11, 1996.

Table 1: Summary of 10 "First Principles" for EU/US contribution to global harmonization (April 1996 Transatlantic Automotive Industry Conference on International Regulatory Harmonization).

- Commit to global regulatory harmonization by becoming Contracting Parties to 1958 Agreement; participate in developing new UN–ECE regulations with the intent of adopting and implementing them.
- Work through/strengthen Working Party 29 to expand it to a broadly recognized body for developing *global* vehicle regulatory requirements.
- Establish work program to contribute to *global* harmonization of regulatory differences.
- Continue process of *global* harmonization of vehicle regulatory requirements and expand discussions to all countries.
- Establish mutually recognized certification processes.
- Globally establish means to incorporate functional equivalence of alternative regulatory requirements; establish means to achieve mutual recognition of corresponding requirements.
- Coordinate pre-regulatory research on need for and development of new regulatory requirements, thereby minimizing the likelihood of future divergence.
- Avoid developing unique new national or regional technical requirements without adequate justification.
- Improve processes for informing public about development of harmonized regulations
- Encourage policy to accept vehicles fully meeting ECE or US or EU requirements as equivalent; avoid adoption of hybrid requirements (do not selectively combine elements of different jurisdictions).

---

vehicle safety with government representatives from other countries and regions. The purpose of the IHRA was to provide the scientific data to enable vehicle safety regulatory agencies around the world to develop future harmonized regulations that minimize regulatory requirement differences among countries. Table 2 lists the six research priorities that were identified.

Following the conclusion of the 15th ESV conference, a seventh topic — Side Impact Protection — was added to the list of active IHRA research priorities. The intent of the IHRA was to draw on both private and public sector expertise from all around the world to develop the data, information and test procedures identified

Table 2: IHRA research priorities (1996).

Topic	Description
Biomechanics	Develop injury measurement surrogates and test procedures for all crash modes
Functional equivalence	Develop technical and scientific aspects of a model for determining functional equivalence of existing regulations
Advance offset frontal crash protection	Develop harmonized test procedures based on real world crashes to assess vehicle crash performance and compatibility for frontal offset crashes
Vehicle crash compatibility	Explore car-to-car and truck-to-car crash compatibility of small and large vehicles
Pedestrian safety	Develop harmonized test procedures to assess safety performance of passenger vehicles in their interaction with pedestrians
Intelligent transportation systems	Develop test procedures to assess driver/vehicle interaction of crash avoidance and driver enhancement in-vehicle systems

for each of the established research priorities. Each project was lead by government representatives. Simply stated, the goal of the IHRA was common, state-of-the-art research that would provide the scientific basis for developing globally-harmonized future safety regulations.

While the founding concept seemed solid, only some of the research projects made progress while others did not. Two IHRA topics have actually resulted in providing the anticipated technical foundation for future harmonized global technical regulations. Those two are the pedestrian protection IHRA, chaired by the government of Japan, which provided the technical foundation for the current draft global technical regulation being finalized in Geneva through WP.29, and the side impact IHRA, chaired by the government of Australia, which resulted in the development of a state-of-the-art side impact test device, namely, WorldSID. Surprisingly, the remaining IHRA topics, which were chaired by the US or European governments, have not provided sufficient substantive data to be used as the basis for a global technical regulation.

7.1. *Industry petitions for functional equivalence determinations*

Recognizing the functional equivalence principle from the April 1996 conference, a cooperative regulatory comparison action was undertaken by the automobile industry. The American Automobile Manufacturers Association (AAMA), the European Automobile Manufacturers Association (ACEA), and the Japan Automobile Manufacturers Association (JAMA)[8] put significant effort into comparing five similar but separate US, EU, ECE and Japanese motor vehicle safety regulations for the same vehicle systems: windshield wiping/washing, windshield defrosting/defogging, headlamp concealment devices, head restraints, and seat belt assemblies. These subject areas were chosen based on the industry's assessment that they were reasonable test cases for favorable determinations of functional equivalence by regulatory authorities. The comparisons were submitted in 1997 to the regulatory authorities requesting that determination.

Subsequently, the US government's motor vehicle safety regulatory agency, NHTSA, established a policy and regulatory process for functional equivalence determinations. Establishing the process itself was consistent with one of the principles from the April 1996 conference. However, the industry's initial examination of the functional equivalence determination requirements indicated that there was unlikely to be enough existing or envisioned future evidence (i.e., data) for the submitted regulatory comparison items that could satisfy the relatively stringent requirements of the new US process.

In the end, both the EU and NHTSA rejected the industry's functional equivalence arguments on the submitted vehicle safety regulatory comparisons and no favorable equivalence findings were obtained.

---

[8]Participation by the Japanese auto industry was considered to be essential for real global progress on motor vehicle regulatory items.

While the real-world safety performance of vehicles designed and built in compliance with the total package of either US or European regulations demonstrate a high level of safety, it is much harder to generate or provide data to substantiate the comparable performance assignable to an individual US and corresponding European regulation. Thus, for industry, the functional equivalence determination hurdle appeared to be very high. With this "lesson learned," the industry turned its focus to another regulatory harmonization action that it believed could be more effective.

8. 1998 Agreement Administered by WP.29

The most significant, tangible success to come out of the TABD effort was the drafting and ratification of the "Agreement Concerning the Establishing of Global Technical Regulations for Wheeled Vehicles, Equipment and Parts Which Can Be Fitted And/Or Be Used on Wheeled Vehicles, Done at Geneva on 25 June 1998" (1998 Agreement). That action established a world forum to develop global technical regulations (GTRs) for motor vehicle safety, environmental protection, energy efficiency and anti-theft performance. That forum is now called the World Forum for Harmonization of Vehicle Regulations (WP.29). It is a subsidiary body of the United Nations Economic Commission for Europe (UN ECE) Inland Transportation Committee (Figure 3).

For four decades, until 1998, WP.29 developed motor vehicle technical regulations under one agreement, commonly known as

Figure 3: UN ECE Inland Transport Committee.

the 58 Agreement.[9] This agreement was regionally focused on harmonizing motor vehicle technical requirements, known as ECE regulations, within Europe. There are currently 140 ECE regulations annexed to the 58 Agreement. Over time other jurisdictions outside of Europe have adopted ECE regulations into their own national requirements.

With growing recognition of the need for global harmonization, the US government (with NHTSA and EPA representation) proposed and co-led negotiations with the EC and Japan that in 1998 officially transformed WP.29 from a largely regional forum into a true world forum. The transformation was completed by the formal adoption of the 1998 Agreement. Among the Agreement's statements of purpose is this one clearly identifying the global focus:

> To establish a global process by which Contracting Parties from all regions of the world can jointly develop global technical regulations regarding the safety, environmental protection, energy efficiency and anti-theft performance of wheeled vehicles, equipment and parts which can be fitted and/or be used on wheeled vehicles.

The 1998 Agreement permits countries that are either not ready to, or legally cannot, adopt and implement obligations of the 1958 Agreement to engage in developing harmonized GTRs. For example, two obligations of the 1958 Agreement — vehicle type approval certification[10] and mutual recognition of regulations[11] — preclude some

---

[9] "Agreement Concerning The Adoption of Uniform Technical Prescriptions For Wheeled Vehicles, Equipment And Parts Which Can Be Fitted And/Or Be Used On Wheeled Vehicles And The Conditions For Reciprocal Recognition Of Approvals Granted On The Basis Of These Prescriptions."

[10] Type approval certification: the manufacturer must prove to a government agency, typically through testing witnessed by or inspection by a regulatory authority or its representative, that applicable regulatory requirements are satisfied before the vehicle is offered for sale. The regulatory authority grants the type approval certification for the vehicle model/line.

[11] Mutual recognition of regulations: each jurisdiction recognizes regulations created and administered by other jurisdictions, even where such regulations vary from their own regulations. It is based on the premise that regulations in one jurisdiction meet community expectations and are acceptable in other jurisdictions.

countries from signing on to the 1958 Agreement. It is in fact these two particular provisions that resulted in the determination that the United States could not legally sign the 1958 Agreement. The US legal regulatory system of manufacturer "self-certification" to Federal Motor Vehicle Safety Standards (FMVSS)[12] does not permit vehicle type approval or mutual recognition of another country's vehicle safety regulations. However, under the 1998 Agreement, the United States has fully participated as a Contracting Party[13] to help develop GTRs.[14] Evidence of the global involvement and reach of the WP.29 activities is illustrated by the continued ramp-up of the number of signatories (currently 30 jurisdictions worldwide) to the 1998 Agreement and their participation in WP.29 activities (Figure 4).

8.1. *1998 Agreement accomplishments and lessons learned*

So how effective has the 1998 Agreement been? To date, 7 GTRs have been established through the WP.29 process, three applicable to light duty passenger vehicles, two covering motorcycles, and two related to heavy-duty vehicle requirements. Some Contracting Parties to the 1998 Agreement are in the process of introducing these global regulations into their own regulatory systems. A number of other GTRs are under development or being contemplated. Assessment of the effectiveness the GTR efforts often depends on the point of view of the observer. However, two observations are undeniable: first, the process has been deliberate if not slow at times and second, both government

---

[12] Self-certification: the manufacturer must certify on its own that every one of the vehicles it produces (not just a model line for example) meets applicable regulatory requirements, without testing witnessed or conducted by or inspection by authorities, before the vehicle is offered for sale. The regulatory authority is not involved in the certification.

[13] A Contracting Party is a signatory to the 1998 Agreement.

[14] Once a GTR is established through the WP.29 process, it still needs to be adopted into the Contracting Party's own regulatory system before it takes effect in that country or region.

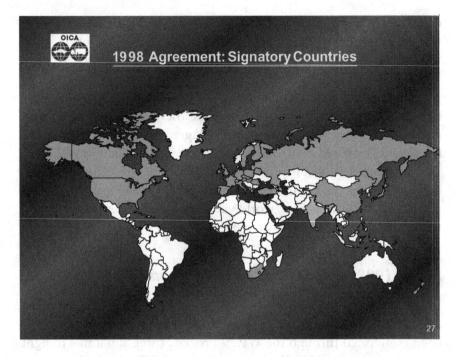

Figure 4:   Global contacting parties to the 1998 Agreement.

and industry parties involved in this work have demonstrated commitment to it by investing substantial time, money, and resources into making a success of the 1998 Agreement since its inception.

9.   Discussion of Several GTR Efforts, Successes and Unsuccessful Outcomes to Date

9.1.   *Lighting installation GTR*

This was one of the first candidates for GTR consideration, because it is a subject (headlamps, brake lamps, turn signals, etc.) regulated by many countries and was expected to be relatively easy due to the similarities among requirements for many lighting devices. Agreement on requirements for approximately 90% of all the lighting devices was achieved; however the remaining lighting devices were either mandated, optionally-permitted, or expressly prohibited by one or more contracting party. Compromise could not be achieved and it was proposed to allow governments to choose what lighting components they would allow or disallow. Major vehicle manufacturers who market vehicles internationally already provide specific vehicle lighting for vehicles that can be sold in various countries around the world. Consequently, the draft GTR's allowance of Contracting Party choice among mandating, allowing optionally, or prohibiting the remaining lighting devices would actually add regulatory burden without providing any benefit to vehicle manufacturers or consumers. Therefore, vehicle manufacturers opposed the Lighting Installation GTR as proposed.

Lesson Learned — Until countries are willing to assess the safety basis for their current requirements and consider changes in order to achieve a harmonized GTR, the best prospects for future GTRs will be relative to those systems that have no, or very few, existing regulatory requirements around the world.

9.2.   *Controls and displays GTR*

Work on a draft GTR on driver controls and displays (e.g., tell tales) started in 2000 under the leadership of Canada. A first draft GTR was prepared in 2002 and, in 2003, NHTSA published a Notice of Proposed Rulemaking (NPRM) based on this draft GTR text. As a result of public comment to the NPRM, NHTSA informed WP.29 of the need for a demonstrated high level of recognition for any symbols or icons contained in the draft GTR. The industry was asked to come up with data (recognition study) and report back to WP.29. The Alliance agreed to perform a study to evaluate all symbols included in the two tables of the draft GTR. The results of this study indicated lower-than-expected comprehension levels for many of the symbols tested. A second study was undertaken to determine if using a slightly different testing method would yield different results. Nine symbols were tested (symbols included in the existing US regulation FMVSS 101 and present in most vehicles in service; symbols not included in FMVSS 101 but present in some vehicles in service; symbols not included in

FMVSS 101 and present in very few or no vehicles currently in service). For some symbols, additional information provided when the symbol was viewed in context helped subjects understand the meaning of the symbol. Other symbols (brake malfunction and lighting) did not communicate their intended messages. For the brake malfunction symbol, comprehension would be higher had the word "Brake" been added to the symbol during testing. The results of the Alliance study were presented to WP.29 in June 2006. As a result of these two studies, NHTSA drafted a new version of the GTR including only 8 symbols (those with a comprehension percent greater than 60%). Canada kept its draft GTR with the 48 symbols. Because neither Canada nor the United States wanted to change their position, WP.29 in November 2007 decided to move the issue off of the active program of work.

Lesson Learned — The technical soundness of any requirement to be included in a GTR must be established ahead of the actual drafting of GTR text. Additionally, while the Alliance provided some basis for assessing symbol- or icon-recognition in the United States, additional data from Europe or other regions were not developed. More data from more countries may have helped to overcome the disagreement that lead to the tabling of this draft GTR.

9.3.   *Pedestrian protection GTR*

Both the EU and Japan placed a high priority on developing a GTR for Pedestrian Protection. Both jurisdictions adopted initial pedestrian requirements for head impact criteria and the EU also adopted leg impact criteria. These requirements were applied to what would be considered a typical passenger car (vehicle mass at or below 2,500 kg). Japan led the IHRA activity (with both government and industry involvement) to develop the test procedures and criteria needed for the GTR. Both US and EU industry members evaluated and analyzed available passenger car accident data to support the IHRA-recommended performance measures. However, the final text for a GTR on Pedestrian Protection is being drafted to extend the application to include larger and heavier types of vehicles that are beyond the scope of the initial technical review.

Lesson Learned — The technical support for the GTR was established by the IHRA work with industry confirmation for typical passenger car vehicles. Industry data for typical passenger car vehicles less than 2,500 kg was developed and used to formulate the draft GTR text. However, applicability of the proposed test protocols has not been demonstrated for vehicles outside the initial scope of the GTR development (i.e., heavier, high-hooded vehicles).

9.4. *Electronic stability control (ESC) GTR*

ESC offers an advanced technology solution for reducing rollover and loss-of-control crashes under a variety of differing road conditions. The underlying technology has been in use for nearly a decade on some vehicle lines, and several government and non-government organizations have developed estimates of real-world effectiveness based on analysis of available accident data. In the United States, close cooperation between NHTSA and the Alliance resulted in a body of research that supported development of an objective, repeatable test procedure and performance criteria that have proven to be acceptable to both regulators and industry around the world. There is clear political pressure in both the EU and United States to quickly reach agreement on a common definition for ESC globally and a draft GTR providing for the optional fitment of ESC has been completed and is scheduled to be for voted on by WP.29 at its June 2008 meeting.

Lesson Learned — The technical soundness for this GTR was established ahead of the drafting of GTR text though a program of cooperative research conducted by NHTSA and Alliance member companies. This resulted in a technically sound final rule in the United States and that has served as the model language for development of the draft GTR.

The above examples are just a few of the GTR activities that the industry has directly participated in, but they are illustrative of the diversity of outcomes and types of actions needed to improve the likelihood that a GTR can be developed successfully. Figure 5 depicts some general observations and "lessons learned" from our experience. Each cell in the matrix is color-coded to indicate the influence

Lessons from the past

	Pedestrian safety	ESC	Emission gtr [iii]	Head restraints	Lighting	Controls & tell tales
Political pressure in key CP s [i]	≥ 2	≥ 2	≥ 2	≤ 1	≤ 1	≤ 1
Existing regulation in EU **or** US [ii]						
Existing regulation in EU **and** US [ii]						
Parallel rulemaking in key CP						
Research available						
Consistent Industry Direction						
Consensus with other NGO s						

(i) If political pressure is high it results in politically active support of AC3 and GR chairs
(ii) So far having an existing regulation in Japan is less problematic as they are generally more committed to harmonization and willing to compromise
(iii) OICA worked pro-actively

Figure 5:   Lessons from the past.

(green/positive, red/negative, or blank/no influence) that the description in the left-hand column had on the development of a GTR. For example, regarding the ESC GTR the green/positive cells indicate: there was political pressure in at least 2 key Contracting Parties (CP), only the US had an existing regulation, supporting research was available, and industry endorsed the drafting of a GTR on this topic. On the other hand, regarding the lighting GTR the red/negative cells indicate: there was no common political pressure, both the US and Europe had competing regulations, there was a lack of relevant research, and industry did not strongly support this work.

10.   Summary of Global Technical Regulation Experience

The following summarizes our experience to date with the process for developing GTR's under the 1998 agreement.

- The 1998 Agreement's stated expectation that a cost/benefit justification be established as a basis for GTR requirements has been pursued with varying degrees of success, depending on the GTR subject.

- A substantial amount of effort and time has been spent trying to reach a compromise position on GTR requirements, especially when there are existing, but differing, regulations on the same subject from at least two different Contracting Parties. The bias among participants toward favoring provisions from their own country's or region's regulations has sometimes necessitated a "compromise" that allows contracting parties to choose among two or more options.

- The tendency to default to Contracting Party "options" within a GTR when a compromise solution cannot be reached is contrary to, and undermines, the harmonization objective. It is specifically problematical for manufacturers, because these "options," which otherwise often consist of the separate provisions from existing, comparable regulations of different countries or regions, require manufacturers to design and/or certify their vehicles according to both options. This invariably entails higher cost and resource burden without measurable benefit for consumers. Thus, when differing GTR "options" can be chosen by different Contracting Parties, the manufacturer is unable to take advantage of the underlying benefit of regulatory harmonization.

- Nearly all efforts to reach final agreement to establish any GTR have taken longer (in some cases much longer) than initial expectations. Many times, the delays are due to the inability of some contracting parties to reach equitable positions on technical requirements. Other times, as is the current case with the pedestrian protection GTR, it is the laborious internal process of the EU to reach agreement with its member states.

- The focus of some national or regional participants in the GTR process is to specify design-specific requirements in a GTR. Others prefer performance-based requirements, which align better with regulatory goals and intentions and ultimately permit more design flexibility and innovation.

- The full value of a GTR, that is, true harmonization, is undermined when Contracting Parties alter the GTR language when adopting the GTR into their respective national or regional regulations.
- Although Special Resolution 1 (adopted under the 1998 Global Agreement) defines vehicle classifications to be used when writing a GTR, a Contracting Party still has to reconcile the GTR to match vehicle classifications applicable in their jurisdiction. National or regional vehicle classifications are often different than those in Special Resolution 1.

Quantitative measures are not available yet of the expected benefits to trade, vehicle development/certification complexity reduction, or consumers from established motor vehicle safety GTRs. Such metrics cannot be calculated at this time because established GTRs have either not taken effect yet, or have not yet been in effect long enough in any jurisdiction. The data simply are not available and may not be for some time.

11. An Additional Initiative: A Competitive Automotive Regulatory System for the 21st Century

A new EC initiative (with input from various stakeholders including auto industry representatives, worker representatives, politicians, etc.) resulted from examination of major policies that affect European auto industry competitiveness. The European auto industry had requested a review of its regulatory environment, and the new initiative was set up to address this objective. The initiative, an integrated approach identified as the Competitive Automotive Regulatory System for the 21st Century, or CARS 21,[15] is intended to advance the European auto industry's global competitiveness and to increase employment while sustaining safety and environmental progress as well as vehicle affordability. The CARS 21 report contains 18 recommendations and

---

[15]CARS 21 — A Competitive Automotive Regulatory System for the 21st century, Final Report December 2005.

a roadmap for EC regulatory reform. Among the many CARS 21 recommendations is "better regulation," including exploring "possibilities for stronger internationalization of the regulatory environment (in particular towards the UN Economic Commission for Europe's international automotive regulations)."

The CARS 21 Report also confirms the recognition (noted earlier) that European regulations are rapidly becoming global regulations through adoption by countries and jurisdictions outside of the EU:

> CARS 21 stakeholders therefore find it important that European standards are being adopted in other markets and would encourage this trend. Policy should therefore continue to actively promote international harmonization.

In summary form, the CARS 21 principles and recommendations that focused on or included some element of regulatory harmonization are:

- Simplify EU legislation (regulations) by strengthening links between the EU regulatory system and the United Nations 1958 and 1998 Agreements. Continue the EC orientation to progressively replace part of EU type approval legislation with corresponding UN Regulations.
- Systematically explore whether developing global regulations is preferable to taking regulatory initiatives within the EU alone. Strive for better harmonization of measures (e.g., test procedures) worldwide to improve market access and reduce costs. Adopt global test methods where feasible.
- Expand self-testing as part of the type-approval process (initially where tests involved are relatively simple). Permit manufacturers to be appointed as testing laboratories after the type-approval authority has determined the manufacturer's competence.

The Alliance supports the CARS 21 recommendations and roadmap, including those beyond the regulatory harmonization items. The Alliance also supports the principles identified in the report focused on the quality of regulations (i.e., that they be objective and based on sound science); simplification of regulations; evidence-based impact assessments (i.e., assuring proper priorities and demonstrating a safety need); stakeholder consultation (i.e., open/transparent process); provision of sufficient lead-time; and the use of alternatives to regulation (i.e., market-driven solutions and voluntary agreements).

Additionally, we note that the design of motor vehicle architectures and safety technology sold in Europe is driven to a great extent by the non-regulatory, consumer information vehicle safety rating program known as EuroNCAP.[16] To have real effect, the CARS 21 principles should also be applied by EuroNCAP, as well as by the process at WP.29. Lastly, the CARS 21 principles are appropriate for application in jurisdictions world-wide.

Consistent with the goals of regulatory harmonization discussed earlier, the Alliance sees the potential for realizing significant progress by adhering to the principles of the CARS 21 report. The real challenge lies in summoning the discipline required to implement and maintain these principles.

12.   Conclusion and Recommendations to Help Achieve Vision for the Future

Harmonization of regulatory safety requirements for automobiles would remove a significant non-tariff barrier to trade for the automotive industry. This, in turn, would lower the cost of doing business throughout the globe and contribute to more affordable vehicles and a greater selection of products.

> *Recommendation:* All governments that regulate the motor vehicle industry should be sensitive to the downside effects of divergent regulations. To share in the benefits of multi-national production and trade, and to enhance the potential for a nation's citizens to have the options to choose affordable vehicles that offer increasing benefits, governments must be willing to modify and harmonize their regulatory policies to facilitate trade.

---

[16]Euro NCAP's aim is to provide motoring consumers — both drivers and the automotive industry — with an independent assessment of the safety performance of some of the most popular cars sold in Europe. Vehicle ratings are based on front and side crash tests, and child protection and pedestrian protection ratings.

Recommendation: Governments, therefore, should carefully analyze existing and proposed vehicle regulations to determine if the national objectives for which they are intended justify the added cost, and provide appropriate benefits while not encumbering the most efficient scale of production, which will allow their manufacturers to compete effectively in the global motor vehicle market. Conflicting and overlapping regulations impede that ability of manufactuers to export to other countries by adding cost and complexity and, in so doing: they hurt consumers by increasing prices and limiting choice.

Looking at the above "lessons learned" during the 10 years since the 1998 Agreement has been in force, one might conclude that the only time a GTR is likely to be successfully finalized and adopted is when there is no current relevant regulation or that only one exists in either the United States or Europe. If, on the other hand, a corresponding regulation exists in both the United States and Europe, the likelihood of a successful, harmonized GTR without "contracting party options" is very low. This might imply that harmonization can only be successful for future regulations and argues against attempting to harmonize the substantial body of existing regulations. However, we believe such a view may be premature.

A "two standards world" scenario was envisioned in a 2004 paper[17] prepared by the Alliance and presented to the US Department of Commerce and NHTSA. That paper acknowledged the US–European competition for global acceptance of their respective regulations that continues to this day. It also noted the concern that this competition could lead to a further divergence of technical requirements around the world as important emerging automotive markets, such as the People's Republic of China and India, start regulatory regimes of their own that may choose some US and some European requirements, thus creating totally unique regulatory schemes. Such proliferation of regulatory schemes does not serve US or European interests. While no one, including industry, believes it necessary to harmonize the entire suite of existing US and European regulations, the opportunity to

---

[17]Wilber, Vann (2004). "A Framework for Technical Regulatory Harmonization". The Alliance of Automobile Manufacturer Association.

develop a single harmonized regulation in those areas of regulation that offers a true cost-benefit advantage, should have a higher likelihood for success.

> *Recommendation*: Successfully completing GTRs and broader implementation of harmonized standards will require a new or at least more innovative approach to the work of WP.29 and collaborative recognition of the lessons learned in GTR development to date. Closer cooperation between the US and Europe is the essential element of this new approach. It will also require careful attention to assure global technical regulation development and adoption to clearly accommodate specific national and regional needs including minimizing the burden on developing markets and economies.

> *Recommendation*: Where new areas of regulation emerge (such as hydrogen as a motor vehicle fuel), all governments should focus efforts on developing a GTR rather than establishing national or regional standards, which will subsequently be difficult to harmonize.

At the June 2005 US–EU Summit, a "Roadmap for US–EU Regulatory Cooperation" was issued. This roadmap calls for annual bilateral meetings between NHTSA and the Directorate-General Enterprise and Industry to identify areas for harmonized safety and fuel economy regulations. In April 2007, the "Framework for Advancing Transatlantic Economic Integration between the European Union and the United States of America" was signed and established the Transatlantic Economic Council (TEC) to "accelerate progress" on transatlantic economic integration. At the first TEC meeting a discussion of regulatory burden resulted in a recommendation that future regulatory impact assessments should take into account the impact of future regulations on trade and investment. Just how effective these recent US–EU initiatives will be in fostering new directions for future harmonized automotive regulation remains to be seen.

Institutional impediments to successful efforts to harmonize automotive regulations range from fundamental disagreements over policy and process to simple bureaucratic reluctance to consider change.

> *Recommendation*: In order to overcome such institutional impediments, responsible government authorities must be willing to think critically

not only of other nation's regulatory frameworks, but of their own, as well.

- By analyzing all proposals for compromise for their effectiveness to meet the specific purpose each regulation attempts to serve.
- Then, ensuring that a firm technical and/or scientific basis exists for the candidate changes to requirements.

Open and substantive dialogue should resolve most differences; however, this can work only when there is common fundamental commitment to the goals of regulatory harmonization. The international framework for this discourse already exists and is starting to function under the 1998 Global Agreement through efforts in the UN ECE WP.29.

At the end of the day, the future vision for true automobile regulatory harmonization comes down to a relatively simple statement that entails much associated hard work — "Tested once, accepted everywhere". This means increased commitment, attention and cooperation globally by regulatory authorities and the regulated industry to do more of what the 1998 Agreement already facilitates, which involves the development and national/regional adoption of useful, beneficial global technical regulations. In this way, we can realize the advantages of harmonization to consumers, manufacturers, governments and economies.

Chapter 7

Systemic Implications of Deeper Transatlantic Convergence in Competition/Antitrust Policy

Robert D. Anderson*

World Trade Organization, Geneva
robert.anderson@wto.org

In the transatlantic context, the field of competition (antitrust) policy has benefited from both: (i) the establishment of formal arrangements to promote cooperation between North American and European enforcement authorities; and (ii) a significant but incomplete and voluntary convergence of substantive enforcement approaches based on mutual learning and experience. These developments have undeniably helped to strengthen enforcement and to minimize inter-jurisdictional conflicts, though they have not eliminated the scope for such conflicts. In the future, however, the most serious policy clashes in the antitrust field are more likely to involve countries outside the transatlantic context. This reflects the proliferation of competition laws across all regions of the world during the past decade and the lack of deep antitrust traditions in some of the relevant countries. The scope for such conflicts may eventually compel reconsideration of multilateral "framework" approaches to competition law that would promote sound economic approaches and

*Counsellor, Intellectual Property Division (for government procurement and competition policy), World Trade Organization (WTO), Geneva, Switzerland and Special Professor, University of Nottingham. Helpful suggestions from/discussions with team leader Simon Evenett, Alberto Heimler, Pierre Arhel, Antony Taubman and Adrian Otten in addition to participants at the conference on Systemic Implications of Transatlantic Regulatory Cooperation and Competition which took place in Ann Arbor on May 8–9, 2008, are gratefully acknowledged. This paper has been prepared strictly in the author's personal capacity. The views expressed should *not* be attributed to the WTO, its Secretariat or any of its Members.

ensure non-discrimination in policy application without entailing forced harmonization. Further efforts at achieving deeper cooperation and convergence in the transatlantic context could provide essential intellectual leadership in this regard.

1. Introduction

Competition (antitrust) rules are a central aspect of the legislative framework within which businesses operate in modern market-based economies. Such rules, which encompass the regulation of mergers, abuses of a dominant position and other forms of firm behaviour in addition to the prohibition of cartels, ensure that consumers enjoy freedom of choice, low prices and good value for money. To an extent, antitrust rules can also serve as an alternative to more intrusive forms of regulation (Melamed 1997; Carlton and Picker 2007).[1] In addition, advocacy activities by competition agencies and related bodies contribute to the evolution of diverse marketplace framework policies (e.g., intellectual property) and industry-specific regulatory regimes (e.g., for telecommunications and other infrastructure sectors) in many jurisdictions (Kovacic 2003a; Anderson and Heimler 2007). In the light of these diverse functions, competition law and policy go a long way to define the business environment and to establish the overall framework for the operation of markets in modern economies.

The field of competition law and policy embodies many of the trends and dilemmas that are at the heart of current debates on international cooperation and inter-jurisdictional competition in economic regulation and policy-making generally. Today, there is broad acknowledgment of the need for cooperation between jurisdictions

---

[1] Indeed, whether antitrust is truly a form of (as opposed to an alternative to) "regulation" can be debated, in that the concept of regulation often implies detailed, ongoing supervision of business conduct (as in energy or telecommunications regulation). For this reason, antitrust authorities themselves often prefer to characterize the rules that they administer as "framework policies and rules" rather then regulation. In this paper, we will accept that antitrust is a form of regulation in a broad sense while also recognizing certain of its attributes (e.g., generality of application; reliance to a large extent on *ex-post* rather than *ex-ante* intervention) that distinguish it from other forms of regulation.

to facilitate effective application of national competition laws (see e.g., Barnett 2008; Kroes 2008; and any number of other speeches by senior representatives of national competition agencies).[2] Formal intergovernmental agreements to facilitate cooperation, mainly but not exclusively of a procedural nature, have been in place for many years.[3] Significant resources are devoted to the administration of these agreements.[4] There is also good evidence that a gradual process of convergence is taking place with respect to the substantive competition law standards of many countries, though important differences in such standards remain (Barnett 2008; Kovacic 2008; and Varney 2010).[5] At the same time, the idea of "harmonization" — or forced convergence of substantive competition law standards — has been strenuously resisted by practitioners, particularly in the US (see, for recent expressions of this view, Barnett 2008 and Kovacic 2008; see also Pate 2004, Melamed 1997 and Klein 1996).[6] The utility of preserving broad scope for individual jurisdictions to choose their own enforcement standards and doctrines has been explicitly defended by reference to the benefits of inter-jurisdictional regulatory competition (see, for example, Kovacic 2003b and 2008; and Barnett 2008).

These trends and dilemmas are illustrated in vivid fashion in the transatlantic context, in which we see both: (i) the existence and regular use of formal cooperation arrangements for the enforcement of competition law that have been in place for a number of years, reinforced

---

[2] Competition/antitrust policy has also been mentioned, but has not figured centrally, in the Merkel initiative. See Simon J. Evenett and Robert M. Stern, "Introduction" to this volume.

[3] The nature of the cooperation that can be undertaken pursuant to these agreements — particularly those applicable in the US–European Community context — will be discussed below.

[4] Nonetheless, whether the actual extent of cooperation in the antitrust field matches the rhetorical commitment to it can be questioned. See Part III, below, and references cited therein.

[5] See Part II below.

[6] By "antitrust standards", reference is made to the doctrinal and analytical approaches governing the treatment, e.g., of abuses of dominant position, mergers or other arrangements.

by extensive contacts between the responsible officials and a gradual process of convergence which has brought the European Union (EU) closer to but not in line with US approaches (see, on this process, Anderson and Heimler 2007); and (ii) periodic conflicts that nonetheless arise in the enforcement stances taken by the US and the EU in major transnational cases (see Part 4.1, below), which arguably call for deeper forms of cooperation and coordination. Calls for substantive harmonization of competition law and enforcement approaches and/or new approaches to the exercise of jurisdiction between the EU and the US nonetheless continue to be rejected.

This paper examines the origins and nature of transatlantic cooperation in the antitrust field, and considers the extent of voluntary convergence in substantive standards that has already taken place. It also reflects on the pros and cons of deeper cooperation/substantive harmonization, the barriers to such developments, and how they might be overcome. The significance of EU–US cooperation and coordination in the wider global context is also considered.

A degree of humility is appropriate in this exercise. The subject of international cooperation and convergence in the antitrust field (often, though not necessarily, with a particular focus on the transatlantic sphere) has for many years been the subject of extensive and insightful study by international organizations such as the International Competition Network (ICN), the Organization for Economic Cooperation and Development (OECD) and (especially in the period from 1997 through 2004) the World Trade Organization (WTO);[7] by high-profile national consultative bodies such as the US International Competition Policy Advisory Committee;[8] and by scholars and practitioners (see, for some of the richer contributions, Evenett et al., 2000; Jenny 2003; Epstein and Greve 2004; and Marsden 2007).

---

[7]See the extensive materials on related topics which are available at the following websites: http://www.internationalcompetitionnetwork.org/ (for the ICN); http://www.oecd.org/topic/0,3373,en_2649_37463_1_1_1_1_37463,00.html (for the OECD); and http://www.wto.org/english/tratop_e/comp_e/comp_e.htm (for the WTO).

[8]See International Competition Policy Advisory Committee (2000).

This paper seeks to build constructively on other contributions by: (i) situating the issue of cooperation in the context of the historical origins, normative approaches and operating modalities of competition policy in the EU and the US; (ii) taking due account of the cooperative measures regarding competition law and policy that have already been put in place in the transatlantic context and relevant officials' own suggestions for deepening such cooperation; (iii) considering the implications of recent conflicts of policy application, e.g., in the *Microsoft* and *GE/Honeywell* cases;[9] and (iv) linking the discussion of EU–US cooperation to the broader global context and the debate on trade and competition policy which occurred in the WTO. In addition, it has benefited from exposure to the insights emerging from studies of other aspects of transatlantic regulatory cooperation at the 2008 conference in Ann Arbor.[10]

The overall perspective of the paper can be summarized as follows. In the transatlantic context, the field of competition (antitrust) policy has benefited from both: (i) the establishment of formal arrangements to promote cooperation between North American and European enforcement authorities; and (ii) a significant but incomplete and voluntary convergence of substantive enforcement approaches based on mutual learning and experience. These developments have undeniably helped to strengthen enforcement and to minimize but not to eliminate inter-jurisdictional conflicts. In the future, however, the most serious policy clashes in the antitrust field are likely to involve countries outside the transatlantic context. This reflects the proliferation of competition laws across all regions of the world during the past decade and the lack of deep antitrust traditions in many of the relevant countries. The scope for such conflicts may eventually compel reconsideration of multilateral "framework" approaches to competition law that would

---

[9]It should be emphasized that no view will be expressed on the substantive merits of the EU and US stances in any of these cases; rather, the focus is on what these cases reveal about the need for deeper cooperation mechanisms.

[10]Too often, cooperation in the antitrust field has been assessed in isolation, without being situated in the broader context of international cooperation on regulatory and other issues.

promote sound economic approaches and ensure non-discrimination in policy application without entailing forced harmonization. Further efforts at achieving deeper cooperation and convergence in the transatlantic context could provide essential intellectual leadership in this regard.[11]

The remainder of the paper is structured as follows. Part 2 examines the differing historical origins and orientations of competition policy in the EU and the US, and the nature and degree of convergence that has already place in the transatlantic context.[12] Part 3 discusses the need for cooperation in the antitrust field in principle, and the cooperation arrangements that have already been put in place by the US and the EU. Part 4 examines several examples of transatlantic conflicts in the application of competition law and considers what they tell us about the limits of existing cooperation mechanisms. The scope for conflicts that go beyond the transatlantic context is also noted, and the road ahead considered. Part 5 provides concluding remarks.

2. The Differing Historical Origins and Orientations of Competition Policy in the US and the EU, and the Process of Convergence Thus Far

In order to better appreciate both the potential gains from deeper transatlantic cooperation on antitrust and the constraints that bear on

---

[11]The importance of ideas and institutional learning processes in the evolution of competition policy standards are stressed in Kovacic (2003a and b), in Barnett (2007) and in Anderson and Heimler (2007).

[12]In this paper, "transatlantic" will refer mainly to the relationship between the United States and the European Community (EU). It is nonetheless worth noting that the US–EU relationship is only the most prominent aspect of a wider transatlantic community encompassing Canada and the non-EU European states, who might also benefit from and wish to take part in initiatives to deepen cooperation and promote further convergence in the competition policy field.

the possibility of such cooperation, it is helpful to briefly review the historical origins and orientations of competition policy in the US and the EU. It is tempting, in this regard, to assume that EU and US competition policy can be easily compared and (if necessary) aligned, on the basis that they are essentially "different ways of doing the same thing". Indeed, as will be discussed below, over time, the competition policies of the EU and the US have grown together in important ways. This is, however, a relatively recent phenomenon; moreover, important differences remain in the details of substantive EU and US policies. As will now be discussed, historically, the competition policies of the US and the EU had different roots and objectives, and have evolved through different deliberative and adjudicative processes (Fox 1997 provides an insightful analysis). These differences continue to bear on the scope for deeper cooperation and convergence. Since the enactment of the first antitrust legislation in the US preceded the adoption of the corresponding provisions of the Treaty of Rome (the founding treaty of what became the European Community and eventually, the European Union) by several decades, we will begin with the former and proceed to the latter.

2.1. *The United States*

The origins of US competition (antitrust) law continue to be debated by scholars. A conventional view holds that the first such legislation, the Sherman Act, grew out of a mixture of populist concerns regarding big business and agrarian discontent, notably with regard to exploitative railroads and industrial trusts. In this view, the Sherman Act of 1890 was passed by the Republican-dominated Congress as a compromise measure which was intended, in part, to head off more extreme proposals (e.g., nationalization/intrusive regulation) by the Granger and similar movements (see, e.g., Thorelli 1955). This view has been questioned by scholars such as Stigler (1985) who, without excluding the role of farmers and small business lobbies as a source of support for the legislation, also stresses the continuity of the Sherman Act with the

English common law on restraints of trade and monopolies, and the desire of legislators to maintain and bolster such a policy with appropriate legislation.[13]

In any event, the substantive provisions of the Sherman Act were deliberately framed in general terms, leaving broad scope for judicial development and refinement of related doctrines and policies.[14] The meaning and content of the legislation had to be and were developed in a series of subsequent Supreme Court and other decisions that elaborated on key concepts such as horizontal and vertical restraints and agreements; monopolization and predation; etc. (Bork 1978 remains an insightful reference to these cases).[15] Further legislative guidance

---

[13] Stigler's view is somewhat at variance with that of Bork (1978), who seems to view the asserted need to codify the common law on restraint of trade as more of a cover story than a true rationale for the legislation.

[14] Sections 1 and 2 of the Sherman Act, the foundational pillars of US antitrust policy, read as follows:

"1. Every contract, combination in the form of trust or otherwise, or conspiracy, in restraint of trade or commerce among the several States, or with foreign nations, is declared to be illegal. . . .

2. Every person who shall monopolize, or attempt to monopolize, or combine or conspire with any other person or persons, to monopolize any part of the trade or commerce among the several States, or with foreign nations, shall be deemed guilty of a felony. . . ."

Neither the concept of a contract "in restraint of trade" nor that of "monopolization" is defined in the legislation — with the result that this task fell to the courts.

[15] Some of the early decisions with particular doctrinal significance were *Trans-Missouri Freight Association*, 166 U.S. 290 (1897), which established the *per se* illegality of price-fixing cartels; *Joint Traffic Association*, 171 U.S. 505 (1898), which introduced fundamental distinctions between price fixing and other inter-firm agreements that have the capacity for creating efficiencies; *Addyston Pipe & Steel*, 85 Fed. 271, which reinforced and elaborated the *per se* illegality of price fixing, while introducing a crucial distinction between "naked restraints" (which serve no purpose other than the elimination of competition) and "ancillary restraints" (in which the limitation of competition makes possible a useful collaborative activity such as a joint venture); the *Standard Oil* and *American Tobacco* cases, 221 U.S. 1 (1911) and 221 U.S. 106 (1911) respectively, which further elaborated the rule of reason and confirmed that the mere possession of monopoly power does not violate the statute; and *Continental T.V., Inc. v. GTE Sylvania Inc.*, 97 S. Ct. 2549 (1977), which over-turned past adverse precedents and established that most non-price vertical market restraints (e.g., exclusive territories)

was provided in the Clayton Act, adopted in 1914 and amended in 1936 and 1950, which dealt with specific types of restraints including exclusive dealing arrangements, tie-in sales, price discrimination, and mergers and acquisitions. However, the basic "common law" approach to the enforcement of competition policy under which the courts (and the Federal Trade Commission) were given broad discretion to formulate enforcement standards and doctrines on the basis of experience and economic learning was retained. Much importance was given to the concept of the "rule of reason", under which the anticompetitive consequences of an allegedly or potentially harmful business practice are weighed against possible justifications and pro-competitive effects, and a judgment is made regarding its reasonableness. To make this approach workable, the courts developed a parallel doctrine of "per se" illegality under which certain practices (e.g., horizontal price-fixing or bid rigging) are conclusively deemed to be illegal; other practices (e.g., exclusive dealing and other "vertical" or "intrabrand" restraints) are judged on a case-by-case basis (Steuer 1999 provides a succinct discussion).

Two results of the common law approach to the elaboration of competition policy in the US are particularly important for our purposes. First, an important consequence of the common law approach has been to permit extensive reliance on economic learning to be incorporated into the judicial decision-making process and, therefore, into antitrust legal doctrines (see, for a definitive discussion, Kovacic, 2003a). In many respects, the practice of antitrust law in the US has become a field of applied economics. As former Assistant US Attorney-General for Antitrust, Hew Pate, stated in 2003 (Pate 2003):

"a common law approach to antitrust has led us toward an objective, transparent and economically based standard for assessing [antitrust policy]. It is the adaptability and incremental approach of case law that has enabled courts and enforcers over time to introduce rigorous economic

---

would be treated under the rule of reason and, therefore, that any anti-competitive effects would have to be weighed against their efficiency benefits. These and other cases continue to be cited in current litigation and to contribute to the evolution of relevant doctrines.

analysis into antitrust law and to continue incorporating better economic thinking as it becomes available."

The influence of economics in the evolution of US antitrust policy is sometimes equated with that of the "Chicago School"; as Kovacic (2007) points out, however, this is misleading. In fact, the importance that has been given to economics in US antitrust policy and the consequent evolution of such policy owes as much to figures such as Philip Areeda, Donald Turner and others associated with the "Harvard School" of antitrust analysis.

A second important consequence of the US common law-based competition law system, which in many respects builds on the first, is that US antitrust rules continue to evolve in ways that are not foreseeable from the statutory framework alone. For example, in just the past two years, the Supreme Court has issued important decisions that have: (i) formally abolished an old presumption that patents necessarily create market power and thereby render tying arrangements involving patented products *per se* illegal (see *Illinois Tool Works Inc. v. Independent Ink, Inc.*, 547 US 28 (2006)); and (ii) overturned a 1911 precedent holding that vertical minimum resale price maintenance (RPM) agreements should be deemed per se illegal under section 1 of the Sherman Act (see *Leegin Creative Leather Products, Inc. v. PSKS, Inc.*, 127 S. Ct. 2705 (2007)).

To be sure, the "economic" approach of the courts to US competition policy has not been welcomed in all quarters. A counterperspective has sometimes been expressed that, in some respects, the reliance on economics has been used to exonerate business arrangements which are, or should be, illegal (see, e.g., some of the postings on the website of the American Antitrust Institute, www.antitrustinstitute.org). Our point for purposes of this paper is simply that the common law approach is a salient feature of the US competition law system to which many US scholars and practitioners attach considerable importance and of which any realistic proposal for a deepening of transatlantic cooperation and convergence in the field of competition law and policy must take note.

2.2. *The European Union*

The origins, architecture and operational modalities of competition policy in the European Union are equally interesting though they differ substantially from those of the United States. The intellectual roots of such policy can be traced back to eighteenth century German liberalism, with its emphasis on the role of law in creating the conditions for economic and political liberty; to fin-de-siècle Austria, where detailed proposals for the regulation of cartels were developed in response to the pressures of industrialization and the felt need to protect citizens from the arbitrary power of industrial interests; and, importantly, to the German "ordo-liberal" school centred around the University of Freiburg.[16] The introduction of a Community-wide competition policy also reflected, very much, a desire to promote economic integration and intra-European trade and thereby to create the necessary conditions for lasting peace and stability in postwar Europe (Gerber 1998 provides a penetrating analysis; see also Anderson and Heimler 2007).

The role of competition policy in the European Community today grew out of specific provisions of the Community's founding Treaties. Provisions to safeguard competition were initially introduced in the European Coal and Steel Community in 1951. Building on the ideas of seminal European figures such as Konrad Adenauer, Jean Monnet and Robert Schuman, the maintenance of undistorted competition was entrenched as a specific objective of the *Treaty of Rome* when it was adopted in 1957.[17] Specific provisions regarding the prevention of anti-competitive practices that could undermine this objective (i.e., cartels and abuses of a dominant position) were included among the substantive provisions of the Treaty. The goal of the founding fathers

---

[16]The latter postulated that competition could provide the basis for a society in which economic progress, social development and individual liberty would flower, but *only where the proper functioning of markets was safeguarded through necessary laws and institutions.*

[17]See Treaty of Rome ("*EU* Treaty"), Article 3(g). The Treaty came into force on 1 January 1958.

was to create a set of rules that would constrain member states from engaging in policies and conduct that could adversely affect other European member states and would thereby ensure that the objectives of the Treaty were not undermined. The special objective of European competition policy to promote market integration had (and, to a lesser degree) continues to have) the result that certain vertical market restraints (i.e., exclusive territories and other practices that limit intrabrand competition) that are not necessarily prohibited in the US are prohibited in Europe (see also Barnett, 2008). This has, traditionally, been recognized as a major point of difference between the two jurisdictions.

The model of competition policy that was incorporated in the *Treaty of Rome* and elaborated over subsequent decades differed from other models (particularly North American models) in other respects, as well. In addition to the core provisions on cartels and abuse of dominance (subsequently reinforced by the introduction of merger control provisions), it incorporated two elements not found in North American models, namely: (i) provisions to deal with the competition-distorting effects of "state aid" (subsidies); and (ii) provisions to address barriers to competition that are introduced through other government measures such as the exercise of regulatory powers. These provisions were deemed necessary to address private and government restraints that segmented national markets, thus potentially undermining the common market.

The Treaty provisions adopted at the Community level had significant repercussions at the level of individual EU member states. Today, fifty years after the signing of the Treaty, all member states have a competition law and an enforcement structure capable of fulfilling their responsibilities within the European competition system. The major driving force behind this development was the example provided by the Union's rules and institutions. The importance given to the competition provisions in the Treaty of Rome and their role in shaping the economic and legal policies and structures of member states have made competition policy part of the "economic constitution" of Europe (see Petersmann 1991 and 2004). Also manifesting this "constitutional" role of competition policy, in recent years competition policy and related institutions and expertise have played an important role in the accession of central and east European states to the European Union (Geradin and Henry 2004).

With respect to substantive competition law standards, three key differences between the EU and the US should be noted at this stage. First, as already noted, due in part to the intended role of the competition provisions of the Treaty of Rome in reinforcing the internal economic union, the EU has traditionally taken a more prescriptive stance toward vertical market restraints (e.g., exclusive dealing and exclusive territories) than has the US, at least for the more than three decades since the US *Sylvania* decision.[18] Second, to many observers competition policy in the EU has also been more concerned than has US competition policy (again, at least for the past thirty years) with the protection of individual competitors as compared to the competitive process *per se* (this difference can be debated and is explored with more subtlety than is possible here in Fox 2003). Lurking behind this has (again, in the view of many observers) been a more "structuralist" approach to competition policy in the EU (i.e., a policy concerned with preventing the accumulation of economic power as such) as opposed to greater emphasis on the maintenance of competition as a dynamic process in the US (see, e.g., Pate, 2003).[19] This has had implications for both merger regulation and the treatment of abuses of a dominant position, and arguably has been the source of several EU–US policy clashes in recent years (see, for discussion, Part 4 below). Third, competition authorities in the European Union have been somewhat more willing than their US counterparts to intervene in cases involving perceived abuses of intellectual property rights, and legal doctrines in the EU have been more supportive of such intervention.[20]

---

[18] See footnote 16, above.

[19] As an example, for many years the legal test for prohibition of mergers under relevant EU regulations was one of "creating a dominant position" — a more static concept than the US approach.

[20] For example, while the refusal to license patented technology in the US is virtually sacrosanct under relevant legal doctrines, such refusals have been successfully challenged in the EU at least in a few cases. See, for discussion, Anderson (2008).

Having noted these historic differences, it is also important to say that, in many respects, EU and US competition policy have recently become more congruent than was the case in the past. This has been due, in no small part, to bilateral discussions between the responsible authorities of the US and the EU, to ongoing autonomous learning processes and to the increasing role of economics in the application of EU competition policy (see Anderson and Heimler 2007 and Kovacic 2008). This process of convergence is the subject of the next subsection of the paper.

2.3.   Recent indications of convergence: The adoption of more economics-based approaches in the EU[21]

The current enforcement programs of the EU Commission and the member states' competition authorities reflect a far-reaching evolution in policy design and enforcement approaches. To take first the most obvious aspect of this evolution, in its early stages, European competition policy was predominantly concerned with vertical market restraints on the basis that they constituted the most obvious threat to the construction of a unified Europe. Such restraints were attacked through the application of Article 81 (then 85) of the Treaty, paragraph 3, to notified agreements and by developing form-based block exemption regulations. This approach, while understandable as a political objective, was extensively criticized over the years on the basis that most vertical agreements do not restrict competition and are, indeed, pro-competitive or at least competitively neutral. As a result, relevant guidelines have been progressively liberalized over the past decade or so, to bring the EU's policies in this area into closer conformity with economic thinking (and, coincidentally, with US approaches). The new block exemption on vertical restraints that was issued in 1999 was an

---

[21] This part of the paper draws, in significant part, on Anderson and Heimler (2007).

important step in this regard.[22] The introduction of the EU (then the European Community's) Merger Regulation in 1989,[23] and the emphasis on economic analysis that it brought with it, reinforced the Commission's movement from form-based to effects-based enforcement (see, for useful background, Neven *et al.* 1994). The Notice on the relevant market which was issued in 1997[24] constituted a further important step in this regard.

Also in furtherance of a more economics-based approach, in December 2005 the Commission issued a "discussion paper on the application of Article 82 of the Treaty to exclusionary abuses." (Commission of the European Communities, DG Competition 2005). The discussion paper proposes the adoption of an "as efficient competitor test" which defines as exclusionary only those practices that exclude potential rivals that are at least equally efficient as the incumbent firm. This represents a change from the past when dominant companies were deemed to have a "special responsibility" to help ensure that competitors remain in the market even if they were not necessarily as efficient as the dominant firm — an approach that was clearly at odds with the standard of economic efficiency.

In the area of merger analysis, the adoption of an economics or effects-based approach has been reinforced by relevant judicial decisions. In *Airtours/First Choice*[25] the Court of First Instance annulled a decision of the Commission[26] on the basis of a lack (in the Court's view) of a sufficiently rigorous economic analysis of the incentives for, and ability to coordinate behaviour as a direct consequence, of the

---

[22] Council Regulation (EU) No 1215/1999 of 10 June 1999 amending Regulation No 19/65/EEC on the application of Article 81(3) of the Treaty to certain categories of agreements and concerted practices *Official Journal L 148*, 15.6.1999, p. 1–4.

[23] Council Regulation (EEC) No 4064/89 of 21 December 1989 on the control of concentrations between undertakings *Official Journal L 395*, 30.12.1989, p. 1–12.

[24] Commission notice on the definition of relevant market for the purposes of Community competition law, *Official Journal C 372*, 09.12.1997, p. 1–12.

[25] Case T-342/99 *Airtours plc v Commission*, Decision of 6 June 2002.

[26] Case IV/M.1524 - Airtours/First Choice, Commission decision, 22.9.1999.

proposed merger. In *Schneider/Legrand*[27] the same Court annulled the Commission's decision[28] on the basis that the Commission had failed to take account of the different degrees of competition in each of the national markets it identified and did not provide Schneider with enough information to offer an appropriate remedy. In *Tetra Laval/Sidel*,[29] the Court of First Instance annulled the Commission's decision on the basis that leveraging market power between two otherwise separate markets, the reason for the Commission prohibition, could have been blocked by ex-post article 82 interventions, a possibility that the Commission did not consider. This decision was subsequently upheld by the European Court of Justice[30] (see, for background and discussion of additional cases, Anderson and Heimler, 2007).

As a result of these judgments, the Directorate-General for Competition has implemented a number of organizational changes, including the creation of the post of chief economist and setting up a "devil's advocate panel" providing an internal critique of arguments provided by case teams. Furthermore, a Commission proposal to change the substantive test of merger control has been approved by the Council. The new approach prohibits all mergers that lead to a "significant impediment of effective competition, in particular as a result of the creation or strengthening of a dominant position." The introduction of a wider test than that of simple dominance was considered appropriate because of the possibility that a merger in differentiated oligopoly markets would lead to a significant increase of market power without necessarily creating a dominant position (Anderson and Heimler, 2007).

---

[27] Case T-77/02, *Schneider Electric SA v Commission*, Commission decision, 22 October 2002.

[28] Case COMP/M.2283 — *Schneider-Legrand*, Commission decision, 30 January 2002.

[29] Cases T-5/02 and T-80/02, *Tetra Laval BV v Commission*, Decision of 25 October 2002.

[30] Case C-12/03 P, *Commission v Tetra Laval BV*, Decision of 15 February 2005.

A further significant change in EU competition policy particularly in the past decade has been a substantially greater focus on anti-cartel enforcement and a progressive toughening of related enforcement approaches and penalties. This, too, was largely the result of developments in economic thinking. Both the Chicago and the Harvard Schools were important sources in this regard. Their influence led both the United States' antitrust authorities and the European Commission to adopt progressively stricter approaches to the repression of cartels and significantly greater resources to this aspect of competition law enforcement.

The need for greater focus on cartels has been reflected in antitrust enforcement procedures as well as substantive law. Following the lead of the United States, in 1996 the European Commission introduced its first "leniency program" for informants in cartel cases.[31] Such programs provide incentives for participants in a cartel or similar arrangement to facilitate prosecutions by cooperating with enforcement authorities and was an important step in strengthening competition law enforcement in this area.[32] The program was strengthened in 2002.[33] Subsequently, the European Commission and all EU member states adopted a model leniency program developed within the European Competition Network (a network linking all competition authorities in the Community).[34] The Commission's program was again amended in 2006, mainly to clarify the type and quality of information to be provided by leniency applicants.[35]

---

[31] Commission Notice on the non-imposition or reduction of fines in cartel cases, *Official Journal C 207*, 18.07.1996, p. 4–6.

[32] The basic principle of such programs is that they offer immunity (whether total or partial) to cartel participants that inform on other members of the cartel.

[33] The main change was that, once a firm was admitted to the program, immunity became automatic. Commission notice on immunity from fines and reduction of fines in cartel cases, *Official Journal C 45*, 19.02.2002, p. 3–5.

[34] http://ec.europa.eu/comm/competition/cartels/legislation/leniency_legislation.html.

[35] Commission notice on immunity from fines and reduction of fines in cartel cases Official Journal C 298, 8.12.2006, p. 17–22.

2.4.   Possible Indications of Further Convergence: Antitrust Policy in the Obama Administration

Clearly, it is too early to be certain whether changes in US antitrust policy initiated under the Obama Administration will result in greater convergence in substantive antitrust policies either between the US and the EU, or globally.It is, however, pertinent to note two developments that arguably point in that direction. First, early in her tenure, Christine Varney, President Obama's appointee as Assistant US Attorney-General for Antitrust, signalled her willingness to take a firmer approach than her recent predecessors in relation to perceived anti-competitive practices by individual dominant firms. Specifically, she repudiated a report on dominant firm conduct prepared by the Division under the previous Administration (the so-called "Section 2 Report"[36] which, in her view, manifested excessive restraint and created uneoessary obstacles to effective competition law enforcement in this area (Varney 2009a). Since, as explained above, competition law enforcement in relation to dominant firm conduct is a key area in which the EU has, at least in some respects, been more pro-active or interventionist than the US in recent years, this clearly opens the door to a further degree of convergence in this area.

Second, while (as we have seen) US efforts to foster voluntary international convergence in substantive competition policies date back many years, recent Administration statements arguably signal an even greater commitment to this process than has been evident in the past. For example, in a speech delivered in New York in 2009, Ms Varney observed as follows with respect to the important issue of convergence in regard to antitrust remedies:

> "With more firms operating on a global scale, our enforcement actions increasingly have an impact beyond the borders of our respective jurisdictions. The likelihood of a broader impact from domestic enforcement action requires us to carefully consider the scope and nature of remedies. Moreover, where multiple agencies pursue an enforcement action

---

[36]"Section 2" refers to section 2 of the Sherman Act, which is principal statutory basis for addressing dominant firm conduct in the US.

with regard to the same conduct, substantial divergence in remedial approaches risks inconsistent results that may undermine one or more jurisdicitons' enforcement, and may also frustrate a firm's good faith efforts to comply with ordered relief" (Varney 2009b).

With regard to the closely related matter of international cooperation, in a speech given in Paris in February 2010, Ms Varney emphasized the importance of all jurisdictions (including the US) being mindful of the possibility of imposing costs on other jurisdictions through the use of competition law remedies having extra-territorial effects. In this context, she advocated what could be taken as tacit endorsement of a kind of "lead jurisdiction" approach under which agencies investigating a particular case having effects in multiple jurisdictions would, to the extent that their statutory mandates permit, consider deferring to the position taken by the agency in the jurisdiction with the most at stake:

> "Thus, while we must all of course adhere to our own mandates and timing requirements, I suggest that we should keep our eyes open, in particular, for the conclusions of that agency with the greatest proportion of commerce and consumers at stake in a particular case. We should be particularly attentive to the opinion of the agency where the principal assets are located or the greatest revenue is earned, where the greatest impact will be felt, and where the thorniest enforcement issues may have already been addressed" (Varney 2010).

While how these views and positions will play out in practice of course remains to be seen, they potentially signal an approach that could contribute substantially to mitigating the potential for international conflicts of jurisdiction in this area.

In sum, a significant degree of convergence between the competition policies of the EU and the US has already taken place. This process of convergence has affected both substantive competition law standards and enforcement procedures. In addition to frequent dialogue between the two jurisdictions' enforcement bodies, the gradual process of convergence has been based, in no small part, on increasing adherence in the EU to the precepts of a body of economic learning that is universal in nature. It should nonetheless be emphasized that important differences in policy implementation and, as a result, potential for conflict remain. This will be the subject of Part 4, below. But first, it is important to outline the procedural arrangements that are in place to facilitate cooperation between the EU and Europe in the implementation of competition law and policy, which have, in turn, been an important underpinning of the convergence process.

3. The Need for Cooperation in Principle, and the Cooperation Arrangements that Have Been Implemented Thus Far in the Transatlantic Context

This section of the paper focuses on the arrangements for procedural cooperation (as distinct from substantive convergence) that are in place between the United States and the European Union. Reasons for cooperation are discussed in sub-section (3.1.); the arrangements in place are elaborated in sub-section (3.2.); and some related observations are made in sub-section (3.3.).

3.1. *Rationales for cooperation in the competition policy field*

The subject of international cooperation in the field of competition law and policy is far from new. It has been discussed at length in numerous academic papers as well as in international organizations and national commissions. An OECD Working Party on the subject has been meeting in Paris for over a decade. It may, nonetheless, be useful to review here some basic aspects of cooperation and related reasons and rationales, before setting out the measures that are in place between the EU and the US.[37]

---

[37] Broadly similar arrangements are also in place between Canada and both the EU and the US. Other cooperative arrangements bring into the "family" both Mexico and the non-EU European states, at least to an extent. Therefore, it may be worth considering whether new initiatives to deepen cooperation the "transatlantic" might also encompass these countries, at least at some stage.

In the field of competition law and policy, the term "cooperation" normally refers to cooperation of a procedural nature — e.g., the giving of notice regarding investigations that may impact on another jurisdiction's interests, consultations regarding such actions, the exchange of information, the possible coordination of investigations, etc. This is in contrast to a broader concept of cooperation which might include substantive commitments regarding the nature and application of competition laws, the establishment of enforcement institutions, etc. It is, nonetheless, clear, as we have already seen, that even cooperation mainly of a procedural nature can have an important impact on the evolution of substantive polices, by exposing the officials concerned to the perspectives and approaches of other jurisdictions. There is no doubt that this has been both an important underlying purpose and an effect of cooperation in the EU–US context (Pate 2003 and Schaub 2001).

Four broad rationales or categories of rationales have been advanced for international cooperation in the field of competition law and policy. A first (and historically, *the* first) concerns the avoidance of conflicts between jurisdictions. Often associated with the notion of "comity"[38], the focus here is on one state providing another with notice of actions that potentially impact on the other state's interests (e.g., on commercial entities based in a foreign jurisdiction). This "defensive" aspect of cooperation was stressed in the first cooperation agreements regarding competition law and policy which were implemented between the United States and Canada[39] and remains an important consideration in EU–US and other agreements.

---

[38] Under the principle of traditional or "negative" comity, one country forebears from an enforcement activity that would affect the other's interests, or at least notifies the other of its intended enforcement action and provides for the possibility of consultation. The principle of "positive comity" allows a country affected by foreign-based anti-competitive activity to request that the relevant authorities in the foreign country take appropriate enforcement actions (see Matte 1996).

[39] The world's first agreement relating to international cooperation in competition law and policy was the so-called "Fulton-Rogers Agreement" between Canada and the United States which was adopted in 1959.

A second important rationale for cooperation in competition law and policy which now receives much greater emphasis from enforcement officials relates to the possibility of improved efficacy of enforcement. Clarke and Evenett (2003) postulate two sources of positive spillovers that provide rationales for international action in this area. First, public announcements of cartel enforcement actions in one country tend to stimulate enforcement efforts in other countries, particularly where there is an established relationship between the relevant enforcement authorities. In this way, trading partners benefit from active enforcement abroad. Second, the investigation and prosecution of arrangements such as international cartels can be greatly facilitated by accessing information about the nature and organization of the arrangement from another jurisdiction that has successfully completed such an investigation. Conversely, a failure to take action against cartels headquartered in a particular jurisdiction may create "safe havens" that make it more difficult for other affected jurisdictions to take such action. These considerations point to the potential benefits of some form of international accord committing the participating countries to take action in this area (Clarke and Evenett 2003: 117–18).

A third set of rationales for international cooperation on competition law and policy relates explicitly to possibilities for mutual learning and/or voluntary convergence in substantive policies. As already noted, such possibilities are widely cited as an important objective and benefit of EU–US cooperation (see, e.g., Pate 2003 and Schaub 2001). In a broader context, they underlie the numerous regular meetings in which competition officials participate under the auspices of the International Competition Network, UNCTAD, the Organization for Economic cooperation and Development and other organizations. Possibilities for mutual learning and the strengthening of institutional capacities were also stressed in the work of the WTO Working Group on the Interaction between Trade and Competition Policy when that body was active between 1997 and 2003.

Still another set of rationales for international cooperation in the field of competition law and policy is "political-economic" in nature. The argument here is that the field of competition policy may be subject to "political market failures" that result in systematic under-investment in related institutions, owing to the diffuse nature of the interests whose welfare is promoted by such institutions (i.e., consumers). International cooperation that elevates the policy significance of competition law and policy and bolsters the role of related institutions may be one way of addressing such failures (this view was expressed on various occasions in the WTO Working Group (see Anderson and Jenny 2005).

In a related vein, Birdsall and Lawrence (1999) observe that a principal benefit of trade agreements aimed at measures beyond the border can be to facilitate domestic policy reforms, by providing a tool for overcoming domestic constituencies that could otherwise block the reform process. They refer specifically to the case of competition policy, observing that (Birdsall and Lawrence 1999: 136):

> "When ...countries enter into modern trade agreements, they often make certain commitments to particular domestic policies — for example, to antitrust or other competition policy. Agreeing to such policies can be in the interests of developing countries (beyond the trade benefits directly obtained) because the commitment can reinforce the internal reform process. Indeed, participation in an international agreement can make feasible internal reforms that are beneficial for the country as a whole that might otherwise be successfully resisted by interest groups."

In making this point, Birdsall and Lawrence focus on its significance for developing countries. It can, nonetheless, be generalized to cover developed countries as well. Even in such countries, political support for competition policy tends not always to be as consistently strong as is sometimes assumed. As an example, in the 1980s, then US Commerce Secretary Malcolm Baldridge, who perceived aspects of US antitrust enforcement as being inimical to US competitiveness, proposed the abolition of section 7 of the Clayton Act (the main statutory basis of US merger policy). Certainly, the establishment of effective competition policies in other jurisdictions (e.g., Canada) has been a long and difficult struggle involving significant political opposition. Conversely, the entrenching of competition rules and the objective of undistorted competition in the Treaty of Rome undeniably provided a major institutional impetus for the establishment of effective competition agencies in the various EU member states (recall the discussion in Part 2, above).

3.2.   Existing transatlantic cooperation arrangements

Cooperation between the competition authorities of the United States and the European Union is built around the following main instruments:[40]

3.2.1.   The 1991 US–EU Competition Cooperation Agreement

The 1991 US–EU Competition Cooperation Agreement provides for:

- notification of cases being handled by the competition authorities of one Party, to the extent that these cases concern the important interests of the other Party (Article II), and exchange of information on general matters relating to the implementation of the competition rules (Article III);
- cooperation and coordination of the actions of both Parties' competition authorities (Article IV);
- a "traditional comity" procedure by virtue of which each Party undertakes to take into account the important interests of the other Party when it takes measures to enforce its competition rules (Article VI);
- a "positive comity" procedure by virtue of which either Party can invite the other Party to take, on the basis of the latter's legislation, appropriate measures regarding anti-competitive behaviour

---

[40]The following summary is based on material available on the websites of both the Antitrust Division of the US Department of Justice (www.justice.gov/atr) and DG Competition of the EU Commission (http://ec.europa.eu/comm/competition).

implemented on its territory and which affects the important interests of the requesting Party (Article V).

The Agreement also provides for regular bilateral meetings to share information on current enforcement activities and priorities; on economic sectors of common interest; to discuss policy changes; and to discuss other matters of mutual interest relating to the application of competition laws. Thus, its objectives clearly encompass the general concerns relating to mutual learning as well both the traditional and positive comity considerations which are referred to above.

3.2.2. The 1998 US–EU Positive Comity Agreement

The US–EU Positive Comity Agreement, which was entered into force on June 4, 1998, was intended to give added force and specificity to the positive comity provision in the 1991 Agreement. Under the rules of positive comity, one party may request the other party to remedy anti-competitive behaviour which originates in its jurisdiction but affects the requesting party as well. In this context, the agreement clarifies both the mechanics of positive comity requests and the circumstances in which they can be made. As noted on the website of DG Competition, "Positive comity provisions are not frequently used as companies (i.e., complainants) prefer to address directly the competition authority they consider to be best suited to deal with the situation."

3.2.3. The Administrative Arrangement on Attendance (AAA)

The AAA sets forth administrative arrangements between the competition authorities of the EU and the US concerning reciprocal attendance at certain stages of the procedures in individual cases, involving the application of their respective competition rules. These arrangements were concluded in the framework of the 1991 Agreement, particularly the provisions regarding co-ordination of enforcement activities.

3.2.4.   The set of best practices on cooperation in merger cases

A further subordinate cooperation instrument regarding competition policy in the transatlantic context is a set of "best practices on cooperation in merger cases" that was adopted in 2002. According to the Europa website, these practices are not legally binding but are intended to set out an "advisory framework" for interagency cooperation. The website further specifies that:

> "The best practices recognize that cooperation is most effective when the investigation timetables of the reviewing agencies run more or less in parallel. Merging companies will therefore be offered the possibility of meeting at an early stage with the agencies to discuss timing issues. Companies are also encouraged to permit the agencies to exchange information which they have submitted during the course of an investigation and, where appropriate, to allow joint EU/US interviews of the companies concerned. The practices designate key points in the respective EU and US merger investigations when it may be appropriate for direct contacts to occur between senior officials on both sides."

3.3.   Use and effectiveness of the above arrangements

Competition officials stress that instruments such as those outlined above merely provide a framework for cooperation; actual cooperation is an informal process that depends importantly on factors such as institutional commitment and trust.[41] In this context, and notwithstanding the occasional conflicts that have occurred, US–EU cooperation on competition law enforcement is viewed by both sides as a major success (see, e.g., Barnett 2008 and Kroes 2008). Indeed, it is only fair to acknowledge the major efforts that have gone into the promoting of transatlantic cooperation in the field of competition law and policy and the important results that have been achieved in this regard. In

---

[41]WTO, Working Group on the Interaction between Trade and Competition Policy (1999).

some respects, the arrangements that are in place to promote transatlantic cooperation on competition law and policy might even serve as a model for cooperation in regard to other aspects of economic regulation.

Nonetheless, it must also be acknowledged (as the relevant officials themselves acknowledge) that the current cooperation arrangements also entail significant limitations. One such important limitation is the inability under the current arrangements to share actionable evidence relating to cartel investigations. In this regard, Neelie Kroes, until recently the EU Commissioner for Competition, has herself observed that (Kroes 2008):

> "Regrettably, at this moment we are still unable to share actionable evidence, the kind of information that is most useful for cartel investigations. The time has come to explore ways to enhance some of our bilateral agreements and to share such information among a small number of enforcers."

Reflecting the same point, the antitrust scholar Spencer Weber Waller has written as follows (Waller 2000):

> "The real story is that, despite considerable success by both sides in individual cases, there has been next to nothing that either the United States or the EU can point to by way of significant formal cooperation in the single most important type of case under any competition law regime [i.e., cartel cases]. What little there is consists of conversation between officials about publicly known facts."

Summing up regarding the state of international cooperation in competition law policy more broadly, but with particular reference to the transatlantic context, Jenny (2003) makes the following observations:

> "– International cooperation (whether formal or informal) between competition authorities in the fight against (international) cartels remains quite limited; it is the exception rather than the norm; however it is considered to be useful by competition authorities which have cooperated.
> – The fact that a formal cooperation agreement exists between two countries is not a guarantee that they will cooperate on every case.

- Most cooperation agreements [and specifically those between the United States and the European Community] do not allow the exchange of confidential information.
- Informal international cooperation has increased somewhat over the last few years; the precise extent of this informal cooperation is still difficult to assess."

Perhaps above all, it should be born in mind that the cooperation called for by these arrangements is voluntary and that the arrangements are, in any case, procedural rather than substantive in nature (i.e., they do not involve the setting of substantive standards). Therefore, while they have undoubtedly contributed to the efficacy of enforcement measures in many ways and have also contributed to and reinforced the long-term process of voluntary convergence, they cannot prevent the policy conflicts that sometimes arise where particular arrangements or transactions are reviewed by both jurisdictions' authorities. Examples of specific instances in which the current cooperation instruments have not sufficed to prevent policy clashes are discussed in the next section of the paper.

4. Are Current/Future Policy Conflicts Manageable Through Voluntary Cooperation/Convergence Alone? and What About the World Beyond the Transatlantic Zone?

This section of the paper delves into some prominent examples of US–EU conflicts in the application of competition law in recent years. No position is taken on the substantive merits of either jurisdictions' position. Rather, the focus is on what these conflicts tell us about the limits of existing cooperation arrangements and the remaining scope for policy differences. Consideration is also given to the (increasing) scope for conflicts in the exercise of competition law and policy that go beyond the transatlantic sphere (i.e., conflicts with countries not in this part of the world). To be sure, such conflicts cannot be eased through deeper cooperation between the EU and the US alone. Enhanced transatlantic cooperation might, however, serve as an important springboard for efforts to manage international conflicts in the application of competition law in the wider global context.

4.1. *Examples of US–EU policy clashes to date*

This subsection of the paper reviews three major examples of transatlantic conflicts in the application of competition law that have occurred in the past decade, namely the *Boeing/McDonnell Douglas* merger (1997); the *GE/Honeywell* merger (2001); and the *Microsoft* cases of the past several years. By way of background, the possibility for such conflicts arises from the fact that both the US and the EU apply their competition laws "extra-territorially." In the US, such application is based on the "effects felt" test — i.e., the US law applies to conduct whose effects are felt by US persons (see, for useful elaboration and qualification, US, Department of Justice 1995). The EU stance on such matters is not identical; however, under the so-called "implementation doctrine," EU law is applicable to arrangements entered into abroad that are "implemented" in the EU. In practice, both doctrines provide robust scope for application of competition law to mergers, abuses of a dominant position and other practices (e.g., cartels) whose impact spans jurisdictions.

A further important point is that, owing to the case-specific nature of modern antitrust enforcement, it should not be expected that any of the cases discussed below will arise again in identical form.[42] They are, rather, presented merely as examples of the continuing scope for conflict between the US and the EU in such matters.

4.1.1. *The Boeing/McDonnel Douglas merger*[43]

The 1997 merger of the Boeing and McDonnell Douglas corporations provided, in some respects, an early example of the kinds of conflicts of policy application that have played out in more recent cases. The merger brought together the two major US-based players in the international civil aircraft industry, leaving only one other major competitor

---

[42] This point was stressed by Kae-Uwe Kuhn at the conference in Ann Arbor.

[43] See World Trade Organization (1997) and other references cited therein.

in the large civil aircraft segment — the European-based Airbus Indus-try consortium.

The EU and US competition authorities initially took divergent positions as to the desirability of allowing the merger to proceed. In the US, the Federal Trade Commission[44] did not oppose the transaction, due partly to a view that, in many respects, McDonnell Douglas was no longer a vigorous competitor and hence its absorption by Boeing would not adversely affect the state of competition in the industry. In contrast, the EU Commission had fundamental concerns about the case and, early in its review process, signalled a disposition to block the merger. This created significant consternation in the US business and policy communities. At one point, then US President Clinton hinted that the US might launch a WTO challenge against the EU on the basis of the position it was taking (Buerkle 1997). Of course, throughout the process there was an ongoing dialogue between the two jurisdictions, competition authorities.

The impasse was resolved when Boeing accepted to make conces-sions regarding various practices that were perceived by the Commis-sion as entrenching its competitive position in the market, in particular a series of long-term exclusive dealing contracts that it had negotiated with major customers. In this sense, the case illustrated the usefulness of existing consultative mechanisms (in particular, the 1991 US–EU Competition Cooperation Agreement) as well as the potential for con-flicts of policy application that could have a major bearing on industrial restructuring in the transatlantic and the global context.

4.1.2.   *The GE/Honeywell merger*

The next major US–EU conflict over the application of competition law also concerned an aspect of the international civil aeronautics

---

[44]In the US, federal jurisdiction over mergers is normally allocated either to the Federal Trade Commission or the Department of Justice based on the agencies' respective expertise and experience in the relevant economic sector.

industry — in this case, the market for jet engines and related electronic components. In particular, the management of General Electric (GE) believed that it could achieve significant efficiencies by integrating its engine-making and aircraft financing division with Honeywell's advanced electronic components business. While the US authorities did not oppose the merger, the EU Commission indicated that it would approve the deal only if GE made substantial concessions regarding access to Honeywell's technology and related matters. This stark clash of viewpoints occurred despite very extensive dialogue and consultation between the two jurisdictions' competition officials on the case (James 2001). Since these requirements were viewed by the GE as clearly excessive and eroding the business justification for the merger, the deal was abandoned.

Again, significant consternation ensued not only in the US business community but on the part of US antitrust officials. President Bush indicated that he was concerned about the issue. Senior officials of the Department of Justice argued that, not only were the proposed concessions excessive, the entire basis for the EU's opposition to the merger (i.e., its "theory of the case") was flawed. As explained by then Assistant Attorney-General Charles James (James 2001):

"The differences between the Justice Department and the EU flowed from an apparent substantive difference, perhaps a fundamental one, between the two agencies on the proper scope of antitrust law enforcement. We concluded that the merged firm would have offered improved products at more attractive prices than either firm could have offered on its own, and that the merged firm's competitors would then have had a great incentive to improve their own product offerings. This, to us, is the very essence of competition, and no principle is more central to US law than that antitrust protects competition, not competitors.

In stark contrast, the EU focused on how the merger would affect European and US competitors, essentially concluding that the very efficiencies and lower prices the transaction would produce would be anticompetitive because they might ultimately drive some of those competitors from the market or reduce their market shares to a point where they could not longer compete effectively. In other words, the EU determined that the fact that customers would be 'induced' to purchase more attractive and lower-priced GE/Honeywell products, rather than those of its competitors, was a bad thing of a sort that its antitrust law ought to prohibit."

Continuing, James (2001) critiqued more specific aspects of the EU's analytical approach in the case:

"In our view, the so-called 'portfolio effects' or 'range effects' analysis as it has recently been employed is neither soundly grounded in economic theory nor supported by empirical evidence, but rather, is antithetical to the goals of sound antitrust enforcement. We fear that it will result in some procompetitive mergers being blocked, and others never being attempted, to the detriment of consumers in many countries. It will dissuade merging parties from talking candidly to antitrust agencies about the efficiencies they expect to realize, out of fear that such efficiencies — even when they would clearly benefit consumers — would be viewed negatively."

It should be noted that the then EU Commissioner for Competition, Mario Monti, vigorously defended the Commission's approach, arguing that: (i) the parties (i.e., the companies concerned) had not provided a clearly articulated and quantified defence in terms of efficiencies that would result from the merger; and (ii) significant foreclosure effects were likely to have occurred as a result of the merger (Monti 2001). In any case, for the purposes of this paper, the point is *not* whether one jurisdiction was "right" or the other "wrong". The point is that, notwithstanding the valuable consultative mechanisms that are in place and the significant degree of convergence that has occurred, significant scope for policy clashes that have a bearing on restructuring and competition in major industries remains. Moreover, the resolution of such conflicts — at least in cases such as this — is likely to involve subtle questions of antitrust and industrial organization theory.

4.1.3. *The Microsoft cases*

Another important — and multi-faceted — example of the scope for US–EU conflicts over the application of competition policy concerns the recent *Microsoft* cases. In the course of these cases, the competition authorities of the United States and the European Communities have taken different positions — though in some respects, only subtly different — regarding aspects of Microsoft's conduct such as the tying of the Windows operating system and various other products such as Microsoft's browser (Internet Explorer) and/or its Media Player. These cases have typically been framed in terms of abuses of dominant position (in the EU) or monopolization (in the US); however, they also implicate issues such as the circumstances in which compulsory access to (potentially proprietary) information and technology may need to be mandated to ensure that markets function competitively. The multiplicity and complexity of these cases precludes more than a summary treatment here. Nonetheless, it is instructive to consider the views that have been expressed regarding aspects of the cases on both sides of the Atlantic.

In its 2004 decision in the case involving the tying of the Windows operating system and Microsoft's Media Player and related practices, the EU Commission required that Microsoft disclose certain information to competitors that was deemed necessary for competitive access purposes, offer for sale a version of its Windows operating system that does not contain the Windows Media Player and pay a fine of 497 million euros (about US$613 million). These remedies went well beyond those that had been imposed in a US case brought against Microsoft in regard to substantially the same conduct. In response to the EU decision, the Antitrust Division of the US Department of Justice issued a press release stating as follows (US, Department of Justice 2004):

> "The EU has today pursued a different enforcement approach by imposing a 'code removal' remedy to resolve its media player concerns. The US experience tells us that the best antitrust remedies eliminate impediments to the healthy functioning of competitive markets without hindering successful competitors or imposing burdens on third parties, which may result from the EU's remedy. A requirement of 'code removal' was not at any time — including during the period when the US was seeking a breakup of Microsoft prior to the rejection of that remedy by the court of appeals — part of the United States' proposed remedy.

Imposing antitrust liability on the basis of product enhancements and imposing 'code removal' remedies may produce unintended consequences. Sound antitrust policy must avoid chilling innovation and competition even by 'dominant' companies. A contrary approach risks protecting competitors, not competition, in ways that may ultimately harm innovation and the consumers that benefit from it ... ."

Subsequently, the Commission's decision was reviewed by the EU's Court of First Instance. The Court's judgment upheld, in all substantive respects, the Commission's decision.[45] In response, the US authorities again issued a press release, this time observing that the decision could "have the unfortunate consequence of harming consumers by chilling innovation and discouraging competition." (US, Department of Justice, 2007). In response, then–EU Competition Commissioner Neelie Kroes stated her view that:

"...it's totally unacceptable [that a representative of the US government] should criticize an independent court's decision. The Commission doesn't pass judgement on rulings in US courts. We expect the same respect." (European Digital Rights 2007).

Without taking any position on the substantive merits of the approach taken by either jurisdiction, the foregoing exchanges further illustrate the continuing potential for EU–US conflicts in such cases and the limited impact that existing cooperation arrangements can have in such cases.

4.2.   The broader global context

Consistent with the focus of the conference for which it was prepared, the foregoing discussion of international clashes in the application of competition law has focused on cases arising in the transatlantic context. It is important, however, not to lose sight of the surrounding global context. In that regard, it should be noted that approximately 100 countries, including such powerhouse "emerging markets" as

---

[45] The Court ruled against the Commission on a potentially important procedural issue relating to delegation to a "monitoring trustee" of certain supervisory responsibilities.

China, India, Brazil and South Africa, now have national competition laws. Perhaps 80 of these laws were adopted in the last 20–30 years. Moreover, a growing number of such countries actually or potentially apply their laws to conduct originating abroad (a wealth of information on individual national laws is provided on the website of the International Bar Association's Global Competition Forum, www.globalcompetitionforum.org). Clearly, the possibility of conflicts in the application of competition law in cases affecting multiple jurisdictions certainly is not limited to the transatlantic zone.

Indeed, such conflicts have already occurred. In early December 2005, in litigation relating to substantially the same conduct as the EU and US Media Player cases discussed above, the Fair Trade Commission of Korea made public an order that requires Microsoft to: (i) sell in Korea a version of its Windows operating system that includes neither Windows Media Player nor Windows Messenger functionality; (ii) facilitate consumer downloads of third party media player and messenger products selected by the Commission; and (iii) not sell in Korea a version of its server software that includes Windows Media Services. The press release issued by the Antitrust Division of the US Department of Justice issued by the US Department of Justice in response to this development was also similar to those issued in response to the corresponding EU decisions (US, Department of Justice 2005):

"The Antitrust Division believes that Korea's remedy goes beyond what is necessary or appropriate to protect consumers, as it requires the removal of products that consumers may prefer. The Division continues to believe that imposing 'code removal' remedies that strip out functionality can ultimately harm innovation and the consumers that benefit from it. We had previously consulted with the Commission on its Microsoft case and encouraged the Commission to develop a balanced resolution that addressed its concerns without imposing unnecessary restrictions. Sound antitrust policy should protect competition, not competitors, and must avoid chilling innovation and competition even by 'dominant' companies."

Apart from important "moral suasion" efforts that are under way in the International Competition Network and other fora, there is

nothing to prevent additional instances of such conflicts from arising at any time. Indeed, prior to the 2008 withdrawal of Microsoft's
attempted takeover of Yahoo, the possibility of China's blocking the
deal was widely noted (Markoff 2008). China's new competition law
came into force on August 1, 2008. In commenting on this possibility, an antitrust specialist based in Beijing suggested that the new
competition law has created the possibility of China becoming "another
[international] regulatory capital contending for influence with Brussels and Washington" (Markoff 2008; see also *Financial Times* 2008).
Possible opposition from China under its competition law was also
mentioned in connection with the possible BHP Billiton/Rio Tinto
merger in the iron ore industry (Corcoran 2008). There are signs
of increasing concern regarding such possibilities in the international
business community (see the websites of the US Council for International Business and the International Chamber of Commerce for
various related submissions and papers).

4.3.   *Summary observations*

The review of various examples of transatlantic conflicts in section 4.1
of this paper has shown that, notwithstanding the significant convergence in substantive competition law standards that has taken place in
the transatlantic zone and the important cooperation mechanisms that
are in place, significant scope for policy conflicts remains. Moreover, as
in the various examples cited, such conflicts can have a major bearing
on the operations of transnational corporations and the structuring of
business arrangements. Often, the effects of the remedies imposed by
one jurisdiction (e.g., barring of a merger or requirements to share
information) will not be confined to that jurisdiction but will "leak
across" into other jurisdictions. Another observation worth making is
that, in conflicts of the type reviewed in this section (where one jurisdiction decides to "give the transaction a pass" or impose less far-reaching
remedies), the tendency is for the jurisdiction having the stricter competition laws to prevail. In some (perhaps most) cases, this may be to
the advantage of consumers. In others, however, it may raise a concern
regarding efficient restructuring being impeded (indeed, at least for

the US authorities, this was a key underlying concern in the examples cited).

Section 4 also showed that the possibility for such conflicts is not at all limited to the transatlantic sphere. In fact, in the future, the most serious policy clashes in the antitrust field are more likely to involve countries outside the transatlantic context. Approximately 100 countries, including such countries as China, India, Brazil and South Africa, now have national competition laws. As seen in the example of Korea's order in the Microsoft case, a growing number of such countries actually or potentially apply their laws to conduct originating abroad.

These observations raise the question of what, if any, additional cooperation mechanisms and/or efforts to achieve policy convergence are desirable. Clearly, this question will require further reflection. A minimum requirement to avoid conflicts in such cases is adherence to the well-known principle of national treatment (one of the founding principles of the WTO), which broadly requires that countries not impose burdens on foreign producers or products that they do not impose on their own firms/products (the application of this principle under various WTO Agreements is discussed in WTO, Working Group on the Interaction between Trade and Competition Policy, 1999).[46]

However, it is not clear that mere application of the national treatment principle, by itself, will answer all possible concerns, particularly where differences in the remedies imposed by particular jurisdictions result not from discrimination as such but from substantive differences in enforcement philosophies and approaches. There may, indeed, be no simple solution. Possibly, the answers can be found in further international discussions aimed at fostering intellectual consensus on the substantive issues involved. However, the potential for conflict that has been identified at least raises the possibility that something more than this — i.e., a system of international coordination, whether voluntary or otherwise — will eventually be needed.

---

[46]The application of the principle of national treatment in the WTO varies as between relevant agreements.

Whatever broader architecture is or is not eventually adopted for the international application of competition law, cooperation and policy dialogue between the United States and the European Communities is likely to provide essential intellectual guidance. As Kovacic (2008) states:

> "The development of competition policy in any jurisdiction is a work in progress... Perceiving the proper role of EU and US competition agency officials to be the continuing pursuit of better practices can focus attention on the need for the continuing reassessment and improvement of competition policy institutions."

5. Concluding Remarks

The field of competition law and policy embodies many of the trends and dilemmas that are at the heart of current debates on international cooperation and inter-jurisdictional competition in economic regulation and policy-making generally. Today, there is broad acknowledgment of the need for cooperation between jurisdictions to facilitate effective application of national competition laws. Formal intergovernmental agreements to facilitate cooperation, mainly but not exclusively of a procedural nature, have been in place for many years. Significant resources are devoted to the administration of these agreements. There is also good evidence that a gradual process of convergence is taking place with respect to the substantive competition law standards of many countries, though important differences in such standards remain.

The state of transatlantic cooperation in competition law and policy must be assessed in the context of historic differences in the nature and objectives of such policy in the EU and the US. In this context, a fair assessment begins by noting that valuable cooperative mechanisms have been in place for a good number of years and that much beneficial convergence in substantive standards has been achieved voluntarily through the exchange of ideas and institutional learning processes. Moreover, as responsible officials have emphasized, forced harmonization of substantive rules would not be without attendant costs. Nonetheless, existing cooperation arrangements have clear limits, and recent case experience suggests that purely voluntary cooperation may not be adequate to address all situations of potential conflicts. In the light of this, consideration may need to be given to the progressive development of deeper forms of cooperation supplemented by further convergence of substantive standards over time, drawing on work already done or under way in various fora.

Moreover, in the future, the more serious policy clashes in the antitrust field are more likely to involve countries outside the transatlantic context. This reflects the proliferation of competition laws across all regions of the world during the past decade and the lack of deep antitrust traditions in many of the relevant countries. The scope for such conflicts may eventually compel reconsideration of multilateral "framework" approaches to competition law that would promote sound economic approaches and ensure non-discrimination in policy application without entailing forced harmonization. Further efforts at achieving deeper cooperation and convergence in the transatlantic context could provide essential intellectual leadership in this regard.

References

Anderson, Robert D. (2008). "Competition policy and intellectual property in the WTO: More guidance needed?". In *Research Handbook on Intellectual Property and Competition Law*, J. Drexel (ed.), pp. 451–474. Cheltanham: Edward Elgar.

Anderson, Robert D. and Simon Evenett (2006). *Incorporating Competition Elements into Regional Trade Agreements: Characterization and Empirical Analysis.* July 2006. Available at: http://www.evenett.com/working/CompPrincInRTAs.pdf.

Anderson, Robert D. and Alberto Heimler (2007). "What has competition done for Europe? An interdisciplinary answer" *Aussenwirtschaft* (the Swiss Review of International Economic Relations), December, pp. 419–454.

Anderson, Robert D. and Frédéric Jenny (2005). "Competition policy, economic development and the possible role of a multilateral framework on competition policy: Insights from the WTO Working Group on Trade and Competition Policy". In *Competition Policy in East Asia*, E Medalla (ed.), pp. 61–85. Oxford: Routledge.

Barnett, Thomas [Assistant US Attorney-General for Antitrust] (2008). *"Antitrust update: Supreme Court decisions, global developments and recent enforcement"*. Washington, D.C.: Address to the Federalist Society, February 29. Available at: http://www.justice.gov/atr/public/speeches/230627.htm.

Barnett, Thomas (2007). *"Competition law and policy modernization: Lessons from the US common-law Experience".* Presentation to the Lisbon Conference on Competition Law and Economics, November 16. Available at: http://www.justice.gov/atr/public/speeches/227755.htm.

Birdsall, Nancy and Robert Z. Lawrence (1999). "Deep integration and trade agreements: good for developing countries?". In *Global Public Goods: International Cooperation in the 21st Century,* Inge Kaul, Isabelle Grunberg and Marc A. Stern (eds.), pp. 128–151. New York: Oxford University Press for the United Nations Development Program.

Bork, Robert H. (1978). *The Antitrust Paradox.* New York: Basic Books.

Buerkle, Tom (1997). *"President hints at retaliation if antitrust officials bar merger: Clinton warns EU Of trade conflict over boeing deal,"* International Herald Tribune. July 18. Available at: http://www.iht.com/articles /1997/07/18/boeing.t_10.php.

Carlton, Dennis W. and Randal C. Picker (2007). *Antitrust and Regulation* (Cambridge: National Bureau of Economic Research, Working Paper 12902). Available at: http://www.nber.org/papers/w12902.

Clarke, Julian and Simon J. Evenett (2003). "A multilateral framework for competition policy?", in State Secretariat of Economic Affairs and Simon Evenett, *The Singapore Issues and the World Trading System: The Road to Cancun and Beyond,* Bern: State Secretariat for Economic Affairs.

Commission of the European Communities, DG Competition (2005). *"Discussion paper on the application of Article 82 of the Treaty to exclusionary abuses,"* Brussels. Available at: http://ec.europa.eu/comm/competition/antitrust/art82/discpaper2005.pdf.

Corcoran, Gregory (2008). *"Rio Tinto, antitrust regulators and black cows,"* Wall Street Journal. January 17. Available at: http://blogs.wsj.com/deals/2008/01/17/rio-tinto-antitrust-regulators-and-black-cows/?mod=WSJBlog.

Elliott, Michael (2001). *"The Anatomy of the GE-Honeywell Disaster,"* Time. July 8. Available at: http://www.time.com/time/business/article/0,8599,166732-1,00.html.

Epstein, Richard and Michael Greve (2004). *Competition Laws in Conflict: Antitrust Jurisdiction in the Global Economy,* AEI Press.

European Digital Rights (2007). *"EU Court confirms the 497 million euro fine against Microsoft".* Available at: http://www.edri.org/edrigram/number5.18/microsoft-decision-tpi.

Evenett, Simon J., Alexander Lehmann and Benn Steil, (eds.) (2000). *Antitrust Goes Global: What Future for Transatlantic Cooperation?* (London: Royal Institute of International Affairs).

Financial Times (2008). "Asian Antitrust Laws 'Threaten Deals'," July 27.

Fox, Eleanor (1997). "US and EU competition law: A comparison". In *Global Competition Policy,* Edward Montgomery Graham and J. David Richardson (eds.), (Washington, D.C.: Peterson Institute).

Fox, Eleanor (2003). "We protect competition, you protect competitors". *World Competition,* Vol. 26., No. 2, June, pp. 149–165.

Geradin, Damien and David Henry (2004). "Competition law in the new member states: Where do we come from? Where do we go?". In *Modernisation and Enlargement: Two Major Challenges for EU Competition Law*, D. Geradin (ed.), (Intersentia Publishers), chapter 13, pp. 273–310.

Gerber, David (1998). *Law and Competition in Twentieth Century Europe: Protecting Prometheus* (Oxford: Oxford University Press).

Inside US Trade (2007). "U.S. Tech Companies To Campaign On EU Antitrust After Microsoft Ruling". *Inside US Trade*, Vol. 25, No. 37, 21 September.

International Competition Policy Advisory Committee (2000). *Final Report*, Washington, D.C.

James, Charles (2001). *International Antitrust in the 21st Century: cooperation and Convergence* (Remarks to the OECD Global Forum on Competition, Paris, October 17).

Jenny, Frédéric (2003). "International cooperation on competition: Myth, reality and perspective", *Antitrust Bulletin*, Vol. XLVIII, Issue 4, April.

Klein, Joel (1996). *A Note of Caution with Respect to the WTO Agenda on Competition Policy* (Remarks to the Royal Institute of International Affairs, Chatham House, London, November). Available at: http://www.justice.gov/atr/public/speeches/0998.htm.

Kolasky, William J. (2002). *Global Competition: Prospects for Convergence and Cooperation* (Remarks before the American Bar Association Fall Forum).

Kovacic, William E. (2003a). "The modern evolution of US competition policy enforcement norms". *Antitrust Law Journal*, Vol. 71, No. 2, pp. 377–478.

Kovacic, William E. (2003b). *Extraterritoriality, Institutions, and Convergence in International Competition Policy.* Paper Based Upon A Presentation Given At The Annual Meeting of the American Society of International Law, Washington, D.C., April 5. Available at: http://www.ftc.gov/speeches/other/031210kovacic.pdf.

Kovacic, William E. (2007). "The intellectual DNA of modern US competition law for dominant conduct: The Chicago/Harvard double helix". *Columbia Business Law Review*, Vol. 1, pp. 1–80.

Kovacic, William E. (2008). *Competition Policy in the European Union and the United States: Convergence or Divergence?* (Bates White Fifth Annual Antitrust Conference, Washington, D.C., June 2).

Kroes, Neelie (2008). *European Competition Policy in the Age of Globalisation — Towards a Global Competition Order?* (Innsbruck: Forschungsinstitut für Wirtschaftsverfassung und Wettbewerb (FIW), 7 February). Available at: http://europa.eu/rapid/pressReleasesAction.do?reference=SPEECH/08/61&format=HTML&aged=0&language=EN&guiLanguage=en.

Markoff, John (2008). *"China law could impede Microsoft deal for Yahoo,"* New York Times. March 28. Available at: http://www.nytimes.com/2008/03/28/technology/28yahoo.html.

Marsden, Philip (ed.) (2007). *Handbook of Research in Trans-Atlantic Antitrust* (Edward Elgar).

Matte, Francine (1996). *Business Across Borders - Competition Law Enforcement in a Global Environment* (Vancouver, Canada: Remarks before the 11th Commonwealth Law Conference, August 27).

McDonald, Bruce J. (2005). *Section 2 and Article 82: Cowboys and Gentlemen*, (Remarks to the College of Europe Global Competition Law Centre Second Annual Conference, Brussels, June 16–17, 2005).

Melamed, A. Douglas (1997). *International Antitrust in an Age of International Deregulation* (Remarks before a George Mason Law Review Symposium: Antitrust in the Global Economy).

Monti, Mario (2001). *Antitrust in the US and Europe: A History of Convergence* (Washington, D.C.: Remarks to the General Counsel Roundtable of the American Bar Association, 14 November). Available at: http://europa.eu/rapid/pressReleases Action.do?reference=SPEECH/01/540&format=HTML&aged=0&language= EN&guiLanguage=en.

Neven, Damien, Robin Nuttal and Paul Seabright (1994). *Merger in Daylight: The Economics and Politics of European Merger Control* (Centre for Economic Policy Research).

Pate, R. Hewitt (2003). *The Common Law Approach and Improving Standards for Analyzing Single Firm Conduct* (New York, Fordham University). Available at: http://www.justice.gov/atr/public/speeches/202724.htm.

Pate, R. Hewitt (2004). *Antitrust in a Transatlantic Context – From the Cicada's Perspective* (Presented at "Antitrust in a Translantic Context" Conference, Brussels).

Petersmann, Ernst-Ulrich (1991). *Constitutional Functions and Constitutional Problems of International Economic Law* (Westview Press).

Petersmann, Ernst-Ulrich (2003). "Theories of justice, human rights and the constitution of international markets". *Loyola University of Los Angeles Law Review*, Vol. 37, No. 2, pp. 407–460.

Posner, Richard A. (2001). *Antitrust Law* (Chicago: University of Chicago Press, second edition).

Schaub, Alexander (2001). *Continued Focus on Reform: Recent Developments in EU Competition Policy* (New York: Address before the Fordham Corporate Law Institute 28th Annual Conference on International Antitrust Law and Policy, October 25). Available at: http://ec.europa.eu/comm/competition/speeches/ text/sp2001_031_en.pdf.

Steuer, Richard M. (1999). *Executive Summary Of The Antitrust Laws* (Mayer Brown LLP: Available at http://library.findlaw.com/1999/Jan/1/241454.html).

Stigler, George J. (1985). "The Origin of the Sherman Act". *Journal of Legal Studies*, Vol. 14, No. 1, pp. 1–11.

Thorelli, Hans (1955). *The Federal Antitrust Policy: Origination of an American Tradition*. Baltimore: The Johns Hopkins Press.

US, Antitrust Modernization Commission (2007). *Report and Recommendations* (Washington, D.C.)

US, Department of Justice and Federal Trade Commission (1995). *Antitrust Guidelines for International Operations* (Washington, D.C.)

US, Department of Justice (2004). *"Assistant Attorney-General for Antitrust, R. Hewitt Pate, issues statement on the EU's decision in its Microsoft investigation"*. Available at: http://www.usdoj.gov/opa/pr/2004/March/04_at_184.htm.

US, Department of Justice (2005). *"Statement of Deputy Assistant Attorney-General J. Bruce McDonald Regarding Korean fair trade commission's decision in its Microsoft case,"* (Press Release, December 7, 2005. Available at: http://www.usdoj.gov/atr/public/press_releases/2005/213562.htm).

US, Department of Justice (2007). "Assistant Attorney General for Antitrust, Thomas O. Barnett, issues statement on European Microsoft decision" (Press Release, September 17).

Varney, Christine (2009a). "Vigorous antitrust enforcement in this challenging era". (Remarks to the US Chamber of Commerce, May 12, 2009).

Varney, Christine (2009b). "Our Progress Towards International Convergence." (Remarks to the 36th Annual Fordham Competition Law Institute Annual Conference on International Antitrust Law and Policy, September 24, 2009).

Varney, Christine (2010). "Coordinated remedies: Convergence, cooperation and the rate of transferences." (Remarks to the Institute of Competition Law, New Frontiers of Antitrust Conference, February 15, 2010).

Waller, Spencer Weber (2000). "Anticartel cooperation," in Evenett *et al.* (2000), chapter 5, pp. 98–116.

World Trade Organization (1997). "Special study on trade and competition policy," in *Annual Report of the World Trade Organization for 1997*, Geneva: WTO, chapter IV.

WTO, Working Group on the Interaction between Trade and Competition Policy (1999). *"The Fundamental WTO principles of transparency and non-discrimination"* (WT/WGTCP/W/114, 14 April. Available at: http://docsonline.wto.org/DDFDocuments/t/WT/WGTCP/ W114.DOC).

Wood, Diane P. (1996). "International standards for competition law: An idea whose time has not come,"*PSIO Occasional Paper, WTO Series No. 2*, Graduate Institute of International Studies, Geneva.

Chapter 8

Transatlantic Regulatory Cooperation on Chemicals — An Idealist's Dream?*

Reinhard Quick

*Professor for International Economic Law, Saarland University
Dr. iur., LL.M (University of Michigan)
Director of the Brussels Office of the German Chemical
Industries Association and Vice Chairman
Trade Committee, Business Europe
quick@bruessel.vci.de*

1. Introduction

There are few areas of transatlantic product regulations where the transatlantic divide is as huge as it is in the area of chemicals. The two sides of the Atlantic have fundamentally different regulations on issues such as hormones, genetically modified organisms (GMOs), cosmetics and the registration and restriction of chemical substances. Two of the four examples mentioned have already been subject to World Trade Organization (WTO) dispute settlement cases, which largely remain unsettled, whilst the other two bear the potential of serious and damaging transatlantic trade disputes with all their negative consequences for transatlantic economic relations. The area of chemicals would obviously be the ideal ground for regulatory

---

*The opinions are those of the author. The author would like to thank Robin Kiera, Christian Bünger, and Dr. Matthias Blum for their support during the preparations of this chapter.

cooperation. If the two sides were able to agree on how to converge the existing divergent regulations, they could ease transatlantic trade tensions and contribute to strengthening the competitiveness of their respective chemical industries. Yet, given the huge divide, the question arises whether regulatory cooperation is at all possible. In order to be successful such cooperation requires not only a political will to accept compromises but also a convergence of value judgments. Unfortunately, notwithstanding many transatlantic summit declarations, on chemicals neither side seems ready to give up its regulatory autonomy.

In the light of the newly found dynamism in transatlantic regulatory cooperation as evidenced by the results of the 2007 Transatlantic Summit, this chapter examines whether there still are possibilities for regulatory cooperation on chemicals. It presents some figures concerning the transatlantic chemical industry, such as trade and investment flows and the industry's position in the world. It then describes the industry's initiatives taken in the framework of the Transatlantic Business Dialogue (TABD) towards greater regulatory convergence and the Governments' reactions to them. It comes to the conclusion that these activities could not stop the EU from adopting the new chemicals legislation REACH, which put an end to all dreams of regulatory cooperation and convergence. The chapter turns next to possibilities for regulatory cooperation notwithstanding REACH. The 2007 Transatlantic Summit Framework for Advancing Transatlantic Economic Integration (referred to as the Merkel initiative) and the activities of the Transatlantic Economic Council (TEC) form the basis for this analysis. The issues discussed show that neither the EU nor the United States engage in regulatory convergence of chemicals legislation. Instead, they discuss the existing transatlantic divide and engage in dispute avoidance. The role of the TEC seems to be reduced to that of a fire-brigade whose mission is to extinguish existing and future "transatlantic fires." Until now it has not been able to promote a process resulting in comparable transatlantic regulation on chemicals. In the conclusion, the way towards a barrier free transatlantic market is discussed.

1.1.   *Some figures concerning transatlantic trade and investment in chemicals*

The chemical industry is a global industry. In 2006 it generated sales worth 2.180 billion Euros, of which roughly 55% was generated in the EU and in the United States — with a slightly larger share for the EU. The remaining 45% was generated in Asia (30%), Latin America (6%), and in the rest of the world. Although within the top ten chemical producing "countries," the United States and Europe are still very strong (Table 1), this strength may not last forever since the emerging countries in Asia, like China or India, are catching up quickly. At the moment, China is the second largest chemical producing country in the world whereas in 2004 it was still in fourth position.

With a population of 489 million and a gross domestic product of nearly 16.8 trillion US Dollars, the EU is the largest economic area in the world, followed by the United States with a population of 304 million and a gross domestic product of 13.8 trillion US Dollars. The two regions account for only about 12% of the world population, yet their economic power is much stronger: they contribute more than half to the world gross domestic product. They are each other's most important business partners in trade and foreign direct investments.

Figures 1 and 2 show the rapid growth of the Asian markets in chemicals. This development could affect the transatlantic relationship: the United States and Europe might lose importance in the long term. In 2006 the volume of trade in chemicals between the United States and the EU was six times higher than in 1988 (Figure 4). As of 2006, about 30% of the extra-EU exports go to the United States. The same applies to imports — more than 30% of the extra-EU imports come from the United States. Moreover, investment activities in chemicals of both sides are nearly as important as the trade relationship: in 2006 the EU chemical industry held a capital stock of 127.5 billion dollars in the United States, constituting 70% of the total chemical industry foreign direct investment (FDI) (183.1 billion dollars).[1] The US industry on

---

[1] Source: Bureau of Economic Analysis: http://www.bea.gov/international/index. htm. (24 April 2008).

Table 1:   ICIS top chemical companies 2007.

Company		Sales ($m)
1	BASF[1]	69,459
2	Dow Chemical	49,124
3	ExxonMobil[2]	48,900
4	Bayer[3]	38,230
5	Shell[2]	36,306
6	INEOS[4]	36,000
7	Sinopec[2]	29,253
8	DuPont	27,421
9	Total[2]	25,234
10	SABIC	23,022
11	Lyondell Chemical	22,228
12	Mitsubishi Chemical	22,037
13	Akzo Nobel	18,137
14	Sumitomo Chemical	15,040
15	Air Liquide	14,456
16	Degussa	14,416
17	Mitsui Chemical	14,183
18	BP[5]	14,000
19	Basell	13,856
20	Asahi Kasei	13,643
21	Huntsman	13,148
22	Yara International	12,773
23	Solvay	12,409
24	Johnson Matthey	12,053
25	Chevron Phillips Chemical[2]	11,839
26	DSM	11,064
27	Shin-Etsu	10,962
28	Linde	10,639
29	ChemChina (CNCC)	10,260
30	LG Chem	10,149
31	Reliance Industries[2]	9,714
32	ICI	9,492
33	Lanxess	9,168

Sales in 2006.
(*Notes:* [1] — *Includes oil and gas;* [2] — *Chemicals only;* [3] — *Includes phar-maceuticals;* [4] — *Includes refining*).
Source: ICIS-News (www.icis.com).

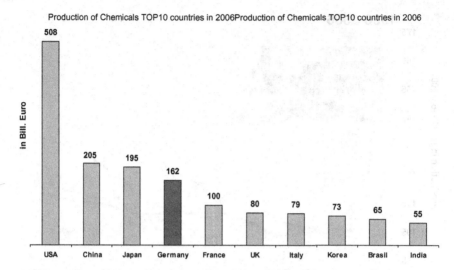

Figure 1:   Production of chemicals top 10 countries in 2006.

Source: CEFIC, Global Insight, VCI, Facts and Figures: http://www.cefic.org/factsandfigures/level02/growthindustry_index.html. (20 March 2008).

the other hand held a capital stock of 75.3 billion dollars in the EU, about 60% of the total chemical industry FDI.[2] To give a more illustrative example: the five biggest German chemical companies (BASF, Bayer, Henkel, Linde and Evonik) employ roughly 50,000 employees in their plants in the United States. Once again, this shows the strong interlinkage between the two regions. Twenty one of the 33 biggest chemical companies in the world are located in either the US or the EU.[3]

Figure 3 shows the European chemical industry's export activities towards the world (excluding pharmaceuticals): notwithstanding the growing importance of Asia, the United States is still Europe's most important export partner.

Such strong interdependence requires regulatory cooperation. It is not surprising that the chemical industry has been a strong supporter

---

[2]Source: American Chemistry Council (ACC).
[3]ICIS Top Chemical Companies 2007. Available at: http://www.icis.com.

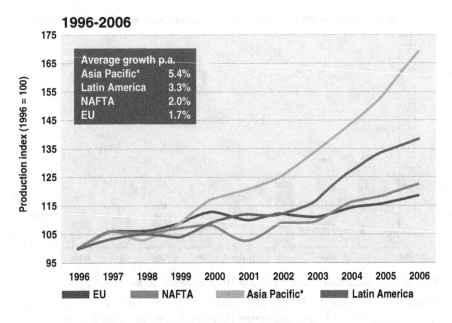

	1996	1997	1998	1999	2000	2001	2002	2003	2004	2005	2006
EU	100.0	106.3	106.1	108.8	113.2	110.1	112.0	111.0	114.3	116.1	118.5
North America	100.0	105.8	105.3	106.7	108.1	102.6	109.1	109.8	116.2	118.8	122.4
Asia Pacific*	100.0	106.4	102.9	108.9	117.8	121.0	125.7	134.1	144.1	154.7	169.1
Latin America	100.0	103.5	105.1	103.7	109.6	112.0	111.9	117.0	127.3	134.3	138.4

Figure 2:   Growth of chemical production (excl. pharmaceuticals) in selected world regions.

Source: Cefic Chemdata International Facts and Figures: http://www.cefic.org/ factsandfigures/level02/growthindustry_index.html. (20 March 2008).

of closer transatlantic economic relations, in particular in the area of chemicals legislation. The industry's will to overcome regulatory barriers goes hand in hand with its proposals to eliminate tariff barriers via the WTO. In the current Doha Round multilateral trade negotiations, the chemical industry has put forward a proposal for a sectoral chemical

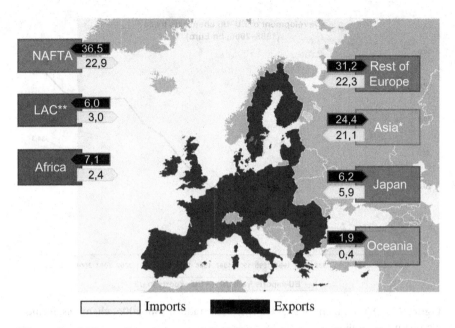

| | Imports | | Exports |

Figure 3: Main trading partners of the EU (trade in chemicals excluding pharmaceuticals) in 2006, billions of euros.

Source: Cefic and Eurostat Facts and Figures: http://www.cefic.org/factsandfigures/level02/growthindustry_index.html (20 March 2008).
*Excluding Japan
**Latin America and the Caribbean

tariff elimination agreement to which all WTO members with a viable chemical industry should adhere.[4]

Although chemical tariffs are low in the OECD countries, the following figures show the importance of tariffs in transatlantic trade in chemicals: in 2006 exports of chemicals (excluding pharmaceuticals) from the EU to the United States amounted to 32.9 billion Euros, whilst chemical exports from the United States to the EU amounted to 20.8 billion Euros.[5] With an average US tariff for chemicals of 3.2%

---

[4]See Reinhard Quick, "Further Liberalization of Trade in Chemicals — Can the DDA Deliver?," 1 Global Customs and Trade Journal, 2006, p. 1 et seq.
[5]Source: Cefic, VCI.

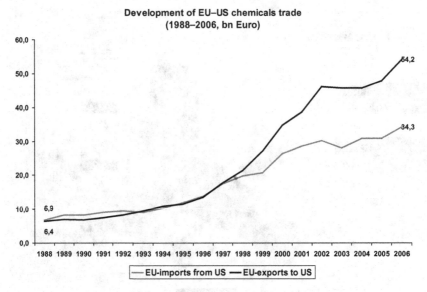

Figure 4:   Development of EU–US chemicals trade (1988–2006, chemicals, including pharmaceuticals).

Source: Cefic, VCI.

and 4.5% in the EU,[6] US importers had to pay around 1 billion Euros per annum into the US budget whilst EU importers had to pay approximately 900 million Euros into the European budget. These are considerable amounts of money which could be invested otherwise — and probably better.

2.   The Chemical Industry's Input to Regulatory Cooperation: The Race against REACH within a Declining and Re-emerging TABD

We now consider the European chemical industry's contributions to regulatory cooperation, in particular in the context of the Transatlantic

---

[6]See WTO, World Trade Report 2005, Tariff profiles, http://www.wto.org/english/res_e/reser_e/wtr_arc_e.htm. (24 April 2008).

Business Dialogue (TABD). The TABD started in 1995, practically came to a standstill in 2002, and was re-vitalised in 2004.[7] In parallel to TABD efforts towards greater transatlantic cooperation, the EU designed and eventually adopted in 2006 a chemicals legislation, called REACH.[8] REACH is a prime example of how unilateral legislative acts can kill any bilateral cooperation. The EU has imposed its views on how to regulate chemicals on its trading partners without taking their views into account. REACH puts in doubt the EU's willingness to engage in regulatory cooperation altogether.

2.1. *Industry's input to TABD*

Given the strong interdependence between Europe and the United States, the chemical industry has always been favorable to closer transatlantic economic ties. After the political initiative had been launched by the late US Commerce Department Secretary, Ron Brown, the industry was influential in making a success of the first TABD meeting, held in November 1995 in Seville, Spain. The European TABD co-chairman at the time was Prof. Jürgen Strube, then CEO of BASF Aktiengesellschaft,[9] the biggest chemical corporation in the world (Figure 5).

---

[7]For an excellent overview of the rise and fall of the TABD, see Green Cowles, "Calming the Waters: the Rebirth of the Transatlantic Business Dialogue," in The Future of Transatlantic Economic Relations: Continuity Amid Discord, Andrews, Pollack, Shaffer, Wallace (eds.), Florence 2005, pp. 275 et seq.

[8]Regulation (EC) No 1907/2006 of The European Parliament and of the Council of 18 December 2006 concerning the Registration, Evaluation, Authorisation and Restriction of Chemicals (REACH), establishing a European Chemicals Agency, amending Directive 1999/45/EC and repealing Council Regulation (EEC) No 793/93 and Commission Regulation (EC) No 1488/94 as well as Council Directive 76/796/EEC and Commission Directive 91/155/EEC, 93/67/EEC, 93/105/EC and 2000/21/EC. O.J. 2006 L 396 p. 1 et seq.

[9]See: http://www.corporate.basf.com/basfcorp/img/ueberuns/aufsichtsrat/Leben slauf_HrStrube_en.pdf?id=eU*epBww*bcp*Hs. (4 March 2008).

The first TABD report[10] did not contain specific sectoral recommendations on chemicals but referred to regulatory cooperation in a more systemic way. TABD Working Group I dealing with standards, certification and regulatory policy put the emphasis on mutual recognition agreements (MRAs), common standards and increased transparency and cooperation in standard setting, compliance requirements, product approvals and certification procedures. The chemical industry was not yet as active in group I as it was in groups II, III or IV that dealt with trade liberalization, investment and third country issues, respectively. Whilst regulatory cooperation in chemicals became a more important TABD subject in the following years, the chemical industry continued to be actively involved in the global activities of the TABD, particularly in the working group dealing with international trade issues.[11]

The first specific references to chemicals concentrated on good laboratory practice, registration of new chemicals, and hazard and risk assessment as the excerpts from the 1996 TABD Chicago Declaration,[12] the 1997 TABD Rome Communiqué[13] and the 1998 TABD Charlotte Statement[14] show:

(Chicago): Industry representatives called for a work plan that identifies the specific measures to reduce regulatory barriers to trade. The first priority is to implement the OECD agreement on GLP (Good Laboratory Practice) and MAD (Mutual Acceptance of Data) by mid-1997. In parallel, EU/US discussions should start on Conditional Equivalence Agreements (CEAs) in the four areas of risk assessment, notification of new chemicals, application and use, and classification and labelling of

---

[10] The Overall Conclusions of the first TABD meeting held in Seville 1995 can be found at http://www.tabd.com/ceo_reports. (4 March 2008). In the following, references will be made to these reports by citation of the year and the city in which the TABD annual conference took place. Also mid-year reports can be found hereunder.

[11] In the early years of the TABD the TABD WTO groups were chaired by representatives from the German chemical industry, i.e., Dr. Hans-Dietrich Winkhaus, CEO of Henkel KGaA and Werner Spinner, member of the Board of Bayer AG.

[12] TABD, Chicago Declaration, Chicago 1996, p. 4.

[13] TABD, Rome Communiqué, Rome 1997, p. 4.

[14] TABD, Statement of Conclusion, Charlotte 1998, p. 7.

chemicals. The agreed end-point of this process should be Unconditional Equivalence Agreements by the year 2000.

(Rome): Industry called for the establishment of joint working groups to resolve non-tariff barriers. Three specific actions were recommended. First, the EU and US sign a MRA regarding Good Laboratory Practice (GLP) and the Mutual Acceptance of Data (MAD) building on the OECD practice in this field. Second, to enhance innovation through modification of the current systems of new chemical introductions for three specific situations: R&D chemicals, low risk chemicals and for polymers. Third, to agree on the methods used for hazard assessment and for risk assessment.

(Charlotte): The chemical industry reviewed the status of its 1997 TABD recommendations to reduce regulatory barriers to transatlantic chemicals trade. As recommended, a joint working group of EU/US industry representatives and government authorities has met since last year to review the issues and to promote the mutual understanding of the differences in the EU and US regulatory systems that is necessary to advance the recommendations. The chemical industry outlined a work plan to advance its recommendations in the coming year. The critical areas of action include the requirements governing the introduction of new chemicals.

The declarations show that the chemical industry approached the subject of regulatory cooperation as a means of finding technical solutions to a highly political issue, namely the regulation of chemicals. Although the industry fully endorsed the TABD's formula "*approved once, accepted everywhere*," its contributions did not consist of big conceptual approaches towards a harmonization of transatlantic regulation. Instead, its suggestions were pragmatic proposals on how to overcome the most important transatlantic differences regarding chemicals legislation, such as the registration requirements for certain low risk chemicals[15] or the development of a common understanding with respect to hazard and risk assessment concerning chemicals. The industry was quite concerned with the different conclusions each side drew

---

[15] Those are chemicals used for research and development or chemicals with low exposure/low release or low risk, such as process intermediates, catalysts or polymers.

on risk assessment, which often led to different regulatory results with
Europe being, in principle, stricter than the United States.

In April 1998, the EU's Environment Council, meeting informally
in Chester, UK,[16] asked the EC (EC) to analyze the functioning of
the EU chemicals legislation. In the autumn of the same year, the EC
presented the requested analysis in a working document.[17] It came to
the conclusion that there was a huge discrepancy between the legislation concerning new and existing chemicals[18]: in the first case, the data
requirements for new chemicals were considered too burdensome, thus
blocking innovation; in the second case, whilst the data requirements
for existing chemicals were not that burdensome, the process of data
gathering was a failure since the competent authorities were unable to
collect the data in a timely manner. Following this report the Environment Council[19] asked the Commission in June 1999 to present a
coherent and integrated EU chemicals policy.

As early as at the Charlotte conference, the business community
expressed concern about both administrations' unwillingness to implement the many TABD recommendations issued until then. The TABD
developed the concept of "scorecards" to check whether the authorities were delivering on the recommendations. The Berlin conference was an impressive demonstration that the TABD process was
fully endorsed by the two business communities: the conference was
attended by 700 participants, many transatlantic working groups met
and agreed on a whole range of generally political and sectorally specific

---

[16]Given the informal nature of this Council, no press release was issued after the
meeting. The first reference to the discussion on chemicals and the future of EU
chemical legislation can be found in the working document of the Commission mentioned in the following footnote. See also: http://europa.eu/rapid/pressReleases
Action.do?reference=IP/98/998&format=HTML&aged=0&language=DE&gui
Language=en. (4 March 2008).
[17]Commission Working Document SEC (1998) 1986 final of 18 November 1998.
[18]Council Regulation (EEC) No 793/93 of 23 March 1993 on the evaluation and
control of the risks of existing substances. O.J. L. 224, p. 34.
[19]2194th Council Meeting — Environment — Luxembourg, 24/25 June 1999; see:
http://www.consilium.europa.eu/ueDocs/cms_Data/docs/pressData/en/envir/
ACF5B.htm. (4 March 2008).

recommendations put together in a 65-page report. The Berlin conference also evidenced one of the big weaknesses of the process, namely the lack of implementation. The other weakness of the TABD was the discrepancy between the work undertaken during the year and the annual CEO conference. The CEOs attending the TABD conference were often not familiar with the technical recommendations prepared by their collaborators, but more importantly, were often also not very interested in the nitty-gritty technicalities of regulatory cooperation. In the following years the CEOs lost interest in the whole process so that the TABD became more concerned with securing CEO attendance at the meetings than with discussing the contents of regulatory cooperation.[20]

On chemicals, though, the Berlin recommendations show that the industry still had confidence in the process and that it was expecting results:

(Berlin): The chemical industry reviewed the status of its 1997 TABD recommendations to reduce regulatory barriers to trans-Atlantic chemicals trade. As recommended, a joint working group of EU/US industry representatives and government authorities has met to review the issues and to promote the mutual understanding of the differences in the EU and US regulatory systems. The joint working group should continue its work for another year, with focus on the tasks outlined in the work plan developed to advance the recommendations in the coming year. The critical areas of action include a workshop on the methods for assessment of hazard, exposure, and risk, and the requirements and socio-economic analysis governing the introduction of new chemicals.

This optimism continued after Berlin and led to a positive assessment of the work on chemicals. The TABD 2000 midyear report[21] gives a realistic but at the same time optimistic view on the work achieved and on the possibility for a common approach on some chemical issues. Again, harmonization of chemicals legislation was considered impossible; mutual recognition of the functional equivalence

---

[20]See also Green Cowles, note 6 above, p. 281.
[21]TABD Midyear Report 2000, p. 20.

of the two systems, however, was seen as a feasible alternative to harmonization:[22]

> At the Berlin Conference, the chemical industry has reviewed the status of its 1997 TABD recommendations to reduce regulatory barriers to trade in new chemicals. It has been agreed that a joint working group of EU/US industry representatives and government authorities should continue to work for another year to advance the recommendations. The priority issues are:
>
> (a) enhancing understanding and acceptance of methods used for hazard assessment and for risk assessment and
> (b) modification of the current systems for new chemicals introductions which include R&D chemicals, low risk chemicals and polymers.
>
> State Of Play:
>
> The regulatory systems governing the introduction of new chemicals differ significantly. Because of their different structure and their interrelation with other legislation, harmonisation is considered to be impossible. Therefore, the chemical industry's objective is mutual recognition of the functional equivalence of the two systems.
>
> Ways to achieve "approved once, accepted everywhere" include the following areas:
>
> • Acceptance of health and environment test data:
>
> Today, there is no MRA between the US and the EU on the acceptance of such test data. However, there is a *de facto* acceptance of test data if the tests follow OECD test methods and are performed in laboratories meeting GLP requirements.
>
> • Modification of the current systems of new chemicals introduction:
>
> Concerning new polymers, the objective is to develop an equivalence agreement between the EU and US that would allow polymers legally produced and marketed in one jurisdiction to be marketed in the other,

---

[22] In 1999, the two sides had concluded mutual recognition agreements (MRAS) on medical devices, pharmaceutical products, telecommunications, electronics, electromagnetic compatibility and sport boats. See O.J. L 31 of 4 February 1999 p. 31. Both sides were still hopeful that these MRAs would also work in practice. The practice however showed that this was not the case. See Reinhard Quick, Regulatory Cooperation — A Subject of Bilateral Trade Negotiations or even for the WTO?, 42 Journal of World Trade, 2008, p. 391 et seq., p. 397, with further references.

without the need for a full notification. Discussions about possibilities of regulatory changes aiming at comparable requirements on both sides of the Atlantic for R&D chemicals and low risk chemicals have achieved some progress.

- Enhancing understanding and acceptance of methods used for hazard assessment and for risk assessment:

The objective is that regulatory authorities develop or utilise scientifically valid methods that lead to assessments of chemicals that are mutually acceptable.

However, the biggest obstacle to progress is the lack of understanding among the authorities concerning the respective other regulatory system. It is envisaged to overcome that barrier with workshops for both authorities and industry. (emphasis added)

Given this positive development, it is all the more astonishing that the 2000 TABD Cincinnati Recommendations lack a section on chemicals. It seems that the warning expressed in the above-cited midyear report, namely that the biggest obstacle to progress was the lack of understanding of the regulatory system, had materialized and that the two sides were unable to come to any agreement whatsoever. It is furthermore interesting to note that the 2001 midyear report was much less optimistic on chemicals and only repeated the earlier recommendations, namely to modify the rules for notifying new substances, to develop mutual understanding on hazard and risk assessment techniques and to consider the mutual acceptance of health and environmental test data.[23] The midyear report also referred to the Commission's "White Paper on the Strategy for a Future Chemicals Policy"[24] which had been adopted in February 2001:

The EU Commission's White Paper on the "Strategy for a Future Chemicals Policy" marks the beginning of a complex decision making process that will result in a new regulatory framework for chemicals' management. These changes to chemicals policy will affect domestic manufacturers and downstream-users, as well as importers from the US and elsewhere.

---

[23]TABD Midyear Report 2001, p. 27 et seq.
[24]Commission White Paper on the Strategy for a Future Chemicals Policy, COM (2001) 88 final of 27 February 2001.

Especially the concept of authorization of substances of high concern and the proposed timetable for registering data packages raise serious concerns with regard to creating unnecessary obstacles to international trade. Therefore, the EU and US chemical industry recommend that EU and US regulators exchange information about contemplated regulatory requirements, examine opportunities to minimize unnecessary divergence in chemical regulations, and strive towards compatible solutions.

The Commission's White Paper analyzed the problems of Europe's dual system for existing and new substances, namely the burdensome requirements for new substances and the lack of data for existing substances whose effects on human health and on the environment were largely unknown. It proposed to change this dual system into a single, efficient and coherent one. Under this new scheme, the industry producing a particular substance would be responsible for supplying data and the authorities would be called on to evaluate the data and to decide on testing programmes. Increased responsibility would also be put on users in the manufacturing chain (formulators and downstream users) who would have to supply data on the particular uses they make of a substance. The White Paper suggested the following three core elements:[25]

- **Registration** of basic information for around 30,000 substances (all existing and new substances exceeding a production volume of 1 tonne) submitted by companies to a central database.
- **Evaluation** of the registered information for all substances exceeding a production volume of 100 tonnes (around 5,000 substances corresponding to 15%) and, in case of concern, also for substances at lower tonnage; the evaluation would be carried out by authorities and include the development of substance-tailored testing programmes focussing on the effects of long-term exposure;
- **Authorization** of substances which are carcinogenic, mutagenic or toxic to reproduction (CMRs) and persistant organic pollutants (POPs).

---

[25] See: http://europa.eu/rapid/pressReleasesAction.do?reference=IP/01/201& format=HTML&aged=0&language=EN&guiLanguage=en (5 March 2008).

TABD had been urging governments to minimize divergence and to achieve progress with respect to the technical recommendations issued. Yet it seemed that in the wake of the EU's overhaul of its chemicals legislation, the chemical industry had given up hope that the TABD process would deliver a meaningful result. The September 11 terrorist attacks in New York gave the TABD process a further, even heavier blow. US policy concentrated on security and the "war against terrorism" leaving little room for transatlantic economic issues. Because of 9/11, no CEO TABD conference was organized in 2001. The TABD just published a report that resumed the already known recommendations on chemicals and urged governments to implement them.[26]

In April 2002, the US and the EU adopted *Guidelines on Regulatory Cooperation and Transparency.*[27] The two sides negotiated these guidelines as part of the Action Plan adopted by the transatlantic summit of May 1998 in the context of the Transatlantic Economic Partnership (TEP).[28] The guidelines were intended to enhance cooperation between EU and US regulators in the development of technical regulations. They specifically referred to regular consultation, exchange of data and information as well as informing one another at an early stage on planned new regulations. Efficient cooperation between regulators was intended to dismantle non-tariff barriers and to defuse potential trade conflicts at a preliminary stage.

In more detail, the guidelines pursued the following goals:

- To improve the planning and development of regulatory proposals, as well as the quality of technical regulation, and minimize divergence in regulation;
- to increase predictability in the development of technical regulation by identifying and exchanging objectives and instruments;

---

[26]TABD 2001 CEO Report, p. 33.

[27]The guidelines can be found at: http://ec.europa.eu/enterprise/enterprise_policy/ gov_relations/interntl_regul_coop_eu_us/regul_coop_guide.htm. (5 March 2008).

[28]On TEP see: http://ec.europa.eu/external_relations/us/economic_partnership/ trans_econ_partner_11_98.htm. (5 March 2008). See also, Eric Frey, Feuding Friends — European Trade Relations in the Clinton Era, 1992–2000, Frankfurt, 2004, p. 71 et seq.

- to grant the regulators of either side the opportunity to take position;
- to promote transparency by early disclosure and access to documents supporting technical regulation;
- to take into account the expertise of either side and discuss alternatives;
- to increase public understanding of technical regulation.

Notwithstanding the successful adoption of the guidelines, the disagreement over regulatory cooperation on chemicals continued. The 2002 TABD midyear report openly criticized that none of the TABD proposals forwarded by the chemical industry had been implemented by the authorities and suggested that the new European chemicals legislation should incorporate the suggestions made so far.[29]

Overall the TABD process began to decline.[30] The 2002 TABD Chicago CEO conference had nothing of the glamor and the pioneering spirit of the earlier CEO conferences. Not only had the TABD difficulties in attracting a sufficient number of "big-name" CEOs, but also the general atmosphere of the conference was dull. There was a general feeling of *déjà vu*, and the discussions were everything but lively. There was however a notable exception to all of this: the break-out session on chemicals. The meeting was attended by a high level delegation from business, two Commissioners and several high-level representatives from the US government. Its purpose was to explore ways and means on how to avoid the ever growing transatlantic divide on chemicals — a divide triggered not only by the Commission's REACH initiative but also by the unwillingness of both sides to implement the earlier TABD recommendations. Nevertheless the Chicago recommendations on chemicals were quite explicitly directed against the EU's legislative unilateralism:[31]

> Consensus recommendations for chemical regulatory policy have been developed by EU and US chemical companies. Chemicals management systems should be:
>
> - Protective of human health and the environment;

---

[29]TABD, Midyear Report, Brussels 2002, p. 31 et seq.
[30]See Green Cowles, note 6 above, p. 290.
[31]2002 TABD Chicago Conference Report, p. 42.

- Workable, practical, and effective;
- Risk based;
- Trade neutral; and,
- Transparent.

The EU White Paper "Strategy for a future Chemicals Policy," unfortunately, does not meet these objectives and indeed moves away from greater convergence of chemical regulatory approaches among countries. The costs, commercial impacts, job losses and trade distortions are likely to be quite significant as chemical substances are used in virtually every other industrial sector as material inputs and in manufacturing.

US and EU chemical companies recommend that the US Government and the EU Commission initiate discussions to examine the impact of the proposals on downstream users and small and medium enterprises. Small- and medium-sized chemicals producers and downstream users may find that the new system hampers innovation by introducing unnecessary regulatory delays and cost increases. Responsibilities of chemical manufacturers & importers and downstream users should be discussed and defined under the US–EU Guidelines for Regulatory Cooperation and Transparency.

US and EU chemical companies further recommend, as a short-term project, the development of appropriate exemptions for low-risk and low-exposure scenarios (e.g., Research and Development, intermediates, polymers, and chemical substances used in controlled environments).

In the long term, US and EU chemical companies recommend a project to develop US and EU cooperative work plans on the latest scientific knowledge and modelling techniques that allow for the assessment of hazard and risk. These techniques are more expeditious, and eliminate the unnecessary, costly testing proposed in the EU White Paper. The US and EU should build on the work of the OECD Chemicals Program.

Throughout its stages, steps and processes, the EU's new regulatory system should be based on an assessment of risk (evaluation of hazards, uses and likely exposures). The new system should also take full advantage of the latest scientific research and the tools and technologies available for use in risk assessment. As the EU develops its new system, it should promote convergence of regulatory systems, and give full credit to international tests, data, and assessments developed under other systems.

Industry urges the EU Commission to increase its efforts to discuss with its partners possible international solutions to the global issues raised in the White Paper.

The Chicago Report was the last attempt to push for regulatory convergence. It came at the wrong time. The TABD process had lost its appeal both to business and politicians. Notwithstanding many recommendations and political summit declarations, there were no results. It almost looked as if political-institutional integration was no longer necessary as the transatlantic market was growing without political support and, notwithstanding the many political difficulties, divergences and tensions between Europe and the United States.

Chicago has also been the last big TABD CEO conference. In 2003, the TABD issued a press release in which it asked for stability in the transatlantic relationship and in which it announced a renewal of the TABD process. Not convergence but divergence was the *leitmotiv* for transatlantic relations at that time.[32] The adoption by the EC of its proposal for the REACH regulation[33] brought any transatlantic attempts towards closer regulatory cooperation in chemicals to an end. The Commission adopted its proposal in full knowledge that it would violate the cooperation requirements contained in the guidelines on regulatory cooperation.

The 2003 reorganization designed to render the TABD smaller and more concentrated on CEO events was not helpful either for the discussion on chemicals. The reports of the new TABD of the years 2004, 2005 and 2006 solemnly announced the creation of a barrier free transatlantic market but did not contain any specific recommendations on how this laudable goal could be materialized as far as chemicals are concerned. These reports barely mention the draft REACH proposal

---

[32] For a more specific analysis of the "seismic shift" in EU–US relations and its effect on the TABD process see Green Cowles, note 6 above, p. 288 et seq.

[33] Proposal for a Regulation of the European Parliament and of the Council concerning the Registration, Evaluation, Authorisation and Restriction of Chemicals (Reach), establishing a European Chemicals Agency and amending Directive 1999/45/EC and Regulation (EC) {on Persistent Organic Pollutants} COM (2003) 644-1 final as well as Proposal for a Directive of the European Parliament and of the Council amending Council Directive 67/548/EEC in order to adapt it to Regulation (EC) of the European Parliament and of the Council concerning the registration, evaluation, authorisation and restriction of chemicals COM (2003) 644-2 final.

and its negative impact on the transatlantic market[34] and fall short of making recommendations on how to solve the problem. It seems that the TABD "chiefs" defined their great transatlantic goals without the technical support of their "indians" working concretely on the nitty-gritty issues. The chemical industry presented some suggestions in 2005[35] in the context of sectoral dialogues convened by the authorities, but these suggestions — though much less ambitious than the earlier TABD recommendations — did not find their way into a TABD document.

At the end of 2006, the Council of Ministers and the European Parliament adopted REACH.[36] The regulation entered into force on 1 June 2007. Given the fact that REACH goes far beyond US legislative requirements for chemicals,[37] both sides' willingness to discuss regulatory convergence in chemicals had been reduced to zero.

The REACH regulation[38] requires manufacturers and importers of substances to provide safety information and puts on industry greater responsibility with respect to risks management. Substances produced or imported in quantities of 1 ton or more per year have to be registered with the European Chemicals Agency (ECHA) accompanied with a technical dossier containing the relevant safety data. The amount of data to be submitted depends on the tonnage produced or imported. The Agency will act as the central point in the REACH system: it will manage the databases necessary to operate the system, co-ordinate the in-depth evaluation of some chemicals and run a public database in which consumers and professionals can find hazard information. REACH also foresees an authorization system aimed at ensuring that substances of very high concern are properly controlled and

---

[34] See TABD Report to the 2005 Transatlantic EU–US Summit, p. 7.
[35] The suggestions are available with the author.
[36] See note 7 above.
[37] Denison, Richard, "Not that innocent. A comparative analysis of Canadian, EU and United States policies on industrial chemicals," Washington D.C. 2007, p. I-1ff.
[38] For a detailed description of REACH see: http://ec.europa.eu/environment/chemicals/reach/reach_intro.htm (11 March 2008). http://ec.europa.eu/enterprise/reach/reach_more_info_en.htm (11 March 2008).

progressively replaced by suitable alternative substances or technologies where these are economically and technically viable. Where this is not possible, the use of substances may only be authorized where there is an overall benefit for society. In addition, EU authorities may impose restrictions on the manufacture, use or placing on the market of substances causing an unacceptable risk to human health or the environment.

REACH seems to respond to some of the TABD recommendations for low risk chemicals: it does not require the registration of polymers if the monomers contained in it have already been registered,[39] provides exceptions for R&D chemicals[40] and allows for a simplified registration of some intermediates.[41] Yet compared to the US Toxic Substances Control Act (TSCA 1976)[42] REACH requirements go far beyond: while the TSCA assumes the innocence of a substance unless proven otherwise (by government institutions), REACH presumes the "guilt" of a substance until proven innocent — by the industry. REACH requires far more data than TSCA and obliges business to publish a certain amount of sensible information whereas TSCA better protects confidential business information. REACH contains clear definitions and a tiered registration system for the submission of risk-relevant information, whilst TSCA allows more flexibility and requires testing only for substances that represent an "unreasonable risk" or that are produced in "substantial quantities." Besides, the US Environmental Protection Agency has a considerable margin of discretion in the application of TSCA.

2.2. Governments' Responses to the New TABD

Whilst the new TABD's activities concerning chemicals went into hibernation, the 2004 transatlantic annual summit[43] gave a new impetus to regulatory cooperation.[44] The US administration and the

---

[39] Article 6 paragraph 3 REACH.
[40] Article 9 REACH.
[41] Article 17–19 REACH.
[42] The Toxic Substances Control Act (15 USC. 2601-2692) of 11 October 1976 (as amended).
[43] http://www.eurunion.org/partner/summit/20030625sum.htm (11 March 2008).
[44] See Quick, note 21 above, p. 400.

EC adopted a comprehensive work program[45] and identified sectoral goals for regulatory cooperation in the areas of pharmaceuticals, cosmetics and chemicals, inter alia. The work programme lists an impressive number of further common fields of activity ranging from energy efficiency and protection of intellectual property rights in third markets to liberalization of FDI and capital market rules, banking supervision, and accounting. Both partners seemed to realize that major transatlantic problems call for complex legal and regulatory modifications on both sides of the Atlantic aimed at convergence, mutual recognition, or equivalence of legislation.

The progress on chemicals is not stunning; what is stunning however is the fact that the Commission and the US Government have taken up the TABD recommendations of the past and work on chemicals legislation even without the constant pressure from the TABD.

The 2005 Roadmap for US–EU Regulatory Cooperation contains the following text on chemicals:

> Objective: Pursue informal cooperative dialogue, in the spirit of the US–EU Guidelines on Regulatory cooperation, between the US Environmental Protection Agency (EPA), DG Environment and DG Enterprise and Industry and DG Health and Consumer Protection and relevant agencies in chemicals related issues of mutual interest.

> Progress/Results: The US EPA hosted the 2nd transatlantic environment conference on chemicals which addressed the EU's proposed REACH legislation, the globally harmonized system (GHS) for the classification and labelling of chemicals, pollution preventing techniques, access to information and genomics. EPA hosted EC experts on its approach to the risk assessment of new chemicals and integrated QSAR modelling programs. Further exchange of experience and training programmes could be explored for respective staff. The US EPA and the EC are also collaborating on the OECD framework on the development of the Global High Production Volume (HPV) chemicals information portal.

> Next Steps: The EC and the United States will continue on the development of the Global HPV Portal.

---

[45] See for example 2005 Roadmap for US–EU Regulatory Cooperation, http://www.eurunion.org/partner/summit/Summit0506/RoadmapAgreed-text.pdf (11 March 2008).

The 2006 Report on the Roadmap for US–EU Regulatory Cooperation says:

> Objective: Pursue informal cooperative dialogue, in the spirit of the US–EU Guidelines on Regulatory cooperation, between the US Environmental Protection Agency (EPA), DG Environment and DG Enterprise and Industry and DG Health and Consumer Protection and relevant agencies in chemicals related issues of mutual interest.
>
> • The US EPA and the EC are together leading and will continue to collaborate in the OECD Chemicals Committee's work on the development of the Global Chemicals Portal, among other pertinent and emerging issues. The US High Production Volume Information System (HPVIS) recently came online and will be one of the national databases contributing to the Portal.

Regulatory cooperation on chemicals has not yet resulted in an exercise of convergence or approximation of chemicals regulations; it merely consists in an exchange of views and a discussion on different transatlantic chemical issues and in a collaboration regarding the OECD Chemicals Committee's work.[46]

2.3.   New Industry Initiatives Towards Harmonization

It is not clear to what extent the adoption of REACH will influence other governments' chemicals policies and legislations. The EC is actively promoting REACH in bilateral consultation, in particular with China and the Russian Federation. At the international level, the International Conference on Chemicals Management (ICCM) has adopted the Strategic Approach to International Chemicals Management (SAICM).[47] SAICM is a non-binding policy framework for international action on chemical hazards. It endorses the goal of the World

---

[46]For a description of the OECD's work on chemicals see infra III.4.
[47]See: http://www.chem.unep.ch/saicm/. (24 April 2008).

Summit for Sustainable Development *that by 2020, chemicals are used and produced in ways that lead to the minimization of significant adverse effects on human health and the environment.* By applying REACH, the EU will satisfy the SAICM goal.

Given the economic importance of Europe and its single market with nearly 500 million people, REACH will have an impact on all big chemical companies in the world. These companies will have to comply with REACH for their production exported to Europe anyway, so they might decide, for efficiency reasons, to apply REACH voluntarily as a global standard. REACH compliance could also be used as a marketing tool to promote their products *vis-à-vis* customers globally. The International Council of Chemical Associations (ICCA), in response to SAICM (and probably REACH), is currently working within its Global Product Strategy initiative on a voluntary project to establish a set of hazard and exposure information for each chemical, sufficient for risk assessment and providing a basis for decisions on risk management. Though not identical with REACH such voluntary initiative could be seen as an exercise of convergence aimed at aligning the chemicals policies of the different countries. If it succeeds, this industry standard could become the benchmark for the implementation of SAICM by all countries having accepted it.

3. Regulatory cooperation on chemicals in the context of the Transatlantic Economic Council

3.1. *The Transatlantic Summit of 2007 and the Transatlantic Economic Council: The re-emergence of a political will to co-operate*

As mentioned earlier, as of 2004 the annual transatlantic summits once again focused on economic integration. Built on these positive developments, the German chancellor's initiative to intensify transatlantic economic integration during her EU Presidency resulted on 30th April 2007 in a *Framework for Advancing Transatlantic Economic*

Integration.[48] The framework is intended to effectively drive forward regulatory cooperation and to reduce existing regulatory burdens. Although neither side accepted a legally binding framework, this summit declaration has a different quality from those preceding it, in that it lays down the conditions for regulatory cooperation. The framework is divided into five sections: Section I: Purpose; Section II: Fostering Cooperation and Reducing Regulatory Barriers; Section III: Lighthouse Priority Projects; Section IV: Transatlantic Economic Council (TEC); and Section V: Work Programme and Cooperation.

Particularly worth mentioning is the cooperation between the US Office of Management and Budget and the Secretariat-General of the EC. Both sides are to develop a methodological framework that ensures the comparability of regulatory reviews and impact assessments, with an emphasis on risk assessments and cost/benefit analyses. The cooperation aims at restraining the other side from adopting unilateral legislative acts and at preventing the creation of new regulatory trade barriers. The use of the above-mentioned guidelines on regulatory cooperation is explicitly prescribed for certain pilot projects with concrete timetables for implementation. The lighthouse projects deal with intellectual property rights, secure trade, financial markets, innovation and technology, as well as the elimination of obstacles to investment.

The framework agreement also establishes the Transatlantic Economic Council (TEC), to be co-chaired, on the US side, by a US cabinet level official in the Executive Office of the President, and, on the EU side, by a Member of the EC. The task of this council is to contribute to the realization of the set objectives and to conduct a targeted approach to the projects. The many areas covered by the framework, ranging from secure trade to cosmetics and from accounting principles to intellectual property, are proof of the existing regulatory divergences that need to be overcome in order to strengthen transatlantic economic integration.

---

[48]The framework agreement and any other documents related to the activities of the Transatlantic Economic Council cited hereafter can be found at: http://ec.europa.eu/enterprise/enterprise_policy/inter_rel/tec/index_en.htm. (5 April 2008).

At its first meeting in November 2007, the Council presented a progress report showing some positive results, and it expressed hope that this positive process would continue in 2008. Besides the many problems that it needs to address, the Council faces a systemic issue: can it really promote a barrier free transatlantic market through concrete suggestions on regulatory convergence or will its role be confined to act as a fire brigade in order to solve problematic issues? For the time being, it seems that the fire brigade role is more prominent than the role of an enabler of regulatory convergence.[49]

Cooperation in the area of chemicals figures prominently in the annexes to the Framework and in the progress report of the first meeting of the Transatlantic Economic Council, as the following excerpts from these documents show:

Framework Annex I: Fostering Cooperation and Reducing Regulatory Burdens:

A. Take the following steps to reduce barriers to transatlantic economic integration posed by new regulations by reinforcing the existing transatlantic dialogue structures:
   1. Pursue development of a methodological framework to help ensure the comparability of impact assessments, particularly risk assessments and cost-benefit analysis.

---

[49] At the first meeting of the TEC, the following two controversial subjects figured prominently at the discussions: the issue of pathogen-reduction treatment for poultry carcasses and the issue of 100% cargo screening in the context of secure trade. The poultry issue relates to an import ban imposed by the EU on US poultry because the US treats poultry carcasses with chemicals that the EU considers dangerous whilst the cargo screening issue results from a new US law imposing such screening. Both cases could result in an EU/US trade conflict and, therefore, need to be solved. The poultry issue grew out of proportion during the second meeting of the TEC and is now considered as a deal breaker by the US about the ability of both sides to advance economic integration transatlantically (see infra note 49). As a consequence to the TEC's position on poultry, the EC presented on 28 May 2008 a proposal for a Commission Regulation that accepts poultry treated with anti-bacterial chemicals under strict conditions. See Commission Press Release IP/08/819 of 29 May 2008, to be found at: http://europa.eu/rapid/pressREleasesAction.do?references=IP/08/819&fornat=HTML. (6 June 2008). Both the Standing Committee of the Member States as well as the US business community rejected the proposal. See, for example letter by Stan Anderson, US Chamber of Commerce, published in *European Voice* of 5 June 2008.

B. Take the following steps to reduce barriers to transatlantic economic integration posed by regulation in specific sectors by intensifying sector-by-sector regulatory cooperation, including through enhanced EC-OMB cooperation, including the following:

   3. Pursue implementation of the Roadmap for Regulatory Cooperation, including the following priority projects to be pursued in 2007 and 2008:

      (a) Collaborating on cosmetics regulation, in particular with a view to reducing the need for animal tests by cooperating on alternative test methods;

      (e) Expanding cooperation on OECD activities relating to risk assessment, Good Laboratory Practices and the Globally Harmonised System of Classification and labelling of Chemicals, study templates, information technology for data submissions, as well as on alternative test methods (QSAR), test methods and risks of manufactured nanomaterials;

Transatlantic Economic Council, Progress Report 2007:

In connection with the first plenary meeting of the Council, the US government and the EC have taken the following steps to reduce barriers to transatlantic economic integration.

• Earlier this year, the US Food and Drug Administration (FDA) and the EC concluded confidentiality arrangements and a joint working plan in the areas of cosmetics and medical devices. . . .

• The FDA and the EC have also agreed to cooperate more closely in the peer review of validation studies of alternative methods to animal testing for cosmetics, which should contribute to reduce animal tests.

• The EC and the United States have underlined their commitment to intensify cooperation on chemicals. They will undertake an analysis of the potential impact of regulations on transatlantic trade in chemicals and chemical products and of how any such impacts might be reduced while maintaining a high level of protection of health and the environment. They will also encourage steps to ensure the transparency of the implementation of regulatory regimes. Working through the US Environmental Protection Agency and its EC counterparts, they will examine the means of increasing cooperation within the OECD with a view to accelerating work on key issues linked to regulation of chemical substances.

It is interesting to note which subjects of cooperation are addressed and which are not. Mention is made of risk assessment methodologies, cosmetics and animal testing, the joint OECD work on chemicals and the impacts of chemicals legislation on transatlantic trade as well as problems of implementation of regulatory regimes. Yet, convergence of chemicals legislation is nowhere to be found in these reports. Apparently, it is illusory to consider regulatory convergence with respect to REACH or GMO legislations.

For the time being the TEC work on chemicals has not produced tangible results. It remains to be seen whether regulatory cooperation will successfully be put into practice with respect to new legislative initiatives and existing legislations. Currently, there is still a wide gap between claim and reality in transatlantic economic integration.

3.2. *REACH and cosmetics: A new transatlantic trade war?*

The results of the second TEC meeting held on 13 May 2008 in Brussels contain two references with respect to the European REACH Regulation,[50] the registration of existing substances and the potential effects of the REACH obligations on animal testing and their relationship to the importation of cosmetic products:

- The EC will take concrete action to ensure that trade in cosmetics and personal care products is not disrupted by REACH implementation. The Commission will undertake the necessary steps within its competence, to ensure transparent implementation, legal certainty, and non-discriminatory trade.
- Cooperation between the US Food and Drug Administration (FDA) and the EC has been intensified in several areas which will facilitate transatlantic trade. These areas include: validation of alternative

---

[50]See Joint Statement of the EC and the United States Second Meeting of the Transatlantic Economic Council, 13 May 2008 to be found at: http://ec.europa.eu/enterprise/enterprise_policy/inter_rel/tec/index_en.htm (8 June 2008).

methods to animal testing for cosmetic ingredients, administrative simplification for medicinal products, and the provision of parallel scientific advice from FDA and the European Medicines Agency (EMEA) to veterinary manufacturers.

3.2.1.   *Registration of existing substances*

REACH requires the registration of substances manufactured or imported on their own or in preparations in quantities of one ton or more per chemical manufacturer or importer per year. Both new and old substances are subject to the registration requirement. Article 23 REACH provides for several transition periods to register so-called *phase-in substances*. These are defined in Article 3 (20) REACH as, inter alia, substances contained in the European Inventory of Existing Commercial Chemical Substances (EINECS).[51] Phase-in substances must first be pre-registered in accordance with Article 28 REACH and then registered by specific deadlines (November 2010, June 2013 and June 2018), depending mainly on the tonnage produced. Substances not contained in EINECS, instead, must be registered by 1 June 2008 at the latest (Articles 6 and 141 REACH); otherwise, they cannot be produced or marketed in the EU (Article 5 REACH). The US cosmetics industry[52] uses quite a number of substances not listed in the EINECS inventory. It claims that corresponding substances used for cosmetics in Europe have an EINECs

---

[51] See O.J. C 146 A of 15 January 1990 and the corrections to EINECS in O.J. C 54 of 1 March 2002 p. 8, as well as the reference to EINECS of the European Chemicals Bureau: http://ecb.jrc.it/esis/index.php?PGM=ein. (9 April 2008).

[52] See: http://www.perfumerflavorist.com/news/17462014.html. (10 April 2008). See also the 2008 National Trade Estimate Report on Foreign Trade Barriers, EU, which says at p. 17: "Another issue of concern relates to the treatment of imported cosmetics. REACH does not appear to provide producers of cosmetics imported into the EU the benefit of any transition period to register inputs, whereas comparable domestic products may benefit from a 3 year to 11 year transition period", available at: http://www.ustr.gov/Document_Library/Reports_Publications/2008/2008_NTE_Report/Section_Index.html. (10 April 2008). See also TABD Recommendations for Action by the Transatlantic Economic Council, dated 13 May 2008.

number and therefore benefit from the transition periods. The US cosmetics industry considers REACH to be discriminatory as US products have to be registered much earlier than the corresponding European products.

To solve this issue, the EU will have to decide whether it can accommodate the US request through flexible interpretation of the REACH provisions, which it seems prepared to do,[53] or not. In the latter case the United States. Will have to decide whether to bring a case against the EU in the WTO. It is not clear whether this is a real case of discrimination or whether the issue has arisen because US firms apply a different nomenclature to their substances than EU companies.

3.2.2. *REACH and animal tests*

The following hypothetical example should illustrate the divergences between REACH and the European cosmetics legislation with respect to animal tests and their potential impact on transatlantic trade. Suppose a famous fashion designer decides to introduce a new colour *lilac-red* for the 2010 summer collection. He consults a chemical company about the production of the lilac-red pigment. After a year-long research, the company can start the production of the new lilac-red pigment in early 2009 at a volume of more than 100 tons. The new pigment is widely used: it constitutes the basis for varnishes for plastic and other materials and, given its special characteristics, it is also used in dyes for textiles. It can also be used for cosmetics products, in particular lipsticks. The chemical company submits a registration dossier on lilac-red together with the necessary test data according to REACH. In its submissions, the company demonstrates the need to conduct animal

---

[53] According to ECHA, this confusion has arisen, in part, from the fact that US firms named their cosmetic ingredients in ways that differed from the International Union of Pure and Applied Chemistry (IUPC) approach accepted in the EU. ECHA director Geert Dancet has stressed that the EU wants to find a suitable solution to this, but still more work needs to be done to address the cosmetics industry's concerns. See: http://www.perfumerflavorist.com/news/17462014.html. (10 April 2008).

tests in accordance with Article 26 REACH in order to prove that the pigment can be used safely for all applications, in particular skin exposure. Suppose that a US cosmetic company now buys the pigment for use in its new lipstick *lilac-red* explicitly designed for the 2010 summer season. Can the lipstick be then exported to Europe?

Article 4a (b) of the European Cosmetics Directive[54] imposes a marketing ban on cosmetic products that contain ingredients that have been subject to animal testing. Article 4a (b) reads:

1. Without prejudice to the general obligations deriving from Article 2, Member States shall prohibit:
    (b) the marketing of cosmetic products containing ingredients or combination of ingredients which, in order to meet the requirements of this Directive, have been subject of animal testing using a method other than an alternative method after such alternative method has been validated and adopted at Community level with due regard to the development of validation within the OECD.

The marketing ban shall, in principle, be introduced after alternative test methods have been validated. However, Article 4a provides for two cut-off dates when the prohibition has to be applied definitively even if alternative test methods have not been developed and validated. These dates are March 2009 and March 2013, depending on the type of animal test that should be replaced by alternative test methods. In its report on the development of alternative test methods, the EC makes the following statements:[55]

The testing ban on finished cosmetic products applies since 11 September 2004, whereas the testing ban on ingredients or combination of

[54]Council Directive 76/768 EEC of 27 July 1976 on the approximation of the laws of the Member States relating to cosmetic products as amended by the European Parliament and Council Directive 2003/15 of 27 February 2003, O.J. L 66 of 11 March 2003 p. 26. A consolidated version of the Cosmetics Directive with all 54 amendments adopted to date can be found under: http://eurlex.europa.eu/LexUriServ/LexUriServ.do?uri=CONSLEG:1976L0768:20070919:EN:PDF. (5 April 2008).
[55]Report from the Commission to the Council and the European Parliament, Report on the Development, Validation and Legal Acceptance of Alternative Methods to Animal Tests in the Field of Cosmetics (2005), COM(2007) 232 of 3 May 2007.

ingredients will apply step by step as soon as alternative methods are validated and adopted, but with a maximum cut-off date of 6 years after entry into force of the Directive, that is, 11 March 2009, irrespective of the availability of alternative non-animal tests. The marketing ban will apply step by step as soon as alternative methods are validated and adopted in EU legislation with due regard to the OECD validation process. This marketing ban will be introduced at the latest 6 years after entry into force of the Directive, that is, 11 March 2009, for all human health effects with the exception of repeated-dose toxicity, reproductive toxicity and toxicokinetics. For these specific health effects, a deadline of 10 years after entry into force of the Directive is foreseen, that is 11 March 2013, irrespective of the availability of alternative non-animal tests.

Several discussions with industry, animal welfare organizations and other stakeholders showed that:

- chemicals are rarely tested on animals solely for their use as ingredients in cosmetics;
- the majority of animal tests are carried out for multiple uses by manufacturers of chemical substances (industry assumes that approximately 80–90% of cosmetic ingredients are tested for multiple uses).

There are currently four alternative in vitro methods in relation to two toxicological endpoints (skin corrosion and acute phototoxicity) listed in Annex V of Directive 67/548/EEC. These alternative test methods are currently the only legally accepted tests at Community level aimed at fully replacing animal tests for toxicological endpoints in the area of chemicals and cosmetic products. However, concerted activities on the development and validation of alternative approaches seem promising for meeting the 2009 deadline provided by Article 4(a) of the Cosmetics Directive. For the 2013 deadline, the situation is much more critical. The replacement of animal test methods by alternative methods in relation to complex toxicological endpoints remains scientifically difficult, despite the additional efforts launched at different levels.

The Commission's report shows that animal tests are normally conducted for multiple uses and that the validation of alternative test methods is not delivering the results that the European institutions had expected when adopting Article 4a of the Cosmetics Directive. It goes beyond the scope of this chapter to describe the many activities undertaken by the EU, OECD, ECVAM and other bodies on developing alternative methods to animal tests. Suffices it to say that the process of validating alternative test methods is complicated and burdensome and might not always lead to the desired results.[56] It remains to be seen whether the ban will in fact be imposed, even if alternative test methods have not been developed let alone validated by the cut-off dates imposed by the directive.

When registering a chemical substance under REACH, the manufacturer or importer must submit a registration dossier in compliance with the provisions of Article 10 of REACH, which lays down the information requirements for registration. Such a dossier requires toxicological data according to Annex VII point 8 of REACH, which, in principle, are obtained through animal tests. Articles 26 and 27 of REACH provide for information exchange and joint use of data obtained through animal tests; if such data do not exist however, the manufacturer of a substance must conduct animal tests.

The comparison between the Cosmetics Directive and REACH therefore leads to the conclusion that REACH mandates animal tests whilst the Cosmetics Directive prohibits them. Article 4a (b) goes even further and introduces a marketing ban on cosmetics whose ingredients have been tested on animals. Since the majority of animal tests are carried out for multiple uses and not for cosmetic purposes alone, the question arises whether the marketing ban of Article 4a (b) can be applied also to animal tests for multiple purposes. The REACH Regulation confirms in Article 2 paragraph 4 (b) that the restrictions of the Cosmetics Directive on testing substances in vertebrate animals continue to apply to substances used in cosmetic products.

One could argue that the wording contained in Article 4a (b) *in order to meet the requirements of this Directive* should result in a narrow interpretation excluding all data obtained through multiple purpose animal tests. Yet this interpretation has not been confirmed. It could even be considered as a circumvention of the ban imposed by the Cosmetics Directive as does Advocate General Geelhoudt in the

---

[56]A description of the situation can be found at the Alternatives to Animal Testing Website: http://altweb.jhsph.edu/regulations/cosmetics.htm. (5 April 2008). Further information can be found at: http://ec.europa.eu/enterprise/cosmetics/html/cosm_ animal_test_de.htm. (5 April 2008).

case French Republic versus European Parliament and Council of the EU (C 244/03). He says[57]:

> First, it seems clear that the ban on animal tests applies equally to tests performed for the purposes of complying with other legislation, in so far as substances that have been the subjects of such tests may not be used as or in a cosmetic products. This interpretation seems necessary for the *effet utile* of the Directive and is consistent with the intention expressed in the preparatory documents leading up to its adoption.
>
> ....
>
> Third, it follows equally from this wording that cosmetic products and ingredients subject to animal tests outside the community are subject to the marketing ban. Such tests would by their nature have been performed in order to meet public health requirements, thus falling within the prohibition.

In its judgment on the above mentioned case,[58] the European Court of Justice dismissed the action by France without addressing the scope of the marketing ban introduced by Article 4a (b). The Advocate General's opinion adds doubts to a broad interpretation of the ban however. Multiple purpose animal tests have the same goal as a specific animal test for cosmetics: health protection. The trigger of the marketing ban is the animal test and not the purpose for which it is conducted. On the other hand, a broad interpretation of the marketing ban could lead to incomprehensive results. That is, suppose an ingredient for a cosmetic product has been in use for many years; suppose that a chemical company has now discovered a new use for that ingredient but that it has some doubts about its toxicity; suppose further that the chemical company now prepares the REACH dossier for the new use of the substance and that the animal tests result in a finding of no toxicity. Would this new animal test now result in a marketing ban of the substance for the use in cosmetic products?

---

[57]Opinion of Advocate General Geelhoudt delivered 17 March 2005 in Case C-244/03 French Republic versus European Parliament and Council of the EU, cif. 82 and 84.

[58]See O.J. C 182 of 23 July 2005, p. 6.

In the transatlantic context, the European marketing ban is also of importance given that no such ban exists in the United States. The United States is also keen on developing and validating alternative test methods,[59] but is not as radical as the EU in its rejection of animal tests. The situation could therefore arise that an ingredient tested on animals in the United States could not be used in a cosmetic product destined for the European market.

The hypothetical cases highlight the danger of yet another transatlantic trade dispute. Again, transatlantic regulations differ so much that it seems impossible to find a common understanding. Creativity and flexibility from both sides will be necessary in order to come to a mutual understanding.[60] If and when alternative test are available and validated, the problem will be solved. It is evident that the two sides are not aiming at regulatory convergence but rather at avoiding a trade dispute.

3.3.   The Globally Harmonized System — Harmonization of classification and labeling of chemicals?

Annex I of the 2007 Framework for Advancing Transatlantic Economic Integration mentions cooperation on the Globally Harmonized

---

[59]See the presentation Framework for Alternative Test Methods in the US presented by Leonard Schechtman and William Stokes at the Conference on Alternative Methods to Animal Testing held in Brussels on 7 November 2005; to be found at: http://ec.europa.eu/enterprise/events/animal_tests/index_en.htm. (10 April 2008). See also the recently adopted tripartite Memorandum of Understanding between different US agencies on High Throughput Screening, Toxicity Pathway Profiling and Biological Interpretation of Findings. This new strategy aims to reduce reliance on animal testing. See: http://yosemite. epa.gov/opa/admpress.nsf/a883dc3da7094f97852572a00065d7d 8/35995a22ceb 67467852573f0006559de!OpenDocument. (10 April 2008).

[60]In its submission to TEC the TABD suggests: "In relation to alternatives to animal testing, the TEC should take stock of the outcome of the April 9–10 meeting of US and EU regulators and, as necessary, direct further actions in order to avoid overly restrictive or non-science-based approaches to alternative validation methods. See TABD submission note 51 above.

System of Classification and Labelling of Chemicals (GHS).[61] GHS is a global initiative to promote standard criteria for classifying chemicals according to their health, physical and environmental hazards. It was initiated in 1992 by the United Nations Conference on Environment and Development and negotiated under the auspices of the Interorganisation Programme for the Sound Management of Chemicals (IOMC). In 2002, the World Summit on Sustainable Development encouraged countries to implement GHS by 2008. GHS was formally adopted by the United Nations Committee of Experts on the Transport of Dangerous Goods and the Globally Harmonized System of Classification and Labelling of Chemicals in December 2002. In 2003, the adoption was endorsed by the Economic and Social Council of the United Nations.[62]

The GHS document consists of recommendations and an explanatory text and is not binding on UN members. Countries with existing legislation are supposed to adapt their legislation according to GHS and countries without legislation should use GHS as the basis for the any forthcoming legislation. GHS uses a building block approach. There is no requirement for countries to use all GHS classes and categories. Yet, for the categories covered in their legislation, countries are expected to comply with GHS. For example, a country could decide to adopt the physical hazard classifications with respect to occupational health and transportation but not with respect to consumer protection. The building block approach therefore allows for national differences and variations in the implementation of GHS,[63] thereby defeating the idea of harmonization. Exporters will have to comply with

---

[61] See note 47 above.

[62] For a description of GHS see: http://www.unece.org/trans/danger/publi/ghs/ghs_welcome_e.html. (10 April 2008). See also Globally Harmonised System of Classification and labelling of Chemicals, First Edition UN Doc. ST/SG/AC.10/30/Rev.1 United Nations New York and Geneva 2005 to be found at: http://www.unece.org / trans / danger / publi / ghs / ghs_rev01 / English / 00e_intro.pdf. (10 April 2008).

[63] For a description of the GHS building block approach with respect to the implementation of GHS for occupational health in the US see Federal Register Vol. 71 no. 176 of 12 September 2006 pp. 53621 et seq.

potentially diverging national legislations. Notwithstanding the building block approach, the UN document on GHS expresses the hope that the GHS implementation will result in harmonization:[64]

> Notwithstanding the fact that an exporter needs to comply with importing countries' requirements for GHS implementation, it is hoped that the application of the GHS worldwide will eventually lead to a fully harmonized situation.

In June 2007, the EC adopted a legislative proposal for the implementation of GHS in the EU.[65] The EU draft legislation follows the building block approach and does not fully translate GHS into EU law, selecting only those hazard classes and categories that are compatible with existing EU legislation.[66] It is expected that the proposal will be adopted by the end of 2008.

GHS will also be implemented in the United States. Key federal agencies with responsibility for regulatory and international affairs have formed an interagency committee to address GHS implementation issues. Participating agencies are: Consumer Product Safety Commission (CPSC), Department of Commerce, Department of State, Department of Transportation (DOT), Food and Drug Administration (FDA), Environmental Protection Agency (EPA), Occupational Safety and Health Administration (OSHA), Office of the US Trade Representative, Department of Agriculture and National Institute of Environmental Health Sciences.

---

[64]See UN doc., above note 61, part I, cif. 1.1.3.1.5.3.

[65]Proposal for a Regulation of The European Parliament and of the Council on classification, labelling and packaging of substances and mixtures, and amending Directive 67/548/EEC and Regulation (EC) No 1907/2006; COM (2007) 355 final of 27 June 2007. For a description of the legislative proposal see Andrew Fasey EU Proposal to Implement the GHS September 2007 at: http://www.chemicalspolicy.org/downloads/SummaryofGHS9-7-07.pdf. (10 April 2008).

[66]Fasey, above note 64, explains that the draft legislation takes up all GHS hazard classifications but does not include categories that are not part of the current EU system, i.e., flammable liquids category 4, acute toxicity category 5, skin corrosion/irritation category 3, aspiration hazard category 2, acute aquatic toxicity category 2, acute aquatic toxicity category 3. The EU proposal also maintains the current level of protection by including aspects currently in the EU system but not yet covered by GHS.

The building block approach of GHS is an invitation to the United States and to Europe to implement GHS differently so that exporters of chemicals on both sides of the Atlantic might yet again be faced with two systems. On the other hand, the TEC activities concerning GHS might provide an opportunity to arrive at a common transatlantic approach. GHS implementation will also be a test-case for both sides to comply with the guidelines on regulatory cooperation. It is not clear yet whether the cooperation on GHS will result in a convergence of national rules or not.

3.4. *Cooperation on chemicals within the OECD*

Expanding the cooperation regarding the OECD work on chemicals is part of the above mentioned Framework.[67] The two sides mention, inter alia, risk assessment, good laboratory practice, and test methods. These subjects are an integral part of the OECD's chemical program,[68] which covers an impressive range of chemical safety issues. The program's main objectives are:[69]

- to assist OECD member countries' efforts to protect human health and the environment through improving chemical safety,
- to make chemical control policies more transparent and efficient and save resources for government and industry,
- to prevent unnecessary distortions in trade of chemicals and chemical products.

The OECD work on chemicals offers a useful tool for regulatory cooperation. Cooperation on test methods, risk assessment and risk management could result in a convergence of chemical regulations. The OECD Guidelines for the testing of chemicals,[70] the principles on good

---

[67] Note 47 above.

[68] See: http://www.oecd.org/department/0,3355,en_2649_34365_1_1_1_1_1,00. html. (10 April 2008).

[69] See: http://www.oecd.org/about/0,3347,en_2649_34365_1_1_1_1_1,00.html. (18 April 2008).

[70] See: http://www.oecd.org/document/22/0,3343,en_2649_34377_1916054_1_ 1_1_1,00.html. (10 April 2008).

laboratory practice,[71] and the Decision on the Mutual Acceptance of Data[72] provide the basis for the acceptance of chemical test data that have been developed for regulatory purposes in one country by all other OECD countries. The OECD development and harmonization of risk assessment methods should help governments to arrive at comparable risk assessments,[73] which, in turn, form the basis for risk management decisions.

The core objective of the OECD's work on risk management[74] *is to support Member countries' efforts to develop national policies and actions, and, where appropriate, international risk management measures.* The work consists in the identification of best practices and new techniques for managing risks, the development of methodologies and even concrete joint action with respect to specific chemicals. Particularly worth mentioning is the OECD program on High Production Volume (HPV) chemicals,[75] as well as the HPV-Manual[76] for hazard assessment. In support of the HPV program, the chemical industry has adopted a voluntary initiative whose aim is to provide an internationally agreed data set and an initial hazard assessment on HPV chemicals.[77] Companies generate and collect the needed health and environment information for the specific HPV chemical. The data will be reported to the OECD and should provide a sound basis for the initial hazard assessment of the chemical and the appropriate actions to be taken as

---

[71]See: http://www.oecd.org/about/0,3347,en_2649_34381_1_1_1_1_37465,00.html (3 March .03.08).

[72]See: http://www.oecd.org/document/41/0,3343,en_2649_34377_1890473_1_1_1_1,00.html (3 March 2008).

[73]See: http://www.oecd.org/department/0,3355,en_2649_34375_1_1_1_1_1,00.html. (18 April 2008).

[74]See: http://www.oecd.org/about/0,3347,en_2649_34375_1_1_1_1_37465,00.html. (18 April 2008).

[75]For a detailed description of the HPV programme see: http://www.oecd.org/document/21/0,3343,en_2649_34373_1939669_1_1_1_1,00.html. (18 April 2008).

[76]See: http://www.oecd.org/document/7/0,3343,en_2649_34373_1947463_1_1_1,00.html (18 April 2008).

[77]See: http://www.icca-at-dubai.org/dbfiles/ICCAHPVChemicalsInitiative_2005.pdf. (18 April 2005).

a consequence thereof. The HPV programme provides for synergies with REACH: European producers and importers of HPV substances will have to comply with the REACH registration requirements but can, in principle, resort to the data set established within the OECD. The programme avoids duplication of efforts, thus minimizing costs for the industry and reducing the number of animal tests.

It is not quite clear what concrete results can be expected from expanded EU/US cooperation on chemicals within the OECD. For the time being, no publicly accessible document exists in which both sides explain what they expect from the process and how they will contribute towards fostering cooperation and reducing regulatory burdens. Even if there is agreement in principle on how to generate test data, there still is a transatlantic divide with respect to risk assessment and in particular risk management. Without convergence also in those areas, further economic integration remains an illusion.

4. Conclusions: How to Achieve a Barrier Free Transatlantic Market

Stronger transatlantic economic integration has been on the political agenda of the EU and the United States for more than 18 years now. Notwithstanding the many summit declarations and political commitments made by US Presidents, EC Presidents, and European Council Presidents, there is still a wide gap between claim and reality with respect to a truly barrier free transatlantic market. The positive initiatives adopted by the summits are brought to nought by the realities of legislation. For the two largest economic areas on this planet, not losing their regulatory autonomy still seems to take priority over achieving legislative convergence. This unsatisfactory situation can be demonstrated nowhere better than in the area of chemicals legislation. There the transatlantic regulatory divide has increased and not decreased over the last 18 years.

In order to remedy this unsatisfactory situation, two issues can be raised: first, how can a barrier free transatlantic market be achieved, and second, what institutional arrangements are necessary to achieve it?

As an answer to the first question two points can be made:

(a) regulatory cooperation *is about doing something better together* and should not be approached from a trade negotiator's point of view. One of the many problems with the lack of success in transatlantic regulatory cooperation is the question of balance and linkages. Do we have to have (real or felt) reciprocity or should both sides recognise regulatory cooperation as having value in itself. Whilst the business communities on both sides of the Atlantic have a clear position on this issue,[78] the governments are still in search of reciprocity and continuously fail to recognise the merits of the approach.

(b) regulatory cooperation should give new impetus to mutual recognition. The transatlantic market is not a single market with common institutions pushing for further economic integration. Since Parliaments on both sides of the Atlantic will continue to adopt divergent legislation, transatlantic regulatory cooperation should bring about a comparability of legislation that enables mutual recognition. Legislation need not be identical, but only comparable in effectiveness so that the old TABD motto "approved once, accepted everywhere" can be applied.

Let us use the example of cooperation regarding the safety of nanomaterials identified in the above mentioned framework[79] to demonstrate how regulatory cooperation should work ideally. For the time being, both sides are studying the regulatory challenges regarding the safety of nanomaterials and work within the OECD on the implications for the safety of human health and the environment of the use of nanomaterials, focusing in particular on testing and assessment

---

[78]The 2008 brochure 'Unleashing Our Economic Potential, A Primer on the Transatlantic Economic Council' written by the US Chamber of Commerce and Businesseurope, on the occasion of the second TEC meeting states at p. 6: "Regulatory Cooperation is not trade negotiation. The political trade-offs that plague trade negotiations should not exist in regulatory cooperation. It is about doing something better together."

[79]See note 47 above.

methods.[80] If, as a result of this work, legislation was envisaged, both sides should work towards mutual recognition. In other words the regulations should provide that a nanomaterial fulfilling the requirements under US law would automatically be considered as fulfilling the requirements of European law with the consequence that it could be marketed in Europe without having to comply with any further requirements. Such mutual recognition would however only be possible if the regulations were comparable in effectiveness.

The answer to the second question is more difficult. The 2007 summit did not propose an institutional overhaul by adopting a binding framework for regulatory cooperation. Rather, it relied on the existing informal institutional architecture entrusting the Transatlantic Economic Council with the realization of the set objectives.

The TEC is exposed to a legislative reality that is quite different from the ideal situation described above. Normally, each side initiates and adopts legislation which, if divergent, excludes mutual recognition. In such a case, in order to succeed, the TEC should be in a position to intervene when the administrations are in the early phase of drafting legislation. Unfortunately, the administrations responsible for the drafting of legislation do not normally take into account the goal of transatlantic economic integration. It would already be a step forward if the TEC could convince them to comply rigorously with the 2002 guidelines on regulatory cooperation. Moreover, the announced TEC agreement regarding the contribution of impact assessment to reducing barriers to transatlantic economic integration will also promote closer cooperation,[81] since it will force the drafters of legislation to take the transatlantic situation into account.

---

[80]For an overview of the OECD work on nanomaterials see: http://www. oecd.org/about/0,3347,en_2649_37015404_1_1_1_1_37465,00.html (18 April 2008).

[81]The document on impact assessment is supposed to be finalised at the meeting of the EU–US High-Level Regulatory Cooperation Forum to be held on 25 April 2008 in Brussels. See: http://ec.europa.eu/governance/better_regulation/impact_en.htm#_ EU_US. (20 April 2008).

A barrier free transatlantic market also faces resistance from Parliaments on both sides of the Atlantic. It is true that, in the *Transatlantic Policy Network (TPN)*,[82] individual parliamentarians advocate the creation of a transatlantic single market in an exemplary manner and have repeatedly been the authors of positive transatlantic parliamentary resolutions.[83] Yet, these positive initiatives are brought to nought whenever new legislative acts are discussed and adopted. The legislators do not strive towards transatlantic comparability of legislation, nor are they bound to the guidelines on regulatory cooperation. From an institutional point of view, legislators should be better involved in the process of transatlantic cooperation. In fact, if the legislators are not convinced that the law they adopt must be comparable to the one on the other side of the Atlantic, no convergence will be achieved. The decision by the 2007 summit to give legislators a mere advisory role as it was given to business and consumers was a wrong signal.[84]

Notwithstanding these weaknesses, the Transatlantic Economic Council can play an important role towards achieving a barrier free transatlantic market if it is able to deliver results. By resolving actual transatlantic conflicts, the TEC will win the confidence of the legislators necessary to promote the broader agenda of economic integration. The TEC must be aware though that it cannot limit itself to the role of a transatlantic fire brigade; instead it must foster economic integration. For example, the TEC could use its influence to transform a future

[82] See: http://www.tpnonline.org/. See also the remarkable TPN Report, 'Completing the Transatlantic Market' of February 2007.

[83] See Resolution of the European Parliament on Transatlantic Relations dated 25 April 2007, to be found at: http://www.europarl.europa.eu/sides/getDoc.do?type=TA&reference=P6-TA-2007-0155&language=DE.

[84] "The Summit Leaders have asked the TEC to convene a Group of Advisers, consisting of the Co-chairs of the three existing dialogues (the Transatlantic Legislators Dialogue, the Trans Atlantic Consumer Dialogue and the Transatlantic Business Dialogue. See EC TEC webpage: http://ec.europa.eu/enterprise/enterprise_policy/inter_rel/tec/index_en.htm. (18 April 2008).

unilateral legislative initiative into a pilot-project for regulatory convergence. If the political leaders were to support such an initiative and the two sides indeed adopted comparable legislation, a breakthrough would be achieved. The success would serve as a catalyst for regulatory cooperation even on issues on which the transatlantic divide is huge, for example chemicals legislation. In such a case, what seems an illusion today could result in real economic integration tomorrow.

Chapter 9

Transatlantic Regulatory Cooperation on Accounting Standards: A 'Varieties of Capitalism' Perspective

Andreas Nölke

Johann Wolfgang Goethe Universität
Frankfurt am Main and Amsterdam Research Center
for Corporate Governance Regulation
a.noelke@soz.uni-frankfurt.de

1. The Puzzle: Successful Transatlantic Regulatory Cooperation on Accounting Standards

In the context of the debate about the advances and difficulties of transatlantic regulatory cooperation, accounting standards clearly qualify as one of the few cases where this cooperation has been feasible. On 15 November 2007, the US Securities and Exchange Commission (SEC) approved rule amendments under which financial statements from foreign private issuers in the United States will be accepted without reconciliation to US Generally Accepted Accounting Principles (GAAP), if they are prepared using International Financial Reporting Standards (IFRS) as issued by the International Accounting Standards Board (IASB). Moreover, the SEC is even considering giving US domestic issuers the same option that foreign issuers now have, i.e., to use either IFRS or US GAAP. Although the SEC has issued a statement in February 2010 that more time might be necessary for making an informed decision on this issue — no doubt a consequence of the financial crisis — many observers assume that the US will adopt in the not-too-distant future, even if the original 2011 deadline is not met. If compared with the long-standing transatlantic quarrels about different types of accounting standards, most notably between rules-based US-GAAP and principles-based IFRS, the recent steps towards regulatory convergence are quite surprising. Even more surprising is the willingness of the US authorities to accept other standards as equivalent to US GAAP, given their long-standing belief in the superior quality of US financial reporting regulations. Moreover, taking into account that the main constituency of IASB standards is the EU, this outcome appears to be very different from the regulatory competition between the EU and the United States in other issue areas.

This chapter contributes to solving this puzzle. Its core argument is that this convergence cannot primarily be attributed to the willingness of the SEC to adapt to EU standards, but rather to the previous convergence of the EU on an Anglo-Saxon accounting regulation model, both with regard to the content and mode of regulation. "Content of regulation" refers to the substantial impact of accounting standards — how do they impinge on economic activity, which actors and activities are favored? "Mode of regulation" refers to the institutional set-up of the development of accounting standards — who is formulating these standards, which actors are involved? Needless to say, content and mode of regulation are strongly inter-related, since standards usually work to the favor of those actors that are most closely involved in their formulation.

In order to support the argument about the convergence on the US model, the paper adopts a "Varieties of Capitalism"-perspective, in particular regarding the distinction between "Liberal Market Economies/LME" and "Coordinated Market Economies/CME," with the first "Anglo-Saxon" model usually illustrated with the case of the United States and the latter "Rhenish" model with Germany. From this perspective, the core question is not whether an accounting standard is rules- or principles-based, but rather what kind of regulatory approach is being followed and what kind of substantial impact changing accounting standards are having. Seen from this perspective, the recent convergence has been made possible by the IASB (and its predecessor IASC) following LME accounting principles, in particular the lead of the FASB in moving from historic-cost to fair value-accounting for some core accounting standards.

As regards the mode of regulation, we need to distinguish between an Anglo-Saxon tradition of regulation by private expertise and a Continental European tradition of regulation by public authorities. Whereas Anglo-American actors favor a model based on private expertise, European Continental voices called for a body composed of nationally delegated (public) actors. Again, convergence has been made possible by the EU adapting a private-expert-based mode of regulation, in contrast to the previous regulation by public authorities.

Together, these developments shift the prime line of contestation from the Transatlantic to the Inner-European space. While British companies and major European multinationals find it easy to adapt to IFRS (and to standard-setting by the IASB), Continental small- and medium-scale enterprises face far more serious problems. Moreover, the latter are lacking access to the experts of the IASB. This, of course, raises a new puzzle, as far as it has to be established why these actors were not able to prevent the shift in both content and mode of regulation. Based on recent studies on the rise of the IASB towards global standard-setter, I am highlighting the role of a number of crucial actors in this process, including the IASC/IASB itself, the proactive role of the United States (SEC), the pressures by major European multinationals, the Commission's preference for a common EU approach, and the limited ability and willingness of some German actors (including the government and the "Mittelstand" Small and Medium Scaled Enterprises (SME)) to defend the Continental model.

Convergence in accounting regulation is not an isolated phenomenon. Also, in the fields of banking-regulation and competition policy, the EU has recently moved to more Anglo-Saxon regulation models, thereby creating problems for Continental SMEs (and the CME model in general), but allowing for much easier transatlantic regulatory cooperation. This raises the question whether the emerging transatlantic consensus might also serve as a blueprint for global regulatory harmonization. So far, not much is known about the

participation of Southern actors in these transnational private governance institutions. However, first studies indicate a still open development, with some actors opposing Western standards, while other actors
increasingly emulate those codes, because of their desire to mobilize
resources on the London and New York financial markets.

2.   Convergence in Substantial Terms: A Variety of Capitalism Perspective on Accounting Standards

Many observers still highlight the differences between IASB accounting standards and US GAAP. IASB standards are principles-based,
whereas US-standards are rule-based. This means that IASB norms
provide some quite general guidelines, whereas GAAP regulate very
specific issues. To be sure, US GAAP and IFRS look very different
with the very detailed US rules being far more voluminous than IFRS.
Moreover, these differences can cause significant difficulty and result in
substantial costs when companies have to prepare two sets of accounts.
However, these differences rather relate to the form of accounting standards and less to their substantial content. Of course, there are many
differences in substantial content if individual IASB and US GAAP
standards are being compared. Still, looking at these individual differences between EU and US regulations is of limited use. Instead,
we should rather look more broadly and try to identify fundamental differences between the two collections of accounting standards.
To do so, we have to put those standards into their broader socio-
economic context. The "Varieties of Capitalism" (VoC) approach provides us with a conceptual framework that is able to make sense of this
context.

The VoC approach has become "canonical" among students of the
comparative economic sociology of Western societies (Blyth, 2003,
p. 215). Pioneered by scholars such as Shonfield (1965) and popu-
larized by Albert (1993), the volume compiled by Hall and Soskice
(2001a) has become a landmark for this research field. The idea that the
basic institutions of capitalism differ from one country to another and

that these differences are not by accident, but are linked by strong institutional complementarities, has led to a very sophisticated and holistic, but still easily understandable picture of the institutional complexity of advanced capitalism(s). Many empirical studies depart from the juxtaposition of Liberal Market Economies (LME) — typically represented by the United States — and Coordinated Market Economies (CME), with Germany as a leading example. Although there are a number of alternatives (e.g., Crouch and Streeck (1997); Whitley (1999); Coates (2000); Amable (2003); and Schmidt (2003)), most authors still prefer to depart from the juxtaposition of the ideal types of Coordinated Market Economies and Liberal Market Economies. Besides offering a rather balanced and comprehensive framework, one of the most important advantages of this typology is its parsimony (Jackson and Deeg, 2006, pp. 31–32). While the two ideal types clearly are unable to give full justice to the intricacies of, e.g., British, French, or Italian capitalism, they still grasp the most important differences between "Anglo-Saxon" and "Rhenish" economies. While the United States and the United Kingdom (and some new EU Member States such as Estonia) lend towards the LME model, most Continental Member States rather share similarities with the CME model.

The main theoretical task of the CME/LME juxtaposition is to explain the marked differences in the competitive advantages of advanced capitalist economies. These advantages are most easily demonstrated if we focus on the different types of innovation processes that are central to the two production systems (Hall and Soskice, 2001b, pp. 38–44). CMEs have a premium on incremental innovation, which is particularly important for the production of capital goods such as machine tools and company equipment, consumer durables, engines, and specialized transport equipment, where "… the problem is to maintain the high quality of an established product line, to devise incremental improvements to it that attract consumer loyalty, and to secure continuous improvements in the production process in order to improve quality control and hold down costs …." Ibid, p. 39). LMEs, in contrast, focus on radical innovation, which is important in fast-moving technology sectors (e.g., biotechnology or software development), and in the provision of complex system-based products and services (e.g., telecommunication or defense systems).

The basic hypothesis of the VoC approach is that the inherent institutional complementarities of the two different types of market economies are able to explain these specific innovation patterns. Furthermore, each element of the two ideal types has strong institutional complementarities with other elements of the same model, and differs clearly from the functional equivalent of the other model. Usually, five interdependent elements can be highlighted (Hall and Soskice, 2001b, pp. 17–33; Jackson and Deeg, 2006, pp. 11–20), namely: (1) the financial system, i.e., the primary means to raise investments; (2) corporate governance, i.e., the internal structure of the firm; (3) the pattern of industrial relations; (4) the education and training system; and (5) the preferred mode for the transfer of innovations within the economy. The first three are most relevant for the study of accounting standards:

(1) The primary means of raising capital for investment in the LME system are bonds and equities to be issued on international capital markets. In CMEs, domestic bank lending plays a much bigger role, together with retained earnings. The two different modes of corporate finance clearly differ regarding the importance of current returns and of publicly available information. Companies in LME economies are strongly dependent on publicly available information and on current earnings for their terms of investments. Dispersed and rather fluid investors need this information in order to value the quality of bonds and shares. In CMEs, the importance of balance-sheet criteria is less prominent, since investors have alternative sources of information, either as owners (family enterprises or concentrated capital) or based on long-term business (banking) relationships, together with diverse channels for reputational monitoring such as business associations.

(2) Correspondingly, the corporate governance systems in the two models differ starkly. The LME model focuses on outsider control by dispersed owners, based on active markets for corporate control (mergers and acquisitions, including hostile takeovers). Managers enjoy a considerable freedom of maneuver, being controlled via incentives

that are strongly geared towards share prices, e.g., via share options. The CME model, in contrast, has rather strong disincentives for hostile takeovers, and is primarily based on insider control by major shareholders (blockholders). Managers have to achieve the consensus of their supervisory boards for major decisions and therefore have to involve blockholders and representatives of workers.

(3) Generally, the relationship between business and labor is far more consensual within the CME model, based on a corporatist system of industrial relations including industry-level wage bargaining and powerful company-level works councils (or even worker representation in supervisory boards as in the German "Mitbestimmung"). This is a necessity for production strategies that are based on continuous improvements in product lines and production processes, based on highly skilled labor. Management needs motivated labor to keep productivity high, whereas labor needs protection against lay-offs to invest into company-specific skills. The LME pattern of industrial relations, in contrast, relies heavily on the market as a coordinating mechanism. Management has full autonomy to hire and fire, based on highly fluid labor markets. Staff, in return, have few incentives to invest in company-specific skills, and instead focus on general skills, transferable across firms.

In each model, accounting standards have specific complementarities with other institutions, in particular in the fields of corporate finance and corporate governance. Accounting information plays a very central role within Liberal Market Economies, where investors are usually outsiders and companies mobilize most of their resources on the financial markets. Here, publicly available accounting information is crucial to the investment decisions of financial market actors. These standards are written on the premise that their key purpose is to provide capital market investors with "decision-relevant" information.

Also in Coordinated Market Economies, accounting standards are an integral part of this particular variety of capitalism. Thus, the rather conservative, creditor-oriented accounting standards in Germany (contained in the "Handelsgesetzbuch"/HGB) have complemented the strong role of the German banks during the development of the CME variety of capitalism in which the HGB was designed. For example, the German accounting standards, which enable the building of substantial "hidden" reserves by German companies, should be seen as an expression of the priority that German banks gave to ensuring the safety of their long-term lending to enterprises. Moreover, "Hausbanken" may be considered as "insiders" to the firm within the Rhenish model — for example they are represented on the advisory board. Because of this, Hausbanken and other block-holders have alternative ways, besides statutory accounts, of gathering information about the internal workings and performance of the firms in which they invest. There is therefore somewhat limited attention given to accounting standards and publicly available accounting information within CMEs. Rather than accounting statements being used to judge the performance of firms, their main purpose in the CME model is to provide prudent valuation of separable assets to reassure bankers that there is sufficient collateral to support their loans. At the same time, these conservative accounting standards allow CME to follow long-term strategies such as investing heavily in human resource development. This has been crucial for maintaining the CME competitive advantage of using highly skilled labor to produce high quality, and often specialized, products.

As far as the substance of accounting standards is concerned, the IASB clearly leans toward the LME model. A telling example is the recent move from historic cost to fair value accounting for a number of important standards (Perry and Nölke, 2006). Historic cost accounting, the traditional approach within most Continental accounting systems, values assets at the cost of acquisition whereas fair value accounting uses current market prices (if no such market exists, a model is used to arrive at a simulated market price). The move from historic cost to fair value is supposed to reduce the discretion of management in valuing assets, especially for assets with active markets. Under fair value-accounting (FVA), the re-evaluation of an asset's worth is an almost continuous process. As such, the current use of the asset has to be regularly justified in terms of its current market value. FVA therefore gives external forces (i.e., influential financial market actors) more leverage with which to set the parameters for economic decision making within the firm, a practice that is in line with the corporate governance relationship between shareholders and managers in the LME variety of capitalism. Correspondingly, the introduction of standards based on fair value accounting techniques — as initiated by the US FASB — is very much in line with basic features of the Anglo-Saxon model, since it is assumed to improve the information basis for capital-market actors. Correspondingly, the recent willingness of the SEC to accept accounts prepared by using IFRS is hardly surprising.

The introduction of FVA standards via the IASB, however, hardly complements the established institutions of the CME model (Perry and Nölke, 2006; Nölke and Perry, 2007a, 2007b). The new financial market-oriented standards make it far more difficult for management to smooth out crises, e.g., by hiding reserves. Instead, these standards increase pressures for maximizing short-term returns upon the assets of a company, measured against international benchmarks. At the same time they increase the earnings volatility as represented in the books, due to their orientation on the fluctuation of current market prices (Ball, 2004, p. 125). Long-term (human resource) investments thus become more difficult to pursue, thereby increasing tensions with labor and demotivating workers to invest into their skills. In defining what constitutes a profitable use, shareholders are likely to adopt a much shorter-term perspective than managers, so that IASB standards can be expected to make conservative (CME) financial planning rather more difficult, and thereby serve to discourage the longer-term business strategies that depend upon it. At the same time, it might put considerable strain on the relationship between management and other stakeholders, since hidden reserves were an expedient option to smooth out good and bad years, thereby avoiding lay-offs and other measures that might create conflicts with workers.

In sum, the recent transatlantic convergence in the field of accounting standards can at least in part be explained by the fact that the EU has implemented a set of standards that — in terms of substance — is very close to the US model. This EU move towards LME-style norms is somewhat surprising because of the tensions between IASB accounting standards and the socio-economic models of the majority of EU member states.

3. Convergence in Institutional Terms: From National Representation to the Rule of Experts

Not only in terms of the substance of accounting standards, but also as regards the institutional mode of the standard-setting institutions, the IASB has moved closely to Angelo-Saxon models. Here we can juxtapose a Continental European and an Anglo-Saxon institutional mode of accounting standard setting. The Anglo-Saxon mode, as exemplified by the US FASB, is based on private professional expertise, whereas the European mode relies on national representation and an important role for public actors. These competing models led to a major confrontation between the SEC and the Commission over the constitution of the IASB (Martinez-Diaz, 2005, p. 19). In the end, the IASB has moved clearly towards a US model, as demonstrated by an institutional analysis of the 2000 and 2005 constitutional changes within the IASB (Botzem, 2007). From this perspective, the 2000 constitutional reform of the IASB was based on the blueprint of an Anglo-American approach towards self-regulation, strongly resembling the US FASB. Furthermore, it replaces a part-time decision-making body that was geared towards representation of the different strands of the profession with an expert-driven organization that is only open to those with the necessary analytical resources, particularly those with experience within one of the Big Four auditing firms. Finally, the revised institutional set-up of the IASB Board of Trustees effectively shields the IASB technical experts from undue external (political) influence. Thus, not only is the content of IASB accounting standards familiar to the SEC, but also the general mode of standard-setting. Again, this contributes to explaining why the SEC has been willing to accommodate IFRS.

Moreover, content and mode of regulation are linked. Regulatory authority works best for those that are prominently represented in its institutions. In the case of accounting standards, both IASB and FASB are working in favor of capital market investors and those (major) companies that cater for investor preferences. A formal analysis of the network involving the various IASB bodies as well as EFRAG (European Financial Reporting Advisory Group, a body that is advising the EU upon the adoption of IFRS) and of the IASB comment-letter process demonstrates this observation most clearly (Perry and Nölke, 2005). The IASB publishes drafts of its proposed accounting standards as well as other programmatic documents on its homepage, usually for 90 days. During this period, everyone can submit a comment-letter that will be published on the IASB site and will be taken as an input in the deliberative process within the IASB committee network. An analysis of all comment letters between 1 April 2002 and 5 August 2004 — a total of 1910 letters written by 900 organizations and individuals — demonstrates a clear pattern of representation: The most prominent group of actors is the Big Four accounting firms. More generally, the comment-letter process is dominated by corporations from the financial sector, whereas non-financial corporations play a minor role. The only active international organization is IOSCO, and other social groups such as labor do not participate at all. A similar picture evolves from a network analysis of IASB/EFRAG committee memberships. Again, the Big Four occupy the most central positions, accompanied by a disproportionate influence of financial sector actors and the complete absence of broad social constituencies such as labor. In terms of nationality, organizations with a background in the United Kingdom are most prominently represented, amplified by the predominantly Anglo-Saxon character of the Big Four. These observations are also broadly in line with other recent studies on the decision-making within the IASB. Other authors highlight the dominance of representatives from Anglo-Saxon countries (Botzem, 2008) and of international organizations that are close to the preferences held by these representatives (Dewing and Russell, 2007).

4. The Politics of Transatlantic Convergence on a US Regulatory Model

Given that both the content and mode of accounting-standard setting by the IASB has become very close to the Anglo-Saxon model, it is comparatively easy for the SEC to accept IFRS as equivalent to US GAAP. At the same time, these findings pose a new puzzle, namely why the EU has settled for an Anglo-Saxon model of accounting standard setting in the first place, i.e., why it has chosen the private standard-setter IASB with its preferences for LME-type accounting standards, in spite of the potentially detrimental effects on its CME-type member state economies. In order to address this question, we can draw on numerous studies that cover the history of the rise of the IASC/IASB towards its current status as global accounting-standard setter.

A number of authors have highlighted the institutional entre-preneurship of the IASC/IASB itself. In 1973, the IASC was formed in the context of British accession to the EU. British accounting bodies were afraid that accession would lead to a transfer of continental stan-dards into the United Kingdom (Hopwood, 1994, p. 243). While this development did not materialize (the EU accounting directives became a mixture of British and German features, Katsikas, 2008, p. 137), the IASC still gradually strengthened its position, most notably by con-cluding agreements with institutional partners (Martinez-Diaz, 2005). These partners include the International Federation of Accountants (IFAC) (1982), the International Organization of Securities Commis-sions (IOSCO) (1995) as well as the members of the Financial Stability Forum. The endorsement by IOSCO and, later, by other international organizations such as the World Bank and the IMF were crucial steps in the rise of the IASB towards a nearly global standard-setter (Martinez-Diaz, 2005). For these IOs, the empowerment of the IASB proved to be an effective way of reaching their regulatory targets. This was oth-erwise not feasible, as indicated by several attempts on the side of the EU and the United Nations, starting in the 1970s.

Two other key players in the process leading to the empowerment of the IASC/IASB were the SEC and the EU. While the EU sealed this process by its endorsement of IASB standards as a formal require-ment for listed European companies, it was the SEC that had a major influence on the early structures and procedures of the IASC/IASB (Martinez-Diaz, 2005; and Katsikas, 2008). Against suggestions that the reformed and renamed IASB should be based on equal represen-tation by its most important constituencies on a geographical basis, it has been modeled according to the US FASB, based on independence and technical skills. Following several failed intergovernmental efforts to harmonize EU accounting standards, the European Commission

(EC) decided to adopt IASB standards for all exchange-listed corporations in the EU from 2005 onwards. Although not all officials were entirely happy with the US blueprint for the work of the IASB, the EU was nervous that more and more European corporations would follow the lead of Daimler-Benz and shift to US GAAP because the adoption of these standards are a basic pre-condition for being listed on the US stock exchange (Katsikas, 2008, p. 154). In order not to become a pure regulation-taker, the EC rather preferred to adopt IASB, and to retain a minimal influence (Dewing and Russell, 2004, pp. 293–94). Moreover, in spite of opposition by EC officials in charge of accounting regulation (Van Hulle 1993), the endorsement of an accounting institution dominated by Anglo-Saxon models fit quite well with the more general goal of the Lisbon-Strategy of modernizing the European economy along LME principles.

Correspondingly, it is not by chance that the privatization of certain facets of EU business regulation has gained ground through a rather depoliticized, professions-based interest constellation that hides the highly political character of these changes (Dewing and Russell, 2004, p. 300). It should not be a surprise that attempts by the EU to introduce Anglo-Saxon business standards in the form of public regulations, such as the European Works Council Directive, the European Company Statute Directive and the 13th Takeover Directive, have led to somewhat uneasy compromises, given the high visibility of these issues and the corresponding political controversy (Cernat, 2004). In contrast, the private governance-based regulations discussed in this chapter have led to a clear decision in favor of the Anglo-Saxon model. Not only is there a strong affinity between these coordination service firms and the workings of LMEs, but private governance also tends to hide its political and distributive consequences behind a veil of professionalism and technocracy (Perry and Nölke, 2006). While more explicit political attacks on the basic institutions of CME capitalism are not (yet) feasible, the utilization of private actors in EU regulation provides an excellent opportunity for the long-term erosion of these institutions. Thus, the choice of the level of regulation — inter-governmental, trans-governmental or private — can be decisive (Pollack and Shaffer, 2001).

However, the choices of actors such as the SEC and EU can only be understood against the more structural backdrop of developments in the financial markets. Without the increasing importance of cross-border listings and capital markets for corporate finance, the impetus for international harmonization of accounting standards would have been much more limited. Traditionally, accounting standards were developed on the national level, under the supervision of national governments. However, international economic integration and the LME-led disintermediation of finance have led to increasing demands for the harmonization of national standards. The assessment of the quality of bonds and stocks traded on international capital markets crucially relies on accounting information. That is, international financial investors not only need transparent company accounts in order to make their resource allocations on a sound basis, but also standardization of such information in order to compare their investment options in different countries without major difficulties. Correspondingly, one of the major driving forces that have supported the harmonization of accounting standards in general and the introduction of IASB standards in particular were mobile trans-border capital investors, most prominently those of Anglo-Saxon origin.

Closely linked to changes in global financial markets and the increasing importance of these investors is the rising prominence of the "symbolic analysts" that provide and interpret specialized information for capital market investors. Thus, the harmonization of accounting standards provides accounting companies with even greater scale advantages in capturing those national markets that so far were regulated by domestic standards (Nölke and Perry, 2007a). At the same time, the harmonization of accounting standards was utterly necessary to preserve the legitimacy of the profession. It increasingly became obvious that different (national) accounting standards lead to dramatically different results for the same company, as was demonstrated when Daimler prepared its accounts not only according to HGB standards, but also to US GAAP in order to become listed on the New York Stock Exchanges (Ball, 2004). The dramatically different outcomes of these two validations tended to undermine the authority of the accounting industry. Given that the most important customers of accounting companies are capital market actors, it is hardly a surprise that these companies plead for a harmonization on the basis of LME-type accounting standards. Based on their strongly increasing resource base, the Big Four and other accounting firms increasingly replace the professions as main accounting representatives within the standard-setting institutions (Botzem, 2008; Dewing and Russell, 2007).

Finally, the shift towards LME-style accounting standards can only be explained against the backdrop of a rather weak and divided opposition. Again, we have to reflect upon the peculiarities of transnational private governance, if compared with, e.g., inter-governmental regulation. Thus we have to take account of the different ability and willingness of different constituencies to mobilize the resources necessary to meaningfully participate in these governance arrangements. Arguably, the choice for transnational private governance in place of public inter-governmental regulation has made it much more difficult for Small and Medium-Scaled Enterprises (SME), the typical representatives of Rhenish capitalism, to influence the outcome of international accounting-standard setting. This move has not only eliminated the veto option for German legislators (and the social constituencies that may mobilize these legislators), but has also weakened the participation by domestic German business interests, if compared to other business interests that are organized on the transnational level. Given the long tradition of close quasi-corporatist interactions among German business, labor, and government, many of these groups strongly rely on the national avenue of interest association for international negotiations. Correspondingly, they are less prepared for the participation in transnational networks, as inter alia indicated the ad hoc formation of an "accounting standard pressure group" funded by a number of major German "Mittelstand" companies in 2006. While it is particularly difficult for the dispersed Rhenish SMEs to mobilize the necessary resources to meaningfully participate in transnational networks, multinational companies with a background in pluralist (Anglo-Saxon) settings, in contrast, find it particularly easy to mobilize these resources. Furthermore, financial sector companies in general, and the Big Four in particular, usually control those analytical resources that are most highly valued in debates about accounting standards. After all, the membership in IASB networks is formally based on the expert knowledge of the representative.

Recently, however, a serious threat to the IASB has emerged in the form of opposition in the European Parliament and some EU member states, who have repeatedly expressed their concern about the lack of democratic legitimacy of EU accounting standard-setting process (Perry and Nölke, 2007b). This has, inter alia, lead to the establishment of a new advisory body, the Standards Advice Review Group (SARG), and to an EC study on IASB governance and funding (both launched in Spring 2007). At the same time, the European Parliament's Economic and Monetary Affairs Committee has forced the EC to conduct additional investigations into the likely impact of a new accounting standard (IFRS 8), by threatening to block its adoption under a new procedure that entitles the parliament to a veto right on such issues. Moreover, it has published a working paper on IFRS and the governance of the IASB with the title "IFRS tested, IASB failed," also in Spring 2007. This document contains strongly-worded statements arguing that the IASB is not transparent and not subject to sufficient democratic control.

At the same time, we have seen an increasing mobilization on the domestic level in Germany. The focus of German protests was the IASB plan to extend its reach from listed companies to SMEs, and thereby to the heart of the Rhenish CME model. Even the powerful German Industry Association (BDI) expressed serious concerns over the direction the IASB was taking and highlighted the lack of SME representation within IASB decision-making bodies. In contrast to previous protests, this increasing mobilization against the IASB has not remained without political repercussions. In April 2007 a delegation of the IASB, led by its chairman Sir David Tweedie, came especially to Germany in order to discuss options on how to resolve the Mittelstand problems with IAS. In July 2007, the EU's Ministers of Finance condemned the undemocratic operating procedures of the IASB and demanded a comprehensive assessment of the economic consequences of both existing and upcoming standards. In September 2007, EC Commissioner McCreevy finally declared that the EU has no intention to make SME-IFRS obligatory for European small- and medium-sized enterprises, even before the comment-letter phase expired by 1 October.

It is not only the European Parliament — led by the conservative fraction — that has massively criticized the work of the IASB. Within the German Bundestag, some factions have openly protested against the London-based organization, including the liberal party (FDP), the socialist party (Die Linke), and the green party (Bündnis 90/Die Grünen). Somewhat ironically, the stand-off between the German Mittelstand and the IASB thus brings together a quite heterogeneous coalition that has Bavarian conservatives and other representatives of German industrial elites on the one side and both the Socialist and Green parties on the other: these two groups are usually found at opposite sides of the political spectrum, certainly on economic issues. Now, however, both are united in their defense of traditional Rhenish economic structures against what they see as increasing pressure exerted by transnational financial market actors. However, given the insular institutional design of the IASB, it remains to be seen whether even this massive political mobilization within one of the most powerful EU member states, together with increasing activism by the European Parliament, the European Commission, and the Council of Finance Ministers, will be able to influence the substantive content of the IASB standards concerned.

5. The Broader Picture: Towards Global Convergence on the Liberal Regulatory Model?

From a VoC perspective, accounting regulation is not an isolated incident. We are able to identify similar developments — shifts from CME towards LME regulation in the EU and, correspondingly, improved perspectives for transatlantic regulatory cooperation — in competition policy (Wigger and Nölke, 2007) and banking regulation (Nölke and Perry, 2007a).

Private enforcement of competition policy has been made possible by a recent EU decision, thereby threatening to create major difficulties for the CMEs within the Union. The main issue at stake here is the legal environment for inter-company cooperation, a crucial mechanism for the spreading of innovations within CME economies. The shift from public regulation (by decisions of the EC) to private regulation (by law firms bringing selected cases to the court) is creating legal insecurity for inter-company cooperation and, more generally, tends to disfavor the SMEs that form the backbone of Rhenish capitalism. Although competition policy is only loosely regulated at the global level, the recent EU shift from the CME towards the LME competition policy model is the outcome of a long-term process of regulatory harmonization and of continuing pressure by the US authorities (Wigger, 2008).

The CME model is based on the principle that capitalism needs to be organized (Albert, 1993, pp. 117–9). Markets are not perfectly self-regulatory, but jeopardized by "market failures." Correspondingly, competition policy is supposed to counter the abuse of excessive market power by very large enterprises and to ensure the economic wellbeing of SMEs. Some forms of inter-firm collaboration between these enterprises may be acceptable (or even desirable), in particular if these serve the diffusion of technology within the economy (Hall and Soskice, 2001b, p. 26). These policy principles are complemented by a form of competition policy enforcement that is mainly based on specialized competition authorities. These authorities usually have far-reaching regulatory powers and due to their public character are supposed to be able to balance the potential of anti-competitive measures against wider socio-economic goals, including the transfer of innovation by inter-firm collaboration. The corresponding systems of ex-ante notification and authorization for mergers and inter-firm cooperation are sometimes bureaucratic and cumbersome, but provide business with considerable legal safety.

Competition policy in LMEs is organized very differently and follows a deviating set of policy preferences. Consistent with the overall model of this variety of capitalism, public market intervention should be kept to a minimum, since markets are mostly self-regulatory. Competition policy follows one overarching principle, i.e., consumer welfare maximization, usually measured by economic modeling based on neo-classical price theory. Thus company size as such is not necessarily a problem, as long as it contributes to low consumer prices, e.g., by economies of scale. In contrast, cartels and other inter-company agreements are under intense scrutiny, in particular if they might nega-tively affect consumer welfare. Broader socio-economic concerns, such as the diffusion of technological innovation through inter-firm collabo-ration, do not play an important role in the LME variety of competition control (Hall and Soskice, 2001b, p. 31). This single-goal orientation fits very well with the mode of enforcement, since in this case the courts are the final decision-makers, whereas intervention by public author-ities should be kept to a minimum. Moreover, in contrast to public competition authorities, courts cannot be expected to balance issues of anti-competitive conduct against broader socio-economic concerns. Thus, the focus on consumer welfare maximization provides the courts with a single measure to base their decisions upon. The courts, how-ever, cannot function without litigants. It is here where the law firms come in. In contrast to the CME model (e.g., Germany), US enforce-ment agencies cannot block anticompetitive cases themselves, but have to litigate their cases before the courts. However, more than 90% of all formal US antitrust actions are based on litigation by private actors. In order for the private law firms to work properly as "watchdogs" of competition policy, the US legal system has a number of systemic features that contain strong incentives for litigation of potential cases of anticompetitive conduct, such as treble damages (plaintiffs do not only get the cost of suing, but also up to three times the damage suf-fered), class actions (law firms collect claimants for a collective claim), and contingency fees (law firms can sell their services under the no cure no pay-condition).

Until recently, the EU system of competition policy closely fol-lowed the (German) CME model, both regarding the rather broad policy considerations, and the enforcement model that was based on ex-ante notification with the EC. The 2004 reform of EU antitrust reg-ulation, however, constitutes a comprehensive shift towards the LME model. The core measure is the replacement of Regulation 17 from 1962 with regulation 1/2003 which abolishes the notification regime. Now companies have to assess themselves whether they — or their competitors, distributors and supplies — have infringed Article 81. If anti-competitive behavior is suspected, companies can appeal to the courts, also on the domestic level. This has led to a major shift of competition policy enforcement from public authorities to the private sector, most notably to the specialized transnational law firms that, together with the Commission, have been the prime driving forces for the reform (Wilks, 2005). Correspondingly, even within the first two years of operation the number of cases brought to the national courts by private actors has increased from 5% to more than 50% (Wigger and Nölke, 2007, p. 497). The reform however, is not yet complete. During the last years, the Commission has consistently pleaded for stronger incentives for private litigants, including damage compensation and class actions, thereby moving further on the road towards the adoption of the US system of adversarial legalism (Kelemen, 2007). At the same time, the EC is moving in the direction of the US policy principles, by taking a "more economic approach" that does not look at a broad array of socio-economic concerns anymore, but focuses on econometric assessments of consumer-welfare implications.

While the reform does not only relate to the CMEs within the EU, the EU will be most seriously affected, although it is yet too early to measure the effects. The replacement of public ex-ante notification by private ex-post litigation creates a high degree of volatility, which is particularly problematic for the long-term strategies that are so typical for CMEs. At the same time, inter-firm collaboration for the diffusion of innovations may become more and more restrained, since it will not be exempted from anti-trust activities anymore. Thus, it does not come as a surprise that large parts of the (Continental) European business community are deeply skeptical regarding the EU plans for furthering recent reforms by supporting private litigation possibilities. Still, they have not been able to mobilize broad-based opposition against the recent reforms, given that the German "Bundeskartellamt" has been induced to accepting the reform — in spite of its opposition to the substantial principles at work — because of a parallel decentralization of Commission competences to the national level and to private actors. (Wilks, 2005).

Similar observations can be made in the case of banking regulation, in which bond rating analysts constitute a central force in the shift towards private business regulation, again based on LME models imported from the United States. The EU has adopted the Basel II rules for banking supervision (Lütz, 2002, p. 202), which mandate rating agency outputs for less sophisticated banks. Although rating competition has intensified since the 1990s, the two major US-based agencies of Moody's Investor Service and Standard & Poor's still largely dominate this profession. Private third-party enforcement of debt rating has an extensive history in the United States (cf. Sinclair, 1994, 2003; Kerwer 2001, 2005; and Mattli and Büthe 2005), but not in Continental Europe. Correspondingly, rating agencies favor the Anglo-Saxon model within their operations, including a rather short-term investment horizon and a preponderance of investors concerns. These most recent developments may further undermine the Rhenish CME model, in particular with regard to the financial basis of "Mittelstand" companies. Due to the limited level of internally generated funds and the strong reliance on debt financing for investment, the German SMEs might be threatened in their core operations. Basle II and the increasing role of rating agencies make it difficult for highly indebted companies. Following from their risk profile, credit costs considerably increase — a process that has already been set in motion during recent years. Many of these companies may be forced to mobilize funding by "going public" or selling shares to private equity companies (Lütz, 2002, p. 198). This may lead to further pressures of "short-termism" that are not compatible with the Rhenish model. Again, there is a certain irony involved here, since the United States has reserved for itself a right to exempt certain groups of banks from the Basel II rules, although this regulation is very much embedded in the more generic Anglo-Saxon model. The Commission, in contrast, makes good use of the opportunity for a harmonized banking supervision within the Union, even if it undermines an important element within Rhenish capitalism.

The recent financial crisis, however, has led many observers to reconsider the wisdom of this approach (also in the concept of the ongoing Basel III negotiations) while the 2010 US financial sector regulatory reforms have decreased the reliance if public regulators on rating agencies.

6. Conclusion

To conclude, there are several signs of convergence in European business regulation towards the US model that are driven by the EU (Dewing and Russell, 2004, pp. 311–2). In all cases, the Commission was one of the core drivers of a process that at least in the short term is to the benefit of (US-based) professional service firms, US institutional investors, and the LME variety of capitalism more general. All of these measures carry the potential to make transatlantic regulatory cooperation easier. But current EU reforms may undermine the comparative advantage of the very variety of capitalism that can be found in large parts of Continental Europe. Both the shift in the mode of regulation (an increasing emphasis on private professional organizations) and in its substance (an increasing affinity with Anglo-Saxon economic reasoning) are instrumental in this regard.

While we may conclude that the increased reliance on private governance (Pollack and Shaffer, 2001) is potentially providing very fruitful avenues for transatlantic regulatory cooperation, we should also note that this type of transatlantic convergence on LME institutions comes at a price, given that it threatens to undermine the institutional complementarities of the continental European CME models. Thus, the recent politicization of the IASB in the EU may already point towards the limitations of this strategy. Furthermore, the current financial market crisis has already highlighted some weaknesses of the LME model, such as the high volatility of financial market earnings under fair value accounting.

References

Albert, Michel (1993). Capitalism Against Capitalism, London: Whurr Publishers.
Amable, Bruno (2003). The Diversity of Modern Capitalism. Oxford, Oxford University Press.
Ball, R. (2004). "Corporate Governance and Financial Reporting at Daimler-Benz (DaimlerChrysler) AG: From a 'Stakeholder' towards a 'Shareholder Value' Model," in: C. Leuz, D. Pfaff and A. Hopwood (eds.), The Economics and Politics of Accounting: International Perspectives on Research Trends, Policy, and Practice, Oxford: Oxford University Press.

Blyth, Mark (2003). "Same as it Never Was: Temporality and Typology in the Varieties of Capitalism," Comparative European Politics 1, pp. 215–225.

Botzem, Sebastian (2007). "Changes in Professional Standardization – The Role of Private Actors in International Accounting Regulation," Paper prepared for the Sixth SGIR Pan-European Conference on International Relations, Turin.

Botzem, Sebastian (2008). "Transnational Expert-driven Standardization: Accountancy Governance From a Professional Point of View, in: Graz, Jean-Christophe and Andreas Nölke (eds.) (2008), Transnational Private Governance and its Limits, London and New York: Routledge.

Cernat, Lucien (2004). "The Emerging European Corporate Governance Model: Anglo-Saxon, Continental, or Still the Century of Diversity?" Journal of European Public Policy 11(1), pp. 147–166.

Coates, David (2000). Models of Capitalism: Growth and Stagnation in the Modern Era, Cambridge: Polity.

Crouch, Colin and Wolfgang Streeck (1997). Introduction, in: Crouch, Colin and Streeck, Wolfgang (eds.), Political Economy of Modern Capitalism: Mapping Convergence and Diversity, Sage: London, Thousand Oaks, New Delhi, pp. 1–32.

Dewing, Ian P. and Peter O. Russell (2004). "Accounting, Auditing and Corporate Governance of European Listed Companies: EU Policy Developments Before and After Enron," Journal of Common Market Studies 42(2), pp. 289–319.

Dewing, Ian P. and Peter O. Russell (2007). "The Role of Private Actors in Global Governance and Regulation: US, European and International Convergence of Accounting and Auditing Standards in a Post-Enron World, in: Nölke, Andreas, Overbeek, Henk and Van Apeldoorn, Bastiaan (eds.), The Politics of Corporate Governance Regulation, (Routledge/RIPE Studies in Global Political Economy) Routledge: London and New York.

Graz, Jean-Christophe and Andreas Nölke (eds.) (2008). Transnational Private Governance and its Limits, London and New York: Routledge.

Hall, Peter A. and David Soskice (eds.) (2001a). Varieties of Capitalism: the Institutional Foundations of Comparative Advantage, Oxford University Press.

Hall, Peter A. and David Soskice (2001b). "An Introduction to Varieties of Capitalism," in: Hall and Soskice 2001a, pp. 1–68.

Hopwood, Anthony (1994). "Some Reflections on 'The Harmonization of Accounting Within the EU'," in: European Accounting Review 3(2), pp. 241–252.

Jackson, Gregory and Deeg, Richard (2006). "How Many Varieties of Capitalism? Comparing the Comparative Institutional Analyses of Capitalist Diversity," MPIfG Discussion Paper 06/02, Cologne: Max Planck Institute for the Study of Societies.

Katsikas, Dimitrios (2008). Transnational Regulatory Authority and Global Economic Governance, Thesis submitted for the Degree of Ph.D. in International Relations, London School of Economics.

Kelemen, Daniel R (2007). "The Americanisation of European Law? Adversarial Legalism a la Europeenne," European Political Science, 7(1), pp. 32–42.

Kerwer, Dieter (2001). Standardizing as Governance: The Case of Credit Rating Agencies, Preprint, Max Planck Project Group Common Goods — Law, Politics and Economics: Bonn.
Kerwer, Dieter (2005). Rules that Many Use: Standards and Global Regulation, in: Governance 18(4), pp. 611–632.
Lütz, Susanne (2002). Der Staat und die Globalisierung von Finanzmärkten: Regulative Politik in Deutschland, Großbritannien und den USA, Frankfurt and New York, Frankfurt: Campus.
Martinez-Diaz, Leonardo (2005). "Strategic Experts and Improvising Regulators: Explaining the IASC's Rise to Global Influence, 1973–2001," in: Business and Politics 7(4), Article 3.
Mattli, Walter and Tim Büthe (2005). "Accountability in Accounting? The Politics of Private Rule-Making in the Public Interest," Governance 18(3), pp. 399–429.
Nölke, Andreas and James Perry (2007a). Coordination Service Firms and the Erosion of Rhenish Capitalism, in: Nölke, Andreas, Overbeek, Henk and Van Apeldoorn, Bastiaan (eds.), The Politics of Corporate Governance Regulation, (Routledge/RIPE Studies in Global Political Economy) Routledge: London and New York.
Nölke, Andreas and James Perry (2007b). The Power of Transnational Private Governance: Financialization and the IASB, in: Business and Politics 9(3), Article 4.
Perry, James and Nölke, Andreas (2005). International Accounting Standard Setting: A Network Perspective, Business and Politics, 7(3), Article 5.
Perry, James and Nölke, Andreas (2006). "The Political Economy of International Accounting Standards," Review of International Political Economy, 13(4), pp. 559–586.
Pollack, Mark. A. and Gregory C. Shaffer (eds.) (2001). Transatlantic Governance in the Global Economy, Rowman & Littlefield: Lanham.
Schmidt, Vivien A. (2003). French Capitalism Transformed, Yet Still a Third Variety of Capitalism, in: Economy and Society 32, pp. 526–54.
Shonfield, Andrew (1965). Modern Capitalism. New York: Oxford University Press.
Sinclair, Timothy L. (1994). Passing Judgment: Credit Rating Processes as Regulatory Mechanisms of Governance in the Emerging World Order, in: Review of International Political Economy 1(1), pp. 133–59.
Sinclair, Timothy L. (2003). Global Monitor: Credit Rating Agencies, in: New Political Economy, 8(1), pp. 147–161.
Van Hulle, Karel (1993). "Harmonization of Accounting Standards in the EC — Is this the Beginning or the End?" in: The European Accounting Review 2(2), pp. 387–396.
Whitley, Richard (1999). Divergent Capitalisms: The Social Structuring and Change of Business Systems, Oxford: Oxford University Press.
Wigger, Angela (2008). Competition for Competitiveness: The Politics of the transformation of the EU Competition Regime, Ph.D. Dissertation, Amsterdam: Vrije Universiteit.

Wigger, Angela and Andreas Nölke (2007). The Privatization of EU Business Regulation and the Erosion of Rhenish Capitalism: The Case of Antitrust Enforcement, in: Journal of Common Market Studies 45(2), pp. 487–513.

Wilks, Stephen (2005). Agency Escape: Decentralization or Dominance of the European Commission in the Modernization of Competition Policy? in: Governance 18(3), pp. 431–452.

Chapter 10

Transatlantic Regulatory Competition and Cooperation in Pharmaceuticals

Keith E. Maskus

Professor of Economics
University of Colorado at Boulder
keith.maskus@colorado.edu

Yin He

Visiting Scholar, University of Colorado at Boulder

1. Introduction

At the 2007 United States–EU Summit, leaders issued the Framework for Advancing Transatlantic Economic Integration between the United States of America and the European Union. This Framework built on the earlier Guidelines for Regulatory Cooperation and Transparency negotiated under the Transatlantic Economic Partnership (TEP). The intention is to reduce regulatory dissonance between the two regions in an effort to limit the associated costs of compliance and conformity assessment that may limit trade and investment. The ultimate goal, as stressed by the European Parliament in 2005 and the US Senate in 2006, is completion of the Transatlantic Market by 2015. The idea was given a boost by Chancellor Merkel in her speech of January 2007 supporting the Transatlantic Market Initiative, or "Merkel Initiative" which seeks to establish barrier-free trade and investment across the ocean.

Discussions to move this bilateral objective forward take place within the Transatlantic Economic Council (TEC), involving senior officials in a number of regulatory agencies. One important sector that falls within the TEC work is pharmaceuticals, wherein the objective is greater cooperation between the US Food and Drug Administration (FDA), the EU Directorate-General for Enterprise (Pharmaceuticals Unit) and the European Agency for the Evaluation of Medicinal Products (EMEA) on matters related to ensuring the safety, quality, and efficacy of pharmaceutical products. This cooperation, which largely involves information and data exchanges and the development of confidentiality agreements, is ongoing. It seeks to make more efficient the "upstream" regulation of drug approvals, thereby bringing newer therapies to the market more rapidly. There is also a bilateral dialogue to identify specific regulatory cooperation projects that promise mutual gains.

The scope of this cooperation, described further below, is modest and achievable in some degree. The TEP and TEC negotiations to date have not focused on broader and deeper areas of regulatory competition and cooperation in pharmaceuticals, in which participation would have fundamental impacts on the global industry. For example, the United States and the EU wish to achieve greater global harmonization of substantive patent standards and examination procedures, an area of considerable interest to their research-intensive pharmaceutical industries. Both the United States and the EU also work to raise intellectual property protection for new medicines in countries with which they negotiate preferential trade agreements (PTAs). These elements are more controversial and difficult to achieve.

With this background, the paper proceeds as follows. In the next section we discuss important regulatory differences in pharmaceuticals between the United States and the EU, permitting us to comment on potential gains from collaboration. In the third section we present an overview of the history of, and analyze the prospects for, mutual cooperation within the narrow confines of the Framework Initiative and within the broader intellectual property rights (IPRs) agenda. In the final section we assess briefly the potential gains from collaboration and discuss structural difficulties that may limit further progress.

2. Regulatory Differences in the United States and European Union

The research-intensive pharmaceutical enterprises in both the United States and the European Union reside in a highly intensive competitive environment and, at the same time, are subject to significant regulation on behalf of public-health. The challenges of developing new drugs and bringing them to the market in the face of these pressures make this a unique industry.

2.1. *Snapshot of the US and EU industries*

The United States spends about 15% of GDP on health care, while in the EU–15 countries this share ranges from 7.5% (Ireland) to 11.1% (France).[1] However, the share of health-care expenditures allocated to medicines is lower in the United States, at around 12.4%, than in most EU nations, where this proportion is generally between 17% and 22%. This difference likely reflects the significant restraints on prices imposed by regulatory authorities in the EU, as noted below.

Global pharmaceuticals production has grown rapidly in recent decades, reaching nearly €720 billion in 2004 (National Science Foundation, 2006). As of 2003, countries in the extended EU accounted for 35% of this production and the United States around 25%. Despite this relatively larger production, worker productivity in the United States is estimated to be more than twice that in the EU. This reflects largely the inclusion of relatively labor-intensive assembly facilities in southern and eastern European member states. Those facilities are less prevalent in the United States, which is more specialized on research and marketing activities.

Increasing globalization in this sector may be seen from the explosion in two-way trade between the United States and the EU. In 1995, each region exported around €3 billion to the other but by 2005 EU imports from the United States reached approximately €12 billion,

---

[1] Organization for Economic Cooperation and Development, Health Data 2007 (data for 2005).

while EU exports in the opposite direction were nearly €20 billion.[2] The United States has experienced a large increase in import penetration, with imports currently over 22% of consumption (US Department of Commerce, 2006). The EU accounts for over 75% of those imports.

This increase in US imports again reflects that country's specialization in R&D activities. Both regions invest heavily in pharmaceutical R&D; in 2005 the US sector invested over €25 billion while firms in Western Europe invested around €21 billion. Perhaps a better measure of relative innovation activity is patents granted in the United States and the European Patent Office. Over the period 2002–2006 the 10 largest EU nations were granted a total of 6,723 patents in technology area 424 (drugs) by the US Patent and Trademark Office, while US inventors were granted 17,289 patents.[3] The figures were more balanced within the European Patent Office, but the United States received the largest number of grants of any individual country. It is noteworthy that the highest numbers of EPO patents received per person employed in pharmaceuticals within the EU were by firms in Germany, the United Kingdom, and the Netherlands, which have the least restrictive price controls and marketing regulations.

In summary, the industry in the EU is somewhat larger and more focused on production, though there is substantial R&D investment underway. American firms are relatively more specialized in R&D and patenting. No doubt there are many factors underlying these differences but one important issue may be the structure of regulation, as noted below.

2.2.   *Competitive structure and challenges*

Traditionally, the pharmaceutical business has consisted of developing chemical molecules that could be shown to control or cure some medical condition. Drug development encompasses laboratory science, animal testing, and several phases of clinical trials. Upon successfully

---

[2] Eurostat data.

[3] http://www.uspto.gov/web/offices/ac/ido/oeip/taf/clsstc/usa_stc.htm

passing through these trials to demonstrate safety and efficacy, firms apply for marketing authorizations in locations where they wish to sell. They may also apply for patent protection. Once developed and approved, these active-ingredient molecules, or "New Chemical Entities" (NCEs), are combined with buffering agents, flavorings, adhesive powders and the like to manufacture medical formulations, the final product sold through pharmacies and hospitals. This highly discrete innovation model still characterizes a significant portion of the industry.

However, recent scientific advances have brought newer technologies to the sector, including biotechnological products, genomic therapies, organic materials, and nutriceuticals. This has generated both more horizontal competition (both pharmaceutical companies and large life-science companies generating new product varieties) and vertical orientation of the industry. In the life sciences, invention generally begins in university laboratories and may involve sophisticated research networks across many locations. Testing in biotechnological products is particularly complex and specialized testing companies have evolved to work with therapies licensed from universities, transforming them into products of interest to pharmaceutical manufacturers.

Developing a new drug and bringing it to market is an expensive and uncertain process. For chemically based medicines it may take up to 13 years and cost an average of over $800 million at current costs in the United States.[4] About half these costs include preclinical discovery research, clinical testing on animals and humans, and regulatory expense for marketing approval, with the remainder reflecting costs of financing. Among the former elements, Phase 3 clinical testing is the most expensive process and only the most promising drugs enter that phase. Because there are substantial economies available from combining research facilities and joint marketing, these high costs have encouraged substantial concentration in the final industry.

---

[4]See "The Value and Benefits of ICH to Industry," paper prepared for the International Federation of Pharmaceutical Manufacturers Associations, and DiMasi, *et al.* (2003).

Pharmaceutical companies are among the most research-intensive firms in any industry, though there is considerable variation in size and firm type. One measure of the number of firms engaged in bringing original products to global markets is the membership of the International Federation of Pharmaceutical Manufacturers (IFPMA). There are 24 members, of which eight are headquartered in the United States, nine in the EU, four in Japan, two in Switzerland and one in India. However, 14 of these firms have truly global reach in terms of massive R&D networks, numerous international production locations, significant product mixes and global sales. The temporary exclusive rights afforded by patents are critical for covering costs of testing and distribution. It is noteworthy that many "blockbuster" drugs currently on patent in the United States and Europe are due to lose protection within the next few years. To some degree this problem is being offset by specialization of R&D into therapies aimed at rare diseases, so-called orphan drugs. Patents in the United States and the EU provide substantial markups on investment in order to bring these drugs to market.

Original manufacturers compete not only with each other in patented and branded drugs, but they also face competition from domestic and foreign generic producers. As discussed below, the ease with which generic products enter markets is determined by patent expiration, limits on patent rights and the prices of patented medicines. Original manufacturers also compete with products imported by parallel trading companies where that activity is legal.

2.3. Comparative regulatory systems

There are an enormous number of regulations in the pharmaceutical sector, ranging from testing protocols to product-specific standards regarding best manufacturing practices. Further, these regulations vary significantly across originator drugs, generics, orphan drugs, and biologics. We attempt only a brief overview here of the major forms of regulation.

2.3.1. *Drug approvals*

Primary regulatory elements are the rules governing testing protocols, submission of clinical test data, certification of safety and efficacy, application procedures for marketing authorization, and certification of good manufacturing practices (GMPs). While such procedures are rarely discriminatory in the sense of favoring domestic applicants over foreign, they vary widely across countries. This has long been the case within the EU, where public-health policy is a national prerogative. Because each national health authority has its own rules and protocols, it can be quite expensive for pharmaceutical companies to achieve marketing authorization throughout the EU or even within a subset of EU countries. In addition to costs of translation, there can be divergent rules governing dossier formats and other application materials. More fundamentally, individual authorities may require separate clinical trials under different protocols regarding animal and human subjects, laboratory procedures and conditions, temperature and humidity, and numerous other factors. The efficiency with which individual offices approve applications also varies considerably, a distortionary factor leading to differential launch strategies across markets. As will be seen in the following section, the EU has made a priority of harmonizing these rules and procedures, sometimes in collaboration with the United States.

Briefly, there are two types of procedures to get a drug approved in the European Union. First is the decentralized procedure (also called "mutual recognition procedure"), which was introduced in 1983. Under this process, manufactures can seek simultaneous marketing authorization in concerned member states, provided that they already have marketing authorization in at least one reference member state. The health authorities in the former are encouraged to recognize the marketing authorization of the latter. If they do not, the matter is referred to European Medicines Evaluation Agency (EMEA) for arbitration.

Second is the centralized procedure through the EMEA, which was adopted in 1995. All biotechnology drug products, medicines for the treatment of HIV/AIDS, cancer, diabetes or neurodegenerative diseases, all designated orphan medicines, and all veterinary medicines intended for use as performance enhancers must go through the centralized procedure, which is optional for innovative chemicals. The manufacturer first submits an application, with information on quality, nonclinical study reports and clinical study reports. A member state is selected to perform the scientific evaluation and to prepare an assessment report, taking into account scientific opinion from the Committee of Proprietary Medical Products (CPMP). When the inspection is done, a written report is issued in conjunction with hearings. If the opinion is positive, the EMEA has 30 days to finalize the initial product assessment report and forward it to the EU, with the application and scientific assessment report for final market authorization. Objections made by other member states to the selected member state's decision are considered by the CHMP, which then makes a recommendation for or against an EU-wide license. This system, which is analyzed further in the next section, has effectively integrated the drug approval process for at least newer therapies and those that might prove controversial across EU markets.

While drug approval procedures used by the US Food and Drug Administration (FDA) are somewhat cumbersome, they are transparent and available to all applicants.[5] The FDA has guidelines for inspecting preclinical (animal) testing and Phase 1, 2 and 3 trials, receiving submission of a new drug application, reviewing the drug's safety and effectiveness, certifying the labels to be used, and inspecting manufacturing facilities. Recent efforts have been made to streamline this process and reduce costs to industry, though not without controversy.

One significant difference between the United States and the EU arises in the approval of generic drugs. The FDA requires a demonstration of therapeutic equivalency and efficacy through scientific testing. Testing costs for demonstrating such equivalency are considerably

---

[5]Procedures are outlined at http://www.fda.gov/fdac/special/testtubetopatient/drugreview.html

lower for generic drugs, since the essential test involves showing that the same active ingredients operate in the generic products as in the patented versions. In principle, this situation exists in the EU as well, except that generic approvals are done by individual countries rather than being centralized, as they are in the United States. This situation fragments the generic market and acts as a disincentive for pan-EU marketing, a significant reason why the generic industry is smaller and its products are higher-priced than in the United States. Only in July 2007 did the EMEA adopt a procedure for granting market authorization for generic drugs for human use.[6]

2.3.2. *Pricing regulations*

Within the EU price controls and profit regulations are left to individual countries as a major component of public-health policy. Maximum prices vary in different countries and are dependent on many factors, such as budget limits, prescribing behavior, patterns of utilization, and importance of the pharmaceutical industry (Mrazek 2002). Some countries, such as France and Spain, set price caps through negotiations, while national authorities of other countries set prices according to defined lists of factors (Mrazek, 2002). Germany and the UK do not directly control prices of on-patent drugs.

Maximum prices may be based on manufacturers' costs. They can also be set by comparing international prices of the same product, but the reference countries and weights are different from one country to another. Some countries, such as Austria, Ireland, Italy and the Netherlands, use an index of international prices. Others, such as Belgium, France, Denmark and Spain, use foreign prices only as a basis for negotiation (Stargardt and Schreyögg, 2006; Rovira and Darba, 2001). The choice of referred countries differs markedly as well (Mrazek and Morrialos, 2004).

---

[6]"Press Release: European Medicines Agency recommends authorization of first generic medicine for human use," http://www.emea.europa.eu/pdfs/general/direct/pr/31672807en.pdf.

The therapeutic value of the drug and the cost of comparable treatments may also be considered in order to balance the costs of using a drug with its benefits. Belgium, Finland, France, Spain and Sweden are examples of countries that apply this principle. Furthermore, the pharmaceutical company's contribution to the economy, such as the number of employees involved, may also be taken into account (as is the case with Belgium and Spain). Finally, in some countries if market volumes pass a threshold the price cap will decrease or companies must pay a cash rebate. This kind of nonlinear price regulation is used in Austria, France, Spain, and Sweden.

The UK relies primarily on profit regulation, with the ceiling profit margin of a new drug negotiated between industry and government. The aim of this policy is to achieve a balance between securing medicines at reasonable prices and encouraging a pharmaceutical industry capable of sustained development of innovative medicines (Jacabzone, 2000). Others nations, including Germany, the Netherlands, Sweden, Denmark, Italy, Spain, Belgium, Portugal and France, control the increase in pharmaceutical expenditures in their budgets by setting reimbursement levels (Heuer *et al.*, 2007).

Demand-side regulation is also applied in the pharmaceutical industry, but to a lesser degree. In these regimes the patient is responsible for paying the price difference between his chosen drug and a reference drug defined by the government. This pricing menu is set to create incentives for patients to be more price-sensitive and therefore decrease the demand for high-priced products. Reference pricing is presumed to stimulate price competition between pharmaceutical firms (Heuer *et al.*, 2007).

Turning to the United States, federal price regulations are virtually absent. Rather, large public procurement programs and private insurance programs seek to limit expenditures through negotiations with pharmaceutical suppliers. However, a few individual states have enacted legislation enabling state authorities to set maximum prices for prescription drugs. For example, in May 2000, Maine passed two laws to establish discounted prices for all residents without prescription drug coverage.

Overall, EU countries regulate pharmaceutical prices much more closely than does the United States. The effect has been considerably less drug price inflation in the EU. From 1986 to 2004 the relative rate of inflation of a standard pharmaceutical index was nearly 50% in the United States but less than 10% in the EU (Golec and Vernon, 2006).

While rigorous price regulation generates consumer benefits, it may raise certain indirect costs, such as reduced research intensity and slower product launches. Kyle (2007) found that in countries with relatively little price regulation, such as the United States, the UK and Germany, the pharmaceutical industries are highly concentrated and research-intensive. The new products those firms develop are launched in more foreign markets and perform more successfully in the global market (Mrazek, 2002). Moreover, new products tend to be marketed more quickly in countries with laxer price regulation (Danzon *et al.*, 2005).

There is evidence as well that strict price regulations diminish R&D expenditures and innovation. Simulation analysis by Vernon (2005) showed that if the United States were to adopt price controls mimicking those in the average EU country it could lead to a decline in R&D intensity of between 23% and 32%. Golec and Vernon (2006) studied how price constraints affect the profitability and R&D spending of EU and US firms. In 1986 R&D investment in the EU exceeded that in the United States by about 24%, but by 2004 EU expenditures trailed those in the United States by about 15%. US-based firms were more profitable, earned higher stock returns, and spent more on R&D than their EU counterparts. According to the authors, EU consumers enjoyed much lower pharmaceutical price inflation but at a cost of 46 fewer new medicines introduced by EU firms and 1,680 fewer EU research jobs. As we describe below, this apparent loss of research competitiveness within the EU industry is one factor driving regulatory reforms.

2.3.3. *Intellectual property rights (IPRs)*

A final form of pharmaceutical regulation is the structure of IPRs. A complete comparison of the United States and the EU in this regard would require a volume in itself. Here we list just the major policy variations that bear discussion of prospects for some cooperation or even harmonization (Maskus, 2006).

Patent standards. The United States clings stubbornly to its principle that the "first to invent" should be awarded the patent, while the EU follows the global "first to file" standard. The United States will need to meet this standard if it hopes to pursue more global or bilateral harmonization. US policy is more likely to grant continuation patents in drugs, new use patents, and patents to combination therapies than is EU policy. The United States has opened up wider areas of medical biotechnology to patents than has the EU. The EU has not yet successfully organized a "Europatent" that would hold in member states, though the European Patent Office provides efficiencies in multiple-jurisdiction applications. Europe appears to have a stronger threshold for demonstrating novelty and hews better to the prior art. The United States offers stronger protection for biotechnological research tools, providing the potential for reach-through royalties on extended licensing to substantial product lines. Europe's protection is considerably less in this context.

Patent Scope. The United States does not recognize a prior-use defense in patent litigation, which generates substantial uncertainty for complex life-science patents. Neither does it generally permit third-party submission of prior art, while the ability to contest the validity of issued patents is essentially nil. The post-grant opposition system in the EU is a useful model for harmonization or convergence deliberations.

Research Exemption. Many countries allow competing firms to use a patented technology in their own research programs for purposes of understanding the technology fully and inventing around the patent. By tradition, the United States has permitted experimental use by noncommercial entities, such as universities, but not by commercial entities. However, the United States has a major statutory exception to exclusive patent-use rights in medicines, the Hatch-Waxman Act of 1984. That Act provided for extended patent terms in drugs, where the approval process reduced effective patent length. To offset this gain in exclusive rights, the Act stated that limited experimental use is possible for testing drugs and medical devices for purposes of regulatory data gathering, the so-called "Bolar exception" to patent rights. The idea was to encourage development of a robust generic industry, which it is widely credited with doing. The Supreme Court upheld this use in a recent court case, essentially exempting from infringement any experimental use associated with the need of firms to gain early marketing approval for generic drugs.[7]

Experimental use of patented technologies in Europe is governed by national patent laws but these are generally more liberal than the US regime. Indeed, all member states of the EU, except Austria, have introduced a general non-industry specific experimental use exception in their patent statutes.[8] Germany, for example, recognizes wide latitude for experimental use. However, there is no consensus across member states regarding a Bolar provision that would permit early experimental use to achieve marketing approval for generic drugs. A number of high-level observers have urged adoption of an EU-wide research exemption to support rapid generic entry.

3. Evolution of Regulatory Cooperation

In light of the regulatory differences described above, industry interests and public agencies in the EU and the United States have engaged for some time in efforts to move some regulatory processes toward convergence. This work has proceeded both in the bilateral (and trilateral, including Japan) arena and within the EU itself.

3.1. *Bilateral regulatory cooperation*

While the history predates it, most observers trace the beginnings of US-EU cooperation in pharmaceuticals to the 1997 Mutual Recognition Agreement (MRA). Firms engaged in bilateral trade and

---

[7] *Integra Life Sciences I, Ltd v. Merck KgaA*, 545 US 193 (2005).
[8] See "Patenting and the Research Exemption", IPR Help Desk, DG Enterprise and Industry of the European Commission, http://www.ipr-helpdesk.org/documentos/docsPublicacion/pdf_xml/8_BP-Patenting-and-the-Research-Exemptio%5B0000003268_00%5D.pdf

investment pushed for this MRA in order to reduce duplicative costs of complying with regulations. American firms were also concerned that without an MRA the ongoing process of regulatory convergence in Europe would erect standards and technical barriers that could be exclusionary and raise their costs (Shaffer, 2002). Businesses on both sides expressed their interests in eliminating regulatory barriers through the Transatlantic Business Dialogue (TABD).

The 1997 MRA included a framework agreement and six sectoral annexes, one of which applied to good manufacturing practices (GMP) in pharmaceuticals. These annexes did not achieve harmonization of transatlantic standards. Rather, they focused on mutual recognition of on-site inspections and examinations of plants by certification bodies in exporting nations undertaken according to the importing country's required standards and processes. Even this achievement was limited in that importer agencies could reject examination reports they found inadequate. Still, the FDA was unwilling to recognize the equivalency of more than a few national regulatory systems because it was burdensome to review the legislation and regulatory processes of multiple EU authorities. The pharmaceuticals annex of the MRA lapsed in due time without achieving much reduction in duplication costs.

To reinvigorate the process the two regions issued in 2004 a "Roadmap for US-EU Regulatory Cooperation and Transparency" to encourage implementation of associated regulatory guidelines. Within pharmaceuticals an initial objective was to enhance ongoing cooperation between the US FDA and the European Agency for the Evaluation of Medicinal Products (EMEA) as regards safety, quality and efficacy of medicines.[9] The roadmap called for expanding the exchange of information and data, engaging in mutual scientific advice, promoting scientific personnel exchanges, sharing guidance documents on drug safety, and examining situations in which US and EU authorities adopted different approval decisions for specific drugs. It advocated also the development of a model confidentiality agreement to encourage information sharing on pharmaceutical testing and data.

---

[9]Cooperation in this regard is described in the next sub-section.

Regarding broader regulatory cooperation, the process was renewed in 2005 with the Transatlantic Economic Integration and Growth Initiative. The emphasis went beyond product standards to include consumer protection, market access in services, financial markets regulation, competition policy, government procurement and intellectual property rights. Further, the European Parliament passed a resolution in 2005 supporting completion of the Transatlantic Market by 2015, while the US Senate adopted a similar resolution in 2006. Each of these focused on the need for sectoral studies to estimate the costs and benefits of removing technical barriers to trade and investment, including regulatory costs.

These proclamations provided the foundation for the current Framework Initiative. With respect to pharmaceuticals, the Initiative seeks to foster cooperation and reduce regulatory costs in the following ways. First, it would promote administrative simplification in the application of regulations in medicinal products. In essence this would mean completing the efficiencies advanced by the International Conference on Harmonization (ICH), discussed in the next sub-section. Next, it would establish closer consultation mechanisms regarding policy options in emerging technologies, such as in nanotechnology, genomic research, cloning, and biopharmaceuticals. It would also encourage interoperability of electronic health records systems, something that has proved elusive even within the United States. A priority would be closer cooperation on the safety of imported products, including medicines, an item of great importance in the wake of recent problems with Chinese medical ingredients and drugs. Finally, the Framework Initiative would expand joint US-EU operations to improve global enforcement of IPRs and would push for international harmonization of patent regimes. These latter elements are controversial and are discussed in section four of this paper.

3.2. Trilateral cooperation: The ICH

While all of these exhortatory documents have been issued at the official level, a significant parallel process toward regulatory cooperation in pharmaceuticals and biotechnology has taken place within the auspices of the International Conference on Harmonization of Technical Requirements or Registration of Pharmaceuticals for Human Use (ICH). This project began in 1990 and brings together regulatory authorities of the EU, the United States and Japan, along with industry experts from those regions. This tripartite structure seeks to develop a single set of technical requirements for the registration of new pharmaceutical products, permitting a more streamlined drug-development process.

As noted earlier, developing a new drug and bringing it to market is expensive, with Phase III clinical testing being especially costly. Where required testing protocols vary across countries, pharmaceutical firms must expend substantial amounts to undertake testing in multiple jurisdictions. Much of these duplicated costs are simply a waste that the firms would rather avoid and offer little in the way of public-health gains to countries that refuse to accept test results done under foreign protocols. Hence there has long been a strong private interest in regularizing approval procedures across jurisdictions.

The ICH process has generated some notable efficiencies, though drug approval procedures in the United States, Japan, the European Medicines Evaluation Agency (EMEA) and individual EU nations remain far from standardized. There is a tripartite Steering Committee that sets overall principles, while Expert Working Groups develop specific guidelines for harmonized policies, which are supposed to be implemented by regulatory agencies. As of April 2008 over 50 such guidelines have been adopted or notified for adoption by the European Commission (Committee of Proprietary Medical Products), the US FDA, or the Japanese Ministry of Health, Labor and Welfare.[10] These guidelines come in three general areas: efficacy, quality and safety. Following are illustrative examples of the potential gains from harmonization.[11]

A significant efficacy guideline is "Ethnic Factors in the Acceptability of Foreign Clinical Data" (E5), promulgated in February 1998 and

[10]http://www.ich.org/cache/compo/475-272-1.html
[11]See "Value and Benefits," above note 4.

implemented by all three regulatory authorities. Under this standard, firms that follow its guidance on the influence of ethnic factors on clinical testing and run their trials using the principles of good clinical practice (guideline E6) may submit its clinical test data in any ICH region. This process permitted Pfizer to gain rapid approval of Viagra in Japan without undertaking repeated clinical trials.

Turning to quality, the ICH guidelines cover the stability and impurities of chemical active ingredients, bulk drugs and drug product quality. For example, prior to the guidelines, a firm that ran stability studies at room temperatures and humidity levels appropriate to its own jurisdiction would need to repeat them under other conditions for foreign marketing approval. ICH harmonization set out standard conditions for stability studies, taking into account the climates of all three regions. Studies meeting the guideline generate stability results that are mutually acceptable in each country, thereby reducing duplicate testing requirements. The ICH is developing similar guidelines for cross-regional stability studies of new manufacturing and packaging arrangements when marketing authorizations are changed. There are also guidelines covering allowable maximum impurities in drug products and biotechnological manufacturing processes.

Safety guidelines refer to preclinical toxicity testing for registration of a new drug. Different countries had significant variations in study length, species requirements, dosage selection and other elements involved in risk assessments. Harmonization here appears to have been particularly effective in defining the safety data that must be achieved before human volunteers or patients may be treated with a new medicine. These definitions exist in particular chemical and biotechnological treatment areas, reducing the need for multiple tests. It is noteworthy that these guidelines adopted the most rigorous best practices among the three regions (typically those in the EU), an example of upward harmonization.

Perhaps the most significant element of ICH harmonization was the 2003 development of the Common Technical Document (CTD). Use of the CTD permits submission of a single dossier covering the data required by regulatory authorities in Japan, the EU and the United States. The single format of this submission is likely to reduce preparation costs considerably and lead to faster review times for marketing approval.

It is fair to say that the pharmaceutical and biotechnological industries in the three regions appreciate the efficiency gains available from the ICH guidelines. As early as 2000, 77% of EU firms had utilized some of the standards, with more than 80% of firms in Japan and the United States doing so. The potential benefits are evident: lower duplication costs, reduced development times, more resources for testing additional new entities, more rapid approvals, and an enhanced ability to coordinate product launches across the three areas. There are regulatory gains as well, including lower examination costs and faster approvals, which bring drugs to market more rapidly. Moreover, some of these guidelines are gaining global acceptance as health authorities in other countries choose to implement them, albeit under some pressure from the EU and the United States.

These are important benefits and, in concert with efforts in the Framework Initiative for greater transparency and information sharing, bespeak real progress in reducing regulatory costs in pharmaceutical approvals. However, there remain significant differences in national review processes within the EU and across the three regions, so harmonization is partial at this time. Put differently, while the costs of applying for approvals have been reduced, authorities in the United States, Japan, the EU and individual EU nations retain significant discretion in how they treat those applications. Neither has there been much progress on post-approval equalization of regulations regarding second uses and new marketing authorizations. One reason for the partial success is that these issues are intensely technical in nature and agreements on the underlying science may be difficult to achieve. Another is that regulatory agencies remain resistant to surrendering much sovereignty in the examination of test results. It seems likely that further progress is likely in coordinating national approval procedures, but that progress will remain slow.

3.3. *Intra-EU coordination*

Mindful of the patchwork quilt of pharmaceutical regulations existing across its member nations, the European Commission has engaged in a process of limited harmonization as well in an effort to reduce regulatory burdens in the industry. An important early policy was the 1989 EC Directive on pricing transparency.[12] The EC recognized that the complexity of pricing regulations in different jurisdictions "…may hinder or distort intra-Community trade in medicinal products and thereby directly affect the functioning of the common market in medicinal products." Accordingly, the Directive set out a series of transparency requirements so that the pricing regimes could be assessed as to whether they constituted restrictions on trade within the single market. The first requirement is for speed: pricing decisions by health authorities must be communicated to marketing applicants within 90 days of the application receipt. Next was transparency: each health authority must publish annually a list of the medicinal products for which prices were fixed in the prior period and the permissible prices. These conditions apply also to applications for price increases in the controlled period. Finally, where there are profitability regulations in place, the means of calculating profits, the range of target profits permitted, and the criteria by which applicants are assigned to particular rate-of-return limitations must be published. There are related transparency stipulations regarding decisions by public-health authorities to include a drug within its national health insurance purchasing programs. The rules in this Directive are widely thought to have reduced the uncertainty involved in marketing pharmaceuticals across the EU.

The European Commission tried to consolidate its many instructions regarding pharmaceutical approvals, packaging, marketing controls and the like in a 2001 *chapeau* directive.[13] The attempt again was to reduce the uncertainty costs of marketing in an environment with multiple jurisdictions and varying regulations in order to improve internal trade prospects. The most significant principles of the document may be described as follows. First, authorities must

---

[12] Council Directive 89/105/EEC relating to the transparency of measures regulating the pricing of medicinal products for human use and their inclusion in the scope of national health insurance systems.

[13] Directive 2001/83/EC on the Community code relating to medicinal products for human use.

pay more attention to scientific risk assessments in order to limit the risk that approval procedures may be impediments to trade. Second, it encourages authorities to develop uniform rules applicable to clinical tests, application dossiers and examination procedures. Third, national health authorities in each member state ought to mutually recognize the marketing authorizations issued by those in other member states. Where a disagreement between countries arises regarding product quality, safety or efficacy, a scientific assessment should be performed according to a Community standard, with a binding uniform decision reached. To achieve this goal, the Committee of Proprietary Medical Products (CPMP) was established within the EMEA.

The Directive also addressed conditions under which specific quality controls could be waived with respect to drug imports from third countries, while requiring EU-wide minimum requirements for the manufacture of such imports. It further refined the rules for distributing products that achieve a Community marketing authorization through the EMEA. Finally, it placed sharp limits on the ability of firms to advertise directly to consumers, reflecting European concerns about the safety implications of such marketing.

Directive 83 has been refined and supplemented by numerous subsequent regulations, most notably a 2003 document pertaining to harmonizing application procedures.[14] This new Directive laid the groundwork for acceptance of the common marketing application dossiers in the Common Technical Document developed by ICH, recognized particular issues as regards approvals of vaccines and biological medical products, and developed a new category of "advanced medical therapies" arising from biotechnology. More broadly, the European Commission now engages in an ongoing review of Community pharmaceutical legislation and in member states.

A further prod to policy convergence came from the recommendations of the high-level "G-10 Medicines Report" prepared by

---

[14]Commission Directive 2003/63/EC.

government and industry experts in 2002.[15] The primary concern of this group was to reduce disparities in regulation and market access in order to encourage innovation in the European industry. The report urged faster regulatory approvals, further convergence in application procedures, greater joint use of information technologies and electronic patient records and more transparency in pricing decisions. As noted above, many of these recommendations have been implemented through Directives or the ICH process.

Beyond these attempts at reducing duplication costs, important modernization strategies have been implemented in the EU as well. For example, in 2007 the European Parliament supported a new set of EU regulations on advanced therapies from genetic technologies. The absence of an EU-wide regulatory system in this area was thought to have impeded investment in the sector, while the new regulations should provide considerably more clarity.[16] For another, the US FDA and the European Commission engaged in extensive consultations before the EC proposed new regulations on medicines for children and medicines for rare diseases (so-called, "orphan drugs"). The new regulatory system in the EU will complement that in the United States as regards these technologies.

To summarize this section, bilateral, trilateral and intra-EU discussions have accomplished quite a bit in terms of reducing duplicate research programs and lowering application costs for international marketing authorizations. These are important achievements, though the systems remain far from fully harmonized. Little of this progress, however, gets at the more fundamental issues of regulating *competition*, as opposed to the management of *technical science*, in the pharmaceuticals area. One exception is a set of recommendations from the G-10 report. It encouraged the development of a more competitive European generics market by considering the implementation of an

---

[15] European Commission, High-Level Group on Innovation and Provision of Medicines. "Recommendations for Action," 7 May 2002.

[16] Gunter Verheugen, "Closing Speech, Transatlantic Business Dialogue," EC SPEECH/07/292, TABD Innovation Conference Health Care, Berlin, 8 May 2007.

EU-wide Bolar exception to patent rights, establishing limits on periods of data exclusivity, and increasing reliance on generic prescribing incentives. It also called for member states to end price controls for medicines that are not included in lists subject to state purchase or reimbursement. The report envisions that increased price flexibility on these uncontrolled products would improve profitability and encourage innovation in Europe.

If they were implemented, these recommendations would push European markets sharply in the direction of those in the United States, with more robust generic competition and additional pricing power for innovative firms. However, little progress has been made in achieving these objectives, because they are controversial and intrude on national policy sovereignty. In this regard, even within the EU there are significant limits on the ability of such soft-law guidelines to achieve significant regulatory convergence that would be meaningful in the competition phase of national markets.

3.4. Cooperation in intellectual property rights

It is worth noting briefly that the EU and the United States share common interests in expanding the scope of patent protection for pharmaceuticals in the global economy. One element involves increasing convergence in the so-called "TRIPS-Plus" agenda for new medicines. The United States has pursued for several years an aggressive pro-patent regime within its bilateral partners in free trade agreements (FTAs) (Maskus, 2006). TRIPS-Plus outcomes may be observed in FTAs with Jordan, Morocco, Australia, and Peru and in the draft treaty with Colombia. In its recent negotiations to establish Economic Partnership Agreements (EPAs) with countries in the Middle East, Central and East Asia and Latin America, the EU has pursued a similarly aggressive policy, though there are differences in approach.

TRIPS-Plus rules go substantially beyond the minimum IPRs standards set out at the WTO. They may require long periods of test-data exclusivity, extended patent terms in pharmaceuticals, the absence of compulsory licensing, and elimination of parallel imports, among other elements. The TRIPS-Plus agenda has met substantial opposition from health, education and agricultural authorities in partner countries, non-governmental organizations (NGOs) and observers within the United States and the EU. Partially in response, the US Trade Representative has scaled back its demands in its most recent and ongoing negotiations. It is likely that both regions will need to moderate their stance on TRIPS-Plus in order to achieve additional trade agreements. The United States and the EU have shown little interest in collaborating on their approaches to date, which would endow pharmaceutical industries with greater power to influence patent policies with FTA partners. An additional question is what policies might be deployed to encourage protection of pharmaceutical patents abroad if the TRIPS-Plus agenda is abandoned. More recourse to improving and encouraging technology transfer in medical technologies bears promise in this context (Foray, 2008).

A second element of potential cooperation is in legal patent harmonization. It has long been an objective of the United States to negotiate a global "Substantive Patent Law Treaty" that would harmonize patent standards and examination procedures around the world, or at least among the major developed and emerging economies. Those negotiations have been underway at the World Intellectual Property Organisation (WIPO) for some years, with little success. The EU shares enthusiasm for this project and has been an active participant in the negotiations. However, virtually no progress has been made because patent standards vary significantly and emerge from varying legal traditions and social preferences. Further progress is possible on mutual recognition of patent examinations, which can reduce the costs of achieving international patent protection. However, additional progress on standards harmonization seems out of reach unless the United States and the European Union contemplate significant domestic patent reforms. The fact that the US Senate in March 2008 pulled back from what would have been a fundamental reform of its patent law, making it more like the EU system (incorporating the first-to-file rule and post-grant opposition) suggests that the politics of harmonization remain difficult (Maskus, 2006). Finding wider agreement with major developing economies will require significant forms of policy compensation, which might be possible within the context of a future WTO trade round.

4. A Concluding Assessment

As this review suggests, there are multiple layers at which regulatory coordination is under consideration in the pharmaceuticals area. There have been notable successes in integrating some aspects of the drug-approval processes between the United States and the EU through the ICH. These changes should generate important economies, which could readily mount to tens of millions of Euros, for the research-intensive drug companies as they escape the need for duplicative and wasteful clinical trials. More progress along these lines seems possible, both within the ICH and the TEC discussions, while ongoing attempts within the EU to achieve convergence in national approval processes should reduce costs of pan-European drug marketing. The most recent TEC negotiations, which aim among other things to facilitate approvals of orphan drugs in both the United States and the EU, could also bring significant benefits in the form of more rapid introduction of medicines for rarified diseases.

Nevertheless, the overall regulatory systems remain far from convergent. For example, policies governing entry of generic drugs are quite different, as are fundamental scientific protocols governing basic research and preclinical testing. At the level of broader regulation, there are no discussions underway to consider whether price controls stand as a barrier to trade and investment, while efforts to achieve even similar patent standards in drugs are unlikely to succeed in the near term.

Crossing these gaps through formal legislation seems unlikely. The existence of substantial regulatory differences between the countries of the EU and the United States reflects numerous complex factors. For example, regulation of competition and innovation in the United States is largely the responsibility of the federal government and there is relatively little scope for state-level variation in price or expenditure controls. Drug approvals are fully centralized within the national authorities, as are nearly all public expenditures on basic medical research. Beyond Medicaid and Medicare, the US government does not purchase medicines for its citizens, reducing the pressure to control prices in order to limit procurement budgets. This concentration of regulatory authority at the national level, along with the traditional antipathy to government as the single payer for drugs, makes it easier for pharmaceutical companies to assert their interests in weaker price regulations and centralized product approvals. Thus, political and economic factors in the United States provide significant weight to the interests of research-intensive pharmaceutical firms.

These pressures exist in some EU countries, particularly Germany and the UK, which have a significant presence of research-based medical companies. However, most EU countries tend to be consumers of new medicines, rather than developers, even if they have substantial capacity to manufacture drugs after they have been introduced. With a lesser presence of firms engaged in R&D, these countries tend to favor consumer interests and to prefer limiting budgetary exposure in medicines. In consequence, they tend to have stricter price controls, profit regulations and limits on patent rights. Further, the authority for new drug approvals remains largely with national governments, rather than with the European Commission.

These two factors — a greater tendency toward strict regulations and considerable variability across EU members in permitting drug introductions — are generally seen by pharmaceutical companies as raising the costs of innovation and drug launches in the EU compared to the United States. Drug companies and biotechnology firms in both locations are interested in seeing more uniformity within Europe, and more collaboration between the EU and the United States, in order to reduce the regulatory burdens they face. However, the differences in regulatory approach are deeply rooted and rationalization will take considerable time and diplomatic energy to achieve.

References

Danzon, Patricia M., Richard Y. Wang and Liang Wang (2005). "The Impact of Price Regulation on the Launch Delay of New Drugs," *Health Economics*, 14(3): 269–292.

DiMasi, Joseph A., Ronald W. Hansen and Henry G. Grabowski (2003). "The Price of Innovation: New Estimates of Drug Innovation Costs," *Journal of Health Economics*, 22(2): 151–185.

Foray, Dominique (2008). "Technology Transfer in the TRIPS Age: The Need for New Types of Partnerships between the Least Developed and Most Advanced Economies," report for The International Center for Trade and Sustainable Development, Geneva.

Golec, Joseph H. and John A. Vernon (2006). "European Pharmaceutical Price Regulation, Firm Profitability, and R&D Spending," *NBER Working Paper* 12676.

Heuer, Alexander, Mulwina Mejer and Jennifer Neuhaus (2007). "The National Regulation of Pharmaceutical Markets and the Timing of New Drug Launches in Europe," *Kiel Advanced Studies Working Paper* No. 437.

Jacobzone, Stéphane (2000). "Pharmaceutical Policies in OECD Countries: Reconciling Social and Industrial Goals," *OECD Labour Market and Social Policy Occasional Papers* No. 40, (Paris: OECD).

Kyle, Margaret K. (2007). "Pharmaceutical Price Controls and Entry Strategies," *Review of Economics and Statistics*, 89(1): 88–99.

Maskus, Keith E. (2006). *Reforming US Patent Policy: Getting the Incentives Right.* Council on Foreign Relations Special Report No. 19, (New York: Council on Foreign Relations).

Mrazek, Monique F. (2002). "Comparative Approaches to Pharmaceutical Price Regulation in the European Union," *Croatian Medical Journal*, 43: 453–461.

Mrazek, Manique F. and Elias Mossialos (2004). "Regulating Pharmaceutical Prices in the European Union". In: Mossialos, Elias and Monique Mrazek (eds.), *Regulating Pharmaceuticals in Europe: Striving for Efficiency, Equity and Quality*, pp. 114–129. Open University Press: England.

National Science Foundation (2006). *Science and Engineering Indicators 2006*, (Washington DC: NSF).

Rovira, Joan and Josep Darba (2001). "Pharmaceutical Pricing and Reimbursement in Spain," *European Journal of Health Economics* 2(1): 39–43.

Shaffer, Gregory (2002). "Reconciling Trade and Regulatory Goals: The Prospects and Limits of New Approaches to Transatlantic Governance through Mutual Recognition and Safe Harbor Agreements," *Columbia Journal of European Law*, 9 (Fall): 29–77.

Stargardt, Tom and Jonas Schreyögg (2006). "The Impact of Cross-Reference Pricing on Pharmaceutical Prices: Manufacturers' Pricing Strategies and Price Regulation," *Applied Health Economics and Health Policy*, 5(4): 235–247.

US Department of Commerce (2006). International Trade Administration. *Trade in HS 30: Pharmaceutical Products, 1989–2005.*

Vernon, John A. (2005). "Examining the Link between Price Regulation and Pharmaceutical R&D Investment," *Health Economics* 14: 1–16.